THE SNOW LEOPARD PROJECT

THE SNOW LEOPARD PROJECT

AND OTHER ADVENTURES IN WARZONE CONSERVATION

ALEX DEHGAN

PublicAffairs

New York

PublicAffairs
Hachette Book Group
1290 Avenue of the Americas, New York, NY 10104
www.publicaffairsbooks.com
@Public_Affairs

Printed in the United States of America

First Edition: January 2019

Published by PublicAffairs, an imprint of Perseus Books, LLC, a subsidiary of Hachette Book Group, Inc. The PublicAffairs name and logo is a trademark of the Hachette Book Group.

The publisher is not responsible for websites (or their content) that are not owned by the publisher.

Print book interior design by Trish Wilkinson.

Library of Congress Cataloging-in-Publication Data

Names: Dehgan, Alex, author.
Title: The snow leopard project: and other adventures in warzone conservation / Alex Dehgan.
Description: First edition. | New York: PublicAffairs, 2019. | Includes bibliographical references and index.
Identifiers: LCCN 2018029065| ISBN 9781610396950 (hardcover) | ISBN 9781610396967 (ebook)
Subjects: LCSH: Wildlife recovery—Afghanistan. | Snow leopard—Conservation—Afghanistan. | Wildlife conservation—Afghanistan. | National parks and reserves—Afghanistan. | War—Environmental aspects—Afghanistan. | Nature—Effect of human beings on. | Afghan War, 2001–
Classification: LCC QH76.5.A3 D44 2019 | DDC 333.95/9755509581—dc23
LC record available at https://lccn.loc.gov/2018029065

ISBNs: 978-1-61039-695-0 (hardcover); 978-1-61039-696-7 (ebook)

LSC-C

10 9 8 7 6 5 4 3 2 1

To Peter Zahler and Pat Wright,
who gave me inspiration and taught me dedication,

To my parents,
who gifted me with great opportunity, and boundless love & support,

And to Kara, Fynn, & Cylus,
who inspired me to be better for them and for the world.

CONTENTS

CHAPTER 1   Bird-Watching with the Taliban   1

CHAPTER 2   The Snow Leopard Start-Up   21

CHAPTER 3   Afghanistan's Biological Silk Road   47

CHAPTER 4   The Ordinary Extraordinary Life in Kabul   63

CHAPTER 5   The Forgotten Peoples on the Roof of the World   87

CHAPTER 6   The Buddhas of Band-e-Amir   115

CHAPTER 7   Vampires in the Land of Light   147

CHAPTER 8   The Search for the Last Afghan Cheetah   169

CHAPTER 9   Adventures in Conservation Diplomacy   191

CHAPTER 10   Back in the CCCP   201

CHAPTER 11   The Snow Leopard Comforter   227

EPILOGUE   The Snow Leopard Project   251

             Acknowledgments   *261*

             Abbreviations   *265*

             Index   *267*

CHAPTER 1

BIRD-WATCHING
WITH THE TALIBAN

FROM MADAGASCAR TO AFGHANISTAN
(WITH A STOP IN BAGHDAD)

A cool mist hung low over the dense reeds as I peered through my scope. Kol-e-Hashmat Khan, a wetland area on the outskirts of Kabul, was once the hunting grounds of Mohammed Zahir Shah, the last king of Afghanistan. Converted in the 1930s by the king into a waterfowl reserve, its name translates as the "lake of the dignified leader." Prior to the Russian invasion in 1979, over 150 species of migratory birds were recorded at the wetland, and it had supported as many as 35,000 waterfowl. Kol-e-Hashmat Khan had long represented an important stopover for one of the planet's great bird migrations between Africa, South Asia, and Eurasia. It was an oasis for birds in the middle of traveling across a vast dry region, and it was also an oasis in the middle of Kabul. But the sprawling capital, particularly after the abdication of the king, suffering through three decades of war, and with the flood of refugees returning to Afghanistan and moving to Kabul, was quickly encroaching.

Today, areas on the edge of the lake are thickly settled—lumberyards, car repair shops, butchers, and houses have crept right up to the water.

The small wetland, just 200 hectares (494 acres), lies just south of Ka-bul, and coming across it is a jarring transition from the dusty, clogged traffic of Logar Road to the serene wetland populated with hundreds of birds just behind a metal gate. A simple, crumbling concrete observation tower stands at the edge of the lake, and King Zahir Shah's steel row-boat, which he used for hunting waterfowl, is still tied up to the shore.

I came to Kol-e-Hashmat Khan in 2006 to start building the Af-ghanistan Biodiversity Conservation Program with the Wildlife Con-servation Society in New York (better known as the Bronx Zoo). I was at the wetlands on that day as part of an effort to monitor the number and diversity of waterfowl, and I wasn't expecting any company other than the birds. But as I peered through the spotting scope, the crunch-ing of footsteps on the reeds broke the silence of the marsh. A young Afghan man in the traditional loose-fitting clothing of the Pashtuns, a shalwar kameez and a turban, approached me from behind. I was im-mediately uneasy. We were far out in the park. I was armed only with my scope, binoculars, and field notebooks. Usually, I did this kind of work with a partner, but today, I was alone. We were shorthanded, so my driver had to help our other projects, and my Afghan ornithologist, Naqib, was away on expedition. I looked up from the scope and turned to greet the young man.

"*Sobh-be kheir.*" (Good morning.)

His only response was a dark glare. We stared at each other for a long while before he asked—first in Pashto, which I didn't understand or speak, and then Dari—"What are you doing?"

I explained to him I was counting birds, part of my work of under-standing what happened to Afghan wildlife.

"I am a Talib," he announced. *Talib* as in a member of the Taliban. He sat back and watched for my reaction.

I looked at him for a moment, shrugged, and turned back to my scope.

He stood silently behind me, and I did my best to ignore him. I ner-vously counted ferruginous pochards, Jacanas, tufted ducks, shovelers, and multitudes of coots floating between the reeds, unsure of what he would do. After a few minutes conducting my awkward survey, I gestured for him to come over and look through the scope.

He looked at me first warily and then, his curiosity getting the better of him, approached and peered through the eyepiece as I showed him how to adjust it. After a few minutes, he turned his head to me and smiled and then peered into the scope again. Before long, I was showing him how to type birds and their names. As we scanned the reeds, I felt the surreality of the moment sink in. How had I found myself bird-watching with the Taliban?

THIS BOOK CHRONICLES the long, strange path that led me, and other conservationists, into some of the world's most dangerous places, all in the service of conservation. In particular, it lays out the story of conservation in postwar Afghanistan, a country that had become nearly a blank slate for conservation. There was a chance, after nearly thirty years of conflict, to start over, to create new and unique protected areas, and the laws, policies, and institutions that protected them, from scratch. This was a country where exploration was still possible and where the unknown had not been exhausted but in fact was refilled.

If we were successful, these would be the first national parks in Afghanistan's history. Afghanistan had come close in 1979 in creating the parks, but that effort was interrupted by the Russian invasion. The country had to wait nearly three decades to try again. But this time, we were starting from scratch—the ecosystems and their flora and fauna had been devastated by the war, and we didn't know what we would find and whether what was left was even worth saving. And there was a bigger question: When the country faced so many other challenges, why should we care about a few snow leopards and big mountain sheep?

We would be founding a start-up in the middle of a post-conflict war zone, and we had a singular window, before Afghanistan imploded again, to take advantage of the relative peace and safety, to accomplish our goals for the country. However, this meant that we would need to build everything from the ground up and get ourselves out into the field in thirty days. The project, funded by the US Agency for International

Development (USAID), was under tremendous pressure to show results, and as a result, almost immediately we would have international
staff coming into Kabul and starting on our initial surveys. This required a fast start-up. We would need to learn how to deal with the
complexities of Afghan society and government bureaucracy, navigate
remote terrains, and create the infrastructure, security, and logistics behind the entire project.

We had an extraordinary plan—a set of comprehensive surveys of
three major regions in Afghanistan for their fauna and flora; assessment
of the underlying threats driving their species extinct and the creation
of solutions to address those threats; the constitution of the governance
structures at the village, regional, provincial, and national levels to enforce the rule of law; the development of programs to build community support and ensure they benefited from future protected areas; the
formation of the support infrastructure for those protected areas; and
finally, the establishment of the areas themselves and the bringing together of other governments to partner with Afghanistan in the transboundary management of these remarkable and unique places. This plan
would take decades with other countries, but we only had three years of
funding from USAID and an unknown window of safety in which to
operate. And the project was already six months behind schedule.

The unknowns would be the hardest part of the project—not knowing the status of the wildlife, the safety of the roads, or whether we
would have the support of the people and the governments. However,
while Afghanistan operationally was a difficult place to work, it was
also an extraordinary place to be. First, the Afghan people are among
the loveliest you could hope to meet. For people who have suffered so
much, they are cheerful and hospitable, and this was even true of many
of its government officials with whom we dealt. Second, Afghanistan
attracts an inherently interesting set of people from outside its borders.
The journalists, humanitarians, and development officers that Afghanistan attracted in the early years after the US conflict were among the
most extraordinary, warmhearted, and intellectually rich people you
could meet.

Finally, perhaps because we were in Afghanistan to do science, as conservation diplomats, we did not have to deal with the kind of corruption or bureaucracy most other programs did. The majority of Afghans were remarkably enthusiastic about our work and supported us in doing it. This may have been because, as an Iranian American, I may have been less of an outsider to their society, more familiar to them than the other foreigners that flooded into their country. But I think there was another reason—for people who had spent much of the previous three decades as refugees in other countries, protecting the unique and charismatic wildlife of the country was a way to help restore their identity. The protection and renewal of wild Afghanistan, of its flora and fauna, represented a restoration of the country's own ferocity and identity. This was an essential component of postwar reconstruction. Although Afghanistan's national character always tended toward generosity, friendliness, and warmth, our work in conservation seemed to generate even greater kindness and support.

How I GOT to Afghanistan is a long and unlikely story. It took me through studying extinction among endangered lemurs in the dwindling eastern forests of Madagascar, to science diplomacy work for the State Department focused on the Middle East, including a foray into Iraq, before being invited to help establish the Wildlife Conservation Society's first national park in Afghanistan. My career might sound a bit haphazard, but it prepared me perfectly for the role that I played in Afghanistan. Law, lemurs, and diplomacy comprised a curriculum not found inside any graduate school. A sense of adventure and a dose of serendipity kept sending me down different paths, and they ultimately led me to that wetland outside Kabul.

I started out as a lawyer, although not the typical kind. In the summer after my first year in law school, I flew to the collapsing Soviet Union with several hundred dollars and a credit card that didn't seem to work anywhere in the country except for a telephone booth in a floating brothel on the banks of the Moscow River, from which I called my family once a week. I had gotten an opportunity to work with the

Russian government on improving their environmental laws after the collapse of the Soviet Union. My position was to help rewrite environmental law and support the Ministry of Environment for the newly created Russian Federation as well as help build the country's civil society. The economic and political impact of the war in Afghanistan, coupled with the suffocating administrative edifice of the former Soviet Union, caused the Communist Party and government to collapse abruptly under their own weight. I jumped at the chance to go to Russia, oblivious to what awaited.

Russian society had fallen into disarray with the collapse of Communism. The Soviet Union was a seventy-year social experiment on an unprecedented scale—a test of whether the drivers of human nature could change—and that experiment had finally failed. The rules for living in Russia, never obvious or simple even under the Soviets, were now changing almost daily. Currency could be rendered worthless by government decree overnight, and inflation ran rampant. Accomplishing anything from buying a train ticket to making a phone call required ingenuity and adaptability. Everything I thought I would be doing in Russia was different from my actual work. Although I had been sent to rewrite environmental laws, ensuring that the laws were enforced was the more needed task. However, the lessons outside my work would be the most valuable to my experiences later. The salary was meager—it included my housing, which I shared first with a hedgehog in the Moscow Zoo, and then a dog at a Soviet block apartment outside of town, plus $300 for the summer—so I had to live as a Russian did and adapt to the society that was in the middle of 30 percent inflation a month and in which even the constitution seemed to change daily. My experience there was like white-water rafting in the dark. Russia was my first training ground for surviving in a foreign land in the midst of chaos. This knowledge proved invaluable more than once on the road to Kabul.

After two summers in Russia, I finished law school and clerked for a federal court in Manhattan. As much as I enjoyed returning to a place where the rule of law maintained the fabric of society, I missed science. Law seemed to be a further refinement of previous interpretations and distinctions, while science provided me a chance to be curious, ask big questions, and seek out their answers in the larger universe. It would be a lecture series on extinction that I had attended at the Wildlife Conservation Society (WCS) in celebration of its one hundredth anniversary that would lure me back to science and adventure.

So I gave up my career in law to begin a doctoral program in evolutionary biology at the University of Chicago. I wanted to answer a critical scientific question: Why, during periods of extreme environmental change, do certain species survive while others go extinct? I sought the answer in the lemur populations in Madagascar. The country had suffered from deforestation and fragmentation of its forests. We asked similar questions years later in Afghanistan. In Madagascar, we were looking at the aftermath of man's war on the environment as part of his survival. In Afghanistan, it was man's war with himself. Both had impacts on the biodiversity of the countries.

I formed a hypothesis in Madagascar that species' adaptability to environmental change, and thus their survival, was directly related to their ability to alter their behavior, and that by quantifying this ability, we could predict the likelihood of species' demise. I proposed that extinction is not a random process, but that species disappear in a predictable order. We could predict species' susceptibility to extinction by measuring their "behavior plasticity," or, in other words, the evolutionary moderated capability of a species to behave differently. In Madagascar, I found two species with different outcomes in response to fragmentation; one species, which was less limited by diet and skeletal structure, was able to cross vast areas of rice paddies to ensure it got sufficient food, while the other was constrained by its evolutionary adaptation to arboreal living and was ultimately trapped on the tiny island of forest.

Before Madagascar, I had never handled the logistics of a large-scale field operation, nor did I have much experience in building and training teams. Our expedition required more than twenty field assistants and researchers, fifty porters, and a shipping container load of scientific equipment and supplies. We had to get every ounce of gear to Madagascar, hardly a travel hub. In the field, we were sometimes a one- to two-day walk from the nearest road, a twelve-hour drive from the capital, with no cellular signal, satellite phones, running water, or electricity. We participated in countless ceremonies for the ancestors and meetings with local kings and elected officials to get nearby villages to buy in. We built and trained our field teams from scratch, working with Malagasy villagers from the forest (the Tanala people) who had little more than grade-school educations. Once the team was assembled, we needed to get to the field sites that I had spotted and measured via satellite imagery and determine whether lemurs still existed in them—and whether their distribution was random or followed our model's predictions.

Nearly every scientific method we used had to be adapted or created de novo. To answer the complex questions we were asking about the behavior of extinction, we needed intensive studies of the soils, trees, aerial and terrestrial predators, and landscape characteristics. Most of all, we needed round-the-clock demographic surveys of the twelve species of the lemurs (half of which were nocturnal) that inhabited the rain forest. Once we had all that together, we could perform behavioral and physiological studies of three of those species. This included the methodologies for surveying lemurs in fragments rather than intact forests, coming up with novel ways to survey predators, finding and darting a lot of lemurs, putting together field teams, and keeping those teams alive in the rain forest.

Moreover, during the two-and-a-half-year expedition, I nearly died from cerebral malaria, contracted regular malaria multiple times, fended off leeches and enormous poisonous spiders, contracted schistosomiasis and dysentery, lost a motorcycle in quicksand, walked seventy kilometers to find an off-road vehicle to save the life of one of my research guides who had been bitten by a poisonous spider, managed an international group of field assistants, some who slowly went crazy from their anti-malarial meds, dived with oceanic sharks, outwitted corrupt officials, and uncovered Madagascar's deep environmental history of previous cycles of deforestation buried in its soil. We confronted constant breakdowns of our Land Cruisers and trucks, liquefying roads, roads that were more potholes than tarmac, and structurally unsound bridges. We were battered by violent cyclones during the rainy season. The powerful storms left rivers clogged with red silt and occasional dead lemurs, washed away roads and bridges, and swallowed vehicles whole. My time in Madagascar taught me a set of entrepreneurial and logistics skills that were incredibly valuable in my later endeavors. In the end, like all my adventures, I had a love-hate relationship with the island. It had been a place of considerable challenge to me physically and emotionally, but looking back, it defined my core identity and who I became.

Within a few days of my return to Chicago from almost two and a half years of living in the Madagascar rain forests, still in culture shock from the transition, al-Qaeda attacked New York and Washington. Along with the rest of the country, the attacks of 9/11 stunned me into numbness. I watched the tragedies unfold for hour after hour, not moving from a simple wooden village chair that I had brought from Madagascar. It became clear that the country I had returned to was very different from the one I had left. The mood was dark, isolationist, nationalistic, and foreboding.

I turned down a position at the Yale School of Forestry in favor of joining the State Department, hopeful that I could leverage my power as a scientist to help steer the direction of the country. I was concerned that the country was becoming more fearful, less optimistic, and less welcoming, and that this would play out in our foreign policy. I wanted to provide another voice in our engagement with the Islamic world. I decided to leave the relative comfort of tropical biology—not the serenest room in the ivory tower, but still academia—for the deserts of Iraq and the perilous landscape of foreign policy. Russia and Madagascar put me to the test, but the chaotic world of a post-conflict war zone was an even greater challenge.

FROM THE RAIN FOREST TO THE DESERT

A year after defending my doctoral thesis in January 2003, I found myself in Iraq's "Green Zone." Tracking lemurs was tricky, but at least we never had to worry about improvised explosive devices (IEDs). Getting from Baghdad's airport to the heavily fortified Green Zone took you down Route Irish, a heavily barricaded seven-mile road. The trip was short, and the road was extensively patrolled by US forces. But Route Irish was still deadly. Targets became a magnet for snipers, rocket-propelled grenades (RPGs), and hidden IEDs.

Gorgeous, towering palms in the median ticked past, but no one was paying much attention to the landscaping. The unarmored bus was filled with employees of the State Department and the Department of Defense, all of us quiet, tensely scanning every overpass for snipers and eyeing every dead animal or bag of garbage as a potential IED. The drivers along Route Irish eyed each other nervously, scanning for fanaticism on the faces of the other drivers, since cars themselves were sometimes used as suicide bombs.

We arrived fifteen minutes later at the gate of the palace—a gaudy, vulgar monument to excess. Its very architecture projected Saddam's absolute power. For many, the palace stood for torture and death. It became the nerve center of the occupation government—*Imperialis Americae*—the Coalition Provisional Authority (CPA). Saddam's throne room in the palace would become my bedroom, among hundreds of other staffers, soldiers, and contractors, all sleeping in bunk beds under the throne room's perpetually lit dome.

The State Department had assigned me to the work of redirecting Iraqi weapons scientists, running one of the first State Department programs under what had been an entirely DOD-Intelligence operation. Although the mission was hard enough on its own—I was working in an active war zone where the landscape and security climate was constantly shifting—it was made harder by the lack of support from the Department of Defense and intelligence agencies as well as my own lack of experience with nonproliferation. I was a lemur biologist, not a specialist in nuclear, chemical, or biological weapon systems. Although my work in Baghdad could not have been more different from my jungle sojourn in Madagascar, I once again found myself building a scientific ecosystem out of chaos.

The program I co-ran with Dr. Carl Philips, an adventurous and tough fellow evolutionary biologist from Texas Tech who had spent a career in the tropics, was only the third redirection project in American history. In the wake of World War II and in the shadow of the escalating Cold War, the United States brought over 1,500 German military scientists and engineers to work on US nuclear and space programs, and also to keep their knowledge out of Russian hands. After the fall of the Soviet Union, Senators Sam Nunn and Dick Lugar created the Cooperative Threat Reduction Program, which worked with former Eastern bloc and Soviet countries to decommission nuclear, biological, and chemical weapons sites and redirect former weapons scientists.

Cooperative threat reduction in Iraq proved very different from efforts in post-WWII Germany and the post-Soviet republics, however. War and looting had destroyed much of the country's infrastructure, the civilian science sector had collapsed due to militarization and sanctions, and there was a shocking lack of information available on the status of Iraqi weapons efforts. And while Russian and German cultures shared religion and history with the US, Iraq did not—not to mention there was a smoldering civil war about to explode. While the US put billions into a fruitless search for Saddam's alleged weapons of mass destruction, it overlooked the very people whose knowledge posed the true threat and then left them at home without a salary.

Early on, it was clear that the redirection effort required a civilian scientific community, since without it, there was nowhere to redirect the former weapons scientists. Rebuilding a robust civilian scientific community would also help rebuild the nation at large. In Iraq, I shuttled between two unique and ephemeral communities—the contractors, translators, diplomats, and development officials who rarely left the Green Zone, and the community of Iraqis, journalists, fixers, soldiers, war profiteers, and adventurers who existed outside the Green Zone, which included most of the scientists who had been involved with the weapons programs. Science had a central role in post-war Iraq, not only to reduce the threat through nonproliferation but to rebuild a society ravaged by three wars in a generation. The Iran-Iraq War, Operation

Desert Storm, and the 2003 invasion and subsequent insurgency left a once-cosmopolitan and educated nation reeling. Through the redirection program, we sought to harness Iraq's greatest natural resource—not its oil but its intelligentsia—to renew the country that existed beyond the concrete and razor-wire barriers of the Green Zone.

Of course, this presumed we could actually *find* the scientists. Once we did, we would need to separate those who had truly dangerous knowledge from those who merely assisted in a weapons project but had no conceptual or technical knowledge that would allow another country to develop a weapon. This required identifying scientists at universities through their scholarly publications, interviewing them, and making decisions about the nature of what they knew and whether they could put it to use. We had to accomplish all this without the assistance of the acting wartime sovereign government that had been established by the Department of Defense—the Coalition Provisional Authority—and sometimes in spite of the outright hostility and direct interference of other parts of our government. Our mission took us outside the safety of the Green Zone without armored vehicles, security contractors, IED-jamming devices, or helicopter escorts. But this actually proved to be an advantage since the insurgency was using the extent of the security protection as a way of prioritizing their targets.

As I later saw in Afghanistan, wars create dialectics within them— they are simultaneously both safe and dangerous, stable and chaotic, rich with life and opportunity and barren, desolate, and devoid of hope. The restaurant filled with diners where you ate the day before might be bombed the following day, killing all the staff who cooked and served the dinner you had eaten. The streets that were filled with children playing one day were eerily empty the next, making you look at every dead dog and wonder whether it had been made into an IED.* You

---

*Much like post-Katrina New Orleans, the Green Zone was filled with abandoned, now feral, dogs and cats.

wondered whether the guard at the checkpoint labeled with the words KILL ZONE, who tonight protected you, might also fire upon you the following night because you approached too fast or failed to dim your headlights. One night, we ate at an outdoor kabob restaurant in Baghdad, lounging on the grass, and watched mortars and rockets fall upon the Green Zone, where I would be returning a few hours later, as if they were a fireworks display on the Fourth of July. This wasn't true for just the foreigners but the local people as well. Which world you got depended on chance, and the boundaries that delineated safety frequently shifted. The wrong turn, the wrong stop, leaving five minutes earlier, may result in death. However, for the Iraqis and other denizens of war zones, there was no choice, no option, other than to continue to live life and seek and cherish the moments of normalcy.

The work in Iraq was also the subject of a bureaucratic skirmish between the Department of Defense (DOD) and Department of State (DOS) over control of the redirection program, and a larger battle between which institution, the DOD or the DOS, Rumsfeld or Powell, would reign supreme. The DOD, with more musicians in army bands than the State Department had employees, would tend to have the upper hand.

The internecine infighting manifested in strange ways. The DOD would not handle, hold, or transfer DOS funds for our program. Since Iraq was under sanctions, there was no way to get government funds into the country other than carrying them directly. So I flew in and out of Baghdad on a C-130, climbing like a corkscrew straight up above the airport to stay out of range of shoulder-mounted surface-to-air missiles and random bullets, bound for the US embassy in Kuwait—the closest State Department facility. At the embassy's cashier office, I filled up a backpack with as much as $30,000 in cash, signed a personal guarantee for the funds, and turned right around for Baghdad to run my program. This happened every few weeks.

Bringing sacks of hard cash back to the war zone was just the first step in keeping the operation running. Because the DOD refused to store the funds inside Saddam's giant safe in the basement of the palace, I had to hide the money under my pillow in my trailer. I ran the $2 million program—soon to expand to $62 million—entirely in cash. This included cars, equipment, buildings, weapons, salaries, and even training a militia. To get the equipment and materials I needed from the Coalition Provisional Authority, I bartered favors and acquired what we needed on the Iraqi gray markets that existed outside the Green Zone. Building a science center turned me into an unlikely entrepreneur. My success was measured not in profits but in my ability to redirect former weapons scientists. In the end, these programs endured beyond me not because they only served US interests on nonproliferation but because they also served Iraqi interests in rebuilding their country. By selling science in a country that helped advance humanity's progress in math, engineering, astronomy, and medicine eight hundred years earlier, I was welcomed everywhere in Iraq where the embassy was not. Sadly, these initiatives were later sidelined in internal power struggles between Shiites and Sunnis, Kurds and Arabs, and in the face of the battle against ISIS a few years later.

When the Coalition Provisional Authority shut down, I returned to Washington, recalled to the mundane world of my science fellowship at the State Department. Before long, I was moody and restless again, even more so than before I had left for Iraq. The adrenaline and freedom generated by war and chaos were addictive, despite the toll they took on me. Even after getting promoted to the Secretary of State's policy planning staff, I was bored with the State Department's bureaucratic factory of paper and the hypocrisy of the divide between our internal values and our actions. I sat through endless meetings in identical bland conference rooms where men and women in dark suits sought to assert their importance. And outside, men in headphones robotically pushed carts of espionage detection equipment through the hallways.

Beyond boredom, I felt powerlessness. America dived headfirst into the tangled politics of the Middle East. Even from the office of the Secretary of State, I felt like I couldn't shift our heading. I was silently screaming, listening to classified briefings on interrogation and incarceration policies that violated human rights and produced no good outcomes.* I needed to return to the new front lines of diplomacy, where science and conservation made a difference on the ground. My résumé was a bit unusual: environmental law in the wreckage of the Soviet Union, a comprehensive and complex field-based research program that studied lemurs in remote Malagasy forest fragments, lugging cash and building a scientific community on the treacherous streets of Iraq. But the work of building Afghanistan's first national park was unusual too.

IN SEARCH OF SNOW LEOPARDS

Once again, through serendipity—in the form of my presentation on Iraq's environment at the Society for Conservation Biology meetings at Columbia University—I met Peter Zahler, the assistant Asia director for the Wildlife Conservation Society. He had come to the meeting, I found out later, specifically to see my session and recruit me. WCS sought to create a national park in Afghanistan and needed a country director. Peter asked if I would be interested. "Of course," I replied before thinking. This seemed like just the opportunity to actually *do* something that I had been looking for.

The viability of actually creating the park hinged on three areas—first, whether sufficient wildlife still existed in the country. We really had no idea beyond a few preliminary, rapid assessments Peter conducted with the UN. Second, whether the Afghan government and people would be amenable to creating national parks, given the other competing needs in the country. And third, whether we could accomplish the work, given the challenges facing NGOs in Afghanistan—especially those that were based in the field—a worsening security situation and the extreme isolation of our field sites, and the extraordinary amount

---

*On one of my flights into Baghdad, I sat and conversed with the military investigators who were sent to review the unfolding scandal at Abu Ghraib. While they couldn't tell me much, the worry that was on their faces suggested the severity of the problem.

of unexploded ordnance and number of land mines scattered across the landscapes where we would be doing our fieldwork. After completing the first post-conflict environmental assessment of the country, Peter convinced USAID to fund a national park. Less than a year after my presentation, we met up in Dubai and flew to Afghanistan together.

Peter Zahler was a handsome, dark-haired, lean, neatly bearded, quiet conservationist who looked more suited to a Manhattan book reading than the back of a yak in the Himalayas. But his refined, controlled exterior hid an obsessed, insane adventurer consumed by wildlife conservation. His fixations weren't typical conservation hot spots. Instead he focused on the less glamorous but culturally and biologically unique environments of Western and Central Asia, which frequently were political and military hot spots. These were the lands of the Silk Road. Peter's curriculum vitae included conservation work on the ground in Pakistan, Afghanistan, Tajikistan, Uzbekistan, Iran, Mongolia, the Russian Far East, western China, and the Russian-Alaskan Arctic. He had spent the better part of a decade researching flying squirrels in the tribal areas in Pakistan. Here the mountains of the Hindu Kush (literally *Indian killer*) marked the divide between Russian and British spheres of colonial influence. This was the Pashtun homeland, the birthplace of the Taliban, and the gateway to the graveyard of empires. And it would be our workplace.

Like many people I met at the WCS, Peter preferred to spend his days in the field rather than in Washington or at the WCS headquarters in the Bronx. When Peter was bored at meetings, I leaned over to see him jotting down on the meeting agenda species lists of carnivores and ungulates for a country from memory. The downside of all this dedication was that he worked night and day, sick or healthy. He did not appear to need sustenance. He once confided to me that if WCS stopped paying him, he would still show up to work. This was not an exaggeration. Peter once got mugged, whacked in the head in the middle of a freezing winter night in Ulan Bator, the capital of Mongolia. He woke up in a bloodstained pile of snow early the next morning, abandoned by passersby. He shook off encroaching hypothermia, washed off the blood, and went to the WCS office to start his workday.

TERMINAL 2: THE CONFLICT AIRPORT

In June of 2006, I left Washington with my girlfriend, Kara, a conservation biologist and former Peace Corps volunteer in Nepal, who would oversee our training programs. We had just moved in together when I got the offer to go to Afghanistan. I nervously asked her if she wanted to go with me, not knowing what it might mean for our future. Surprisingly (or perhaps not, as she later became the mother of my children), she said yes. Turns out she's never one to shy away from adventure. We flew to Dubai to meet up with Peter Zahler, who took us the rest of the way into Afghanistan.

To travel to Iraq, I had taken commercial flights to Kuwait, then switched to the military side of the airport to wait for hours for a C-130 flight back to Baghdad. It was there that I came to truly understand the concept of "hurry up and wait." A military chartered bus picked us up at 3:30 in the morning and dropped us off in a dusty room, where we waited for a flight that might not actually leave until 2:00 in the afternoon. Afghanistan was much easier to get to since we were taking a commercial airline, but equally as unglamorous. Commercial flights came and went to Kabul via Dubai's infamous Terminal 2.

Dubai's glamorous and cosmopolitan main Terminal 1 teemed with tourists in shorts on their way to vacation destinations in the Maldives or Thailand, Arab men in blindingly white dishdashas, and South Asian guest workers on their way home, all shopping for Fendi bags, Hermès scarves, and Chanel perfume. You could purchase hundred-dollar lottery tickets to win an Aston Martin. Dubai was part of the modern Silk Road, much as Afghanistan was part of the old one. The main terminal's building was soaring and gleaming, studded with gourmet restaurants filled with endless buffets and expensive shops.

While Terminal 1 represented the future aspirations of the Middle East, Terminal 2 represented its past. This terminal had a far different atmosphere. The flights from Terminal 2 went to the places no one wanted to vacation in—Basra, Kandahar, Erbil, Mogadishu, Beirut, Aleppo, Khartoum, and of course Kabul. Kara and I called it the "conflict airport," since most of the destinations were in war zones of one intensity or another. The space was dark, gritty, and run-down. Terminal 2 wasn't even directly connected to the more glamorous terminals, as if Dubai was unwilling to acknowledge that it was the crossroads between conflict zones and the West. Getting to Terminal 2 required a long and expensive taxi ride that circumnavigated much of the enormous airport. That taxi ride always filled me with dread.

The list of Terminal 2's carriers—Equatorial Congo Airlines, Kam Air, Ariana Afghan Airlines, Kish Airlines, Jubba Airways, Turkmenistan Airlines, Mahan Air, and Samara Airlines—also didn't inspire confidence. Many of them were banned from flying into Europe or the US on their second- or thirdhand (or worse) Soviet-built Tupolevs. Flying into Kabul wasn't exactly puddle-jumping, either. Kam Air flight 904, flying from Herat to Kabul in 2004, slammed into the mountains outside the capital at an altitude of eleven thousand feet. The crash wasn't found until herders came down from the mountains a few days after the crash and told authorities where to look. Recovering bodies from the wreck was difficult, as winter snows and high elevations prevented the teams from getting to the crash until spring. Once the rescuers reached the plane, they found it had crashed in a minefield, which had to be demined before they could recover the bodies. We were flying Kam Air into Kabul.

Terminal 2 had none of the luxury shopping that Dubai was known for. A single restaurant sold overcooked and very dubious-looking, oily beef hot dogs spinning languidly on rollers. However, Terminal 2 did have one feature of interest: hidden in the small duty-free area was a small bookshop with a well-curated collection of books written by humanitarian workers, journalists, and military officers who worked in the very countries served by the terminal. Here you could find accounts of UN work in Somalia, or a war correspondent's history of the Middle East. The conflict airport had a conflict bookstore. Sitting in the terminal would be the very audience that voraciously would read such books and truly appreciate the stories.

Travelers in the terminal eyed each other warily. As Kara and I ate our well-oiled halal hot dogs, we entertained ourselves by imagining the stories of the other passengers: mercenaries, guards, intelligence operatives, war correspondents, aid workers, contractors, and war profiteers. They carried duffel bags and boxes wrapped in rice bags with addresses stenciled in marker, stacked on top of gleaming wheeled suitcases. Even their luggage reflected the schizophrenia of the two worlds.

When the call came for Kam Air, everyone rushed to the boarding door. No zones were called, and none seemed expected. So we joined the scrum, pushing our way through the door. After a short flight across the Persian Gulf, whose blue water glinted through the dust in the air, then across the parched lands of southeast Iran, we were in Afghanistan. Almost exactly two years after returning from Iraq, I touched down at Kabul International Airport. And once again, remembering similar first flights into the Soviet Union, Madagascar, and Iraq, I stared out the plane window, wondering how I had found myself again in a foreign place with a daunting mission.

My romantic visions of the storied Silk Road, magnificent wildlife, and majestic landscapes quickly gave way to despair and concern as the gray-and-beige fabric that enveloped Kabul came into view. Wrecked airplanes and land mines lined the sides of the pockmarked runway. The views outside the window of our vehicle on the way in to the guesthouse where we stayed—the Park Palace—were not much more inspiring. Bullet holes punctuated the walls of yellowed Soviet-era concrete block apartments. Some buildings looked as if a giant had taken a large bite out of them, with half-crumbled walls and missing roofs. Gutted tanks and abandoned armored personnel carriers littered the city. In one part of Kabul, the wrecked carcasses of destroyed buses were heaped four stories high, like toy blocks for a child giant. Some parts of Kabul were still in ruins, and the entire city was cloaked in a thick Persian carpet of dust.

Although war had shattered the human landscape, it may have inadvertently protected the natural one. Much of the country was seen as too dangerous to inhabit because of the land mines and constant battles, which had turned most of the population into refugees for more than three decades and depopulated the natural environments. The unintended consequence of this was that there was significantly decreased pressure on natural resources. Thirty years of war may have created natural enclaves—much like the demilitarized zone between North and South Korea, or the Chernobyl Exclusion Zone—where the wildlife could return and even flourish. We didn't know—no one did—but we were about to find out.

This hope—that Afghanistan's once spectacular wildlife was still there—became the basis for my work. We were about to launch a start-up to create the first national park in Afghanistan's history and chart the status of endangered species in some of the remotest lands on Earth.

CHAPTER 2

THE SNOW LEOPARD START-UP

WILDLIFE CONSERVATION IN Afghanistan doesn't seem like an obvious thing to do. This was a nation racked by thirty years of war and still fighting a Taliban insurgency. The country was already characterized by profoundly diverse cultures and language, extraordinary biodiversity, and challenging topography. Compounding that was weak leadership and a decentralized government, the disarmament of multiple militant groups, and somewhere between ten and thirty million unexploded land mines.

This was business as usual for Afghanistan. Humans have been living in what is now Afghanistan for fifty-two thousand years and seemed to be fighting for control of the region for just as long. Situated at the crossroads of empires, these lands had been fought by khans and kings, cold warriors and communists. The Afghan people have had little choice but to be resilient in the face of conflict. Invasion and empire brought a patchwork of culture, language, and even religion: Zoroastrianism, animism, Buddhism, Hinduism, and Islam have all found a place in Afghanistan at different points in its history.

For all the invasions, Afghanistan is a difficult—maybe impossible—place to conquer. Although Afghanistan's cities have been destroyed, its peoples slaughtered, its agricultural lands despoiled or mined, foreigners have never truly managed to hold it. The list of invaders is long, and they came to share a respect for the fierceness of the Afghan people. Alexander the Great, who had defeated the Achaemenid Empire, acknowledged Afghanistan was "easy to march into, hard to march out of." After Alexander, empire after empire took their turn. Chandragupta Maurya, the unifier of north and south India, defeated the remnants of Alexander's empire and introduced Buddhism to Afghanistan. His empire was followed by the Greco-Bactrians, the Indo-Scythians, the Parthians, the Indo-Parthians, the Kushans (who would link China and Rome via the Silk Road), the Sassanids, the Kidarites, the Hephthalites, the Kabul Shahi, the Arab tribes from the west who brought Islam starting in the seventh century CE.

The Arab invasion, which brought Islam, was brutal, but it did not succeed in converting all of Afghanistan. As Nancy Dupree wrote in her 1977 travel guide to Afghanistan: "Due to the harshness of the Arab invasion in the mountains, cities submitted, only to rise in revolt and [return] to their old beliefs once the armies passed." Afghanistan was like a field of grass, bending with every windstorm but standing tall again when the storm passed. The Arab invasion wasn't the end. The Mongols were next in line to devastate Afghanistan, destroying many great cities and monuments. They would be followed by the British, the Russians, and finally the Americans.

British concern about growing Russian influence in Western Asia (Iran) and Central Asia led to a disastrous British-Indian invasion of Afghanistan in 1839, setting off the first of three Anglo-Afghan wars. The First Anglo-Afghan War was the beginning of Afghanistan's reputation in the West as the graveyard of empires. After a few years of uneasy occupation, the British were exhausted. They negotiated a retreat from Kabul. But as the retreating invaders passed through the mountains, tribesmen killed 4,500 British and Indian troops, along with 12,000 logistics staff. Only a handful of survivors, and just one British soldier, assistant surgeon William Brydon (with part of his skull sheared off), completed the trek to the British garrison at Jalalabad. Two more Anglo-Afghan wars would follow.

The twentieth century was more of the same. On December 24, 1979, a Soviet army 100,000 strong invaded, igniting yet another global-politics proxy war in Afghanistan. Somewhere between 850,000 and 1.5 million Afghans were killed, and another 6 million became refugees as the result of the Soviet invasion and the subsequent civil war that led to the rise of the Taliban. This long, violent history was the prelude to the US invasion in 2001. America didn't find Afghanistan any easier to subdue than the Soviets, the British, or any of the other countless would-be conquerors, but believed in their exceptionalism. What happened to the Soviets could never happen to the world's sole superpower. In each case, Afghanistan's soil would be soaked in blood as it had been for thousands of years.

For each of these empires, Afghanistan was an intractable situation. When wars are fought between countries, the rules are neat, soldiers wear uniforms, and they fight on battlefields. But invading Afghanistan has always been a war of insurgency, a gray zone of asymmetrical warfare that requires deep understanding of a culture, of the competing factions, interests, and alliances, and of the country's history. For centuries now, land cleared of insurgents has been retaken again and again, and a new generation of soldiers and commanders is forced to hit Repeat.

In 2006, postwar Afghanistan was starting on a pathway to volatility and peril. But it was also a place of extraordinary beauty that few in the West knew. Even after more than a decade of US military involvement in Afghanistan, most Americans view Afghanistan as an inhospitable, dusty land of mud houses, thick clay walls, and bearded, turbaned men and women in burkas. Afghanistan exists for us mostly on television screens as a dun-colored background for action movies and little more. Few understand its history as part of the great Silk Road between East and West. Even fewer grasp its biological importance.

Just as Afghanistan was a crossroads of human cultures and empires, it was also a biological Silk Road that served as a crossroads for the fauna and flora of three of the planet's eight biogeographic realms. Afghanistan's wildlife was shared with the Palearctic (Europe and northern

Asia, including such species as brown bears, wolves, and lynx), the Afrotropic (gazelles and hyenas), and the Indomalayan (leopard cats and giant flying squirrels) regions.

What created this dramatic and largely unappreciated biodiversity? Peter Zahler explained it to me this way: Afghanistan is not just a crossroads of people and wildlife but of terrain. Some of the most dramatic and distinctive mountain ranges in the world converge in Afghanistan. The Wakhan Valley is a fingerlike extension of land that points east on maps of the country, into what geographers colorfully call the "Pamir knot," a pileup of mountain ranges, including the Himalayas, the Karakoram, the Hindu Kush, the Tien Shan, and the Kunlun, all colliding in a slow-motion maelstrom of plate tectonics.

The mountains extend south along Afghanistan's eastern border, under a drape of forests, before burrowing into the vast red-sand dunes of the Registan Desert of the south. They also punch broadly into the heart of the country in the Hazarajat Plateau. Bamiyan Province, which largely contains that plateau, holds the ochre cliffs of Band-e-Amir. These mountain chains create some of the toughest terrain in the world, situated between Europe, Asia, and Africa. As a result, the valleys within Afghanistan's mountains become conduits for wildlife moving between the world's biogeographic realms.

Within Afghanistan, there are a host of different habitats. These include thick coniferous forests reminiscent of the forests of the American Rockies, home to Asiatic black bears, wolves, and flying squirrels. The vast, dry grasslands of the central plateau region and the hot, sandy deserts of the southwest are home to gazelles, bustards, and countless avian and small mammal species. Extensive wild pistachio woodlands once stretched across much of the middle of the country, reminiscent of the great acacia savannas of Africa. Huge shallow lakes and wetlands (Dasht-e Nāwar, Abi-Estada) supported enormous numbers of waterfowl, pelicans, and even breeding flamingos. The Amu Darya River, which runs along the northern border of the country, provides habitat for fish, waterfowl, and otters, and the thick scrub that lines the river's banks and covers its islands contains birds, deer, wild boar, and, long ago, even tigers. The mountains that carve up the country are important ecosystems themselves, separating by elevation the haunts of snow leopards, Marco Polo sheep, markhor, ibex, and golden eagles.

Take these fragile habitats and their denizens, add a quarter century of conflict, and stir furiously; the result is a serious disruption of the ecosystem. Millions of internally displaced people with no food or shelter were suddenly turned out on the land. Unsurprisingly, Afghanistan's land suffered along with the people during the last thirty years of conflict. Grasslands were overgrazed as ancient systems of management broke down. Forests were cut down for fuel and timber. Wildlife was shot for food and fur. Drought and uncontrolled well-digging resulted in a plummeting water table, causing lakes and wetlands to dry up and driving birds to leave for other lands. Our goal was to reverse this disruption, but first, we needed to set up the infrastructure, teams, and creditability among the Afghans and international community to achieve it.

WE SPENT OUR first morning in Kabul walking through the grounds of the Park Palace, an aspirationally named two-story motel in the middle of the city. Behind the dusty tan walls (everything in Afghanistan is tan, khaki, or yellow, save a few garish new houses) were manicured courtyards punctuated with picnic tables, bordered by two stacked rows of single rooms. With the exception of the high outer walls, the Park Palace was straight out of a 1950s American roadside motel. Despite the perception of a verdant and serene oasis, the Park Palace was actually a prison. Development workers, security officials, and war opportunists hid behind its walls, disconnected from life in Afghanistan and locked in by real and imagined security threats that lay beyond. This would become the first headquarters of the Wildlife Conservation Society in Afghanistan—Silk Road Silicon Valley meets Motel 6.

As we toured the grounds, we met a few of the Palace's inhabitants. In one room, a paunchy middle-aged man sat in front of a desk pushed against the window, wearing only a pair of white briefs. A tall, lanky man, possibly European, dressed in shorts, obsessively ran endless loops around the inside perimeter of the Palace. Everyone we encountered looked tense, with good reason. A US military truck accident the month before had resulted in angry crowds attacking the Palace and attempting to break through their barriers before they were dispersed by Palace employees and the UN security forces.

We only spent a month at the Palace, but it was a crucial month. We had only thirty days to find permanent offices and a place to live in Kabul, put together a team of Afghans to staff the program, set up bank accounts, purchase and retrofit vehicles that would be crossing potentially mined roads and fording icy rivers, arrange security and medical evacuation plans, identify potential survey paths, meet with our USAID donors, and get official permission to work in the country, which we did not have yet. We would also need to find an attorney who had the trust of our fickle lawyers in New York to represent our interests. Once we took care of that to-do list, we then had to get our teams into some of the remotest landscapes on Earth and then bring them back alive.

And then came the essential challenge: once the teams were in the field, they would have to assess whether Afghanistan's iconic wildlife— snow leopards and Marco Polo sheep and more—and the habitats they depended on had even survived three decades of war. No one had carried out any surveys of Afghanistan's wildlife in the intervening thirty years, outside the preliminary rapid assessment that Peter Zahler had carried out through the UN Environment Programme (UNEP) Post-Conflict Assessment Unit to justify the fuller program. That assessment delineated the problems but hadn't the resources or time to systematically and carefully verify whether there were sufficient wildlife and habitats remaining to protect. If the answer was yes, WCS needed to determine how to protect these species and set up the infrastructure and capacity for biodiversity conservation within the country. This meant building the national laws and policies, governance and enforcement structures, protected areas, and building the technical capacity of our Afghan counterparts, as well as addressing new challenges that we would encounter along the way. But without the wildlife, all our work would be in vain.

We also faced some larger questions about the relevance of our project—conserving wildlife and establishing a transboundary national park—to the larger goals for Afghanistan, including security, democracy, and economic viability. How much did conservation matter to the rest of the world for a country with more pressing problems? How could we demonstrate that value to the fiercely independent Afghan people? Would the people of Afghanistan care and support our efforts? We had to get into the field to start answering these questions. But at the moment, we were in the Park Palace, and we didn't even have offices, a team, a bank account, or permission. We needed to build all of that.

We started with the basics: finding a staff and an office for the Wildlife Conservation Society. Peter had heard that CHF International, a USAID contractor, was closing down its operations, so we decided to interview their staff who would be otherwise let go. The interviews took better than a week and were completed incongruously at the garden picnic tables of the Park Palace.

Qais* was the first to interview, hoping to get the role of travel and logistics coordinator. He was dressed like the host of an Afghan game show from the 1970s. He wore a cruise ship–white suit, with a dark maroon shirt and striped tie. Formal Afghan shoes—fairylike, pointed, with long tips that curled slightly at the end—completed the outfit. Imagine a genie dressed to work at a Fortune 500 company. We hired him on the spot. As it turned out, Qais was a wedding singer as well. His slightly goofy, insecure persona wondrously transformed into a confident and polished performer once he was behind the electronic keyboard. His skills also included a deftness in handling complex logistical challenges anywhere in Afghanistan and neighboring countries, and he did it with disarming sweetness, eternal optimism, and a polite and genuine deference that extended to every person, no matter his or her rank or position. This charm allowed him to sidestep every administrative barrier, corrupt official, or bureaucrat. His logistical

---

*To protect their identities, I refer to the Afghan members of the team by their first names only.

talents were all the more incredible given that he had never once flown on a plane.

Qais was also full of surprises. He once greeted me as I was getting off a flight with, "Thank God you weren't sitting next to the dead body," offering no explanation as he hurried me to the car, repeatedly throwing worried looks back at the plane. Qais also inadvertently kidnapped and held hostage an American dentist, Jim, who he thought was the environmental law consultant for the Wildlife Conservation Society program (also named Jim and also an American, but that was where the similarities ended). Over Jim the dentist's protests, Qais hustled the American into the WCS Land Cruiser and drove to the office. Only when our acting country director was handed a phone and told to speak to the wrong Jim, while already on the phone with the right Jim, the lawyer, who had been marooned at the airport, did we realize there was a problem.

We also hired Shafiq to lead our office. Shafiq was a tall, stocky Afghan with darker Pashtun features. He was nonchalant and confident with dashes of ennui and reticence. His secret weapon was a pained look, coupled with a tilted head and open hands, reserved for corrupt officials seeking bribes. Zabih became our finance director. He was in his midthirties, with a close-cut beard and an ancient handsomeness. Zabih was eminently cool, almost an Afghan hipster, and dressed in fashionable American jeans and Western clothing, with a kind personality. And Khoja was hired to be our driver. He was sweet and gentle, with fair hair and features that were perhaps a genetic remnant of Alexander the Great's armies. He could have just walked off an ancient Greek amphora. Khoja often drove Kara out to get our favorite snack, *shir-e-yach*, a sweet ice cream, at Shahr-e Naw Park.

We were soon joined by the first of our international staffers, Etienne Delattre, a gaunt French-Belgian conservationist who worked for the WCS Asia Program as a geospatial analyst based out of Thailand, where he lived. Etienne served in a similar function for the Afghanistan program. Etienne was always desperately worried about the number of child sex offenders from Belgium and the effect it had on the reputation of a small country known for fruity Lambic beers, choc-olate, and Tintin. He also had a perpetually unimpressed air. Etienne's moods alternated between being intensely social and happy and deeply introspective and solitary, feeding off his surrounding environment.

In one of his first duties, Etienne, a capable and empathetic man-ager, helped us recruit our full-time GIS (geographic information sys-tems) officer, Haqiq, as Etienne despised the restrictive atmosphere of Kabul and worked with other WCS projects as well. However, Etienne would spend a considerable amount of time devoted to training and mentoring Haqiq, sitting side by side with him at the computer. Through Etienne's effort, Haqiq would be Afghanistan's first conser-vation GIS expert in the country, which would have a powerful impact for Afghan conservation. WCS preferentially committed to training and mentoring conservationists in the development world, rather than hiring short-term expat technical staff and development mercenaries. Our commitment to building local technical capacity would lead to our scolding at our meetings with our USAID technical leads. When we mentioned Haqiq's GIS and computer expertise and our desire to invest in him, the USAID program manager would note that this would take too long and asked, "Why don't you just hire an American instead?"

This team would soon grow—experts, consultants, additional staff—but the program started with Qais, Shafiq, Zabihullah, and Khoja. In the first month of the program, the team we built worked out of the Park Palace. We occupied the guesthouse's picnic tables all day long, and until we could buy computers, Shafiq, Qais, and Zabih took over the Park Palace's meager and dusty computer lab. Kara and I worked out of our guestroom, perched on the bed with our laptops, surrounded by piles of papers. Borrowing from a strategy I used in Iraq for main-taining a lower security profile, we rented Shafiq's Toyota Corolla, un-til the program could get its own vehicles. This was our lean start-up.

Next on the list was to get offices and a dedicated guesthouse. Peter, Kara, and I met up with Richard Scarth and his partner, Torialai Ba-hadery, at the small storefront offices of Property Consultants Afghan-istan, the city's first Western realty company. Richard, a cheerful and kind Brit, had the extraordinary idea to become a Kabul real estate agent after serving as a Royal Navy reservist in Afghanistan. Tor, an entrepreneurial Afghan, was his partner.

Richard patiently explained the unique challenges of being a real estate agent in a war zone. The authenticity of deeds, which have been mostly lost, are constantly in question. Landownership is frequently contested. It is made harder as entire neighborhoods have disappeared into rubble, and the nearly four million people who were displaced are now coming back and seeking their property, which may have been restored by someone else who now was living there. While Kabul already had plenty of real estate agents—eight thousand, to be exact—none of them were versed with dealing with Westerners. All these NGOs, contractors, journalists, and returning Western Afghans wanted housing, but there wasn't a simple way to find it. "That's why we exist," Richard noted—to help this community navigate postwar Kabul with a model the expats understood from the West.

The other reason Richard and Tor's company existed was that there was a lot of money to be made. Just as I'd experienced in other conflict zones and countries in upheaval, Afghanistan's housing prices were incredibly high, often exceeding that of expensive Western cities. A housing construction boom was under way. It was fueled by corruption, the opium trade, and billions of development and reconstruction funds, plus the presence of development and military contractors, humanitarians, war dogs, and journalists from more than forty-three nations who needed places to live and work. Even with the new construction boom, there was a serious shortage of good, sturdy housing. The rent for the house we ultimately chose for our office seemed astonishing for Afghanistan: $6,800 per month, but it was actually a bargain—some of the houses we looked at rented for $15,000–$20,000 a month. Kabul's realty market was among the hottest in Asia, and given the funding that flowed into Afghanistan, gouging was rampant, even if the newly built houses were already starting to crumble and leak from poor construction standards.

Our tour of potential offices was an education in Kabul décor. There were two dominant styles: 1970s pre–Soviet invasion chic, or the Middle East's beloved faux–Louis XIV ornateness, complete with gaudy gold-plated mirrors and crystal chandeliers. The liberal use of glass didn't pair well with IEDs.

Style was not our main concern, though. We needed a headquarters and a secure place to live that wasn't the Park Palace. Within a day of arriving in Kabul, I came down with a fever and debilitating stomach ailments. I lurched from house to house as we assessed each new place's layout, structural integrity, and security risks. Peter viewed the real-estate hunt with roughly the attitude of Genghis Khan's hordes sizing up the next village. He kept driving us forward with little mercy for my illness. When we returned to the Park Palace from our excursions, I threw up and collapsed on a large pile of Richard's colorful housing flyers boasting numbers of bedrooms, bathrooms, and other amenities.

Security was always on our minds as we reviewed each house. State Department travel warnings for Afghanistan laid out the biggest risks: terrorism, IEDs, kidnappings, and land mines. The only thing more ubiquitous than worries about safety was the Toyota Corolla. There was a fundamental conviction in Afghanistan that only one car was strong enough to endure the country's potholed roads: the trusty Corolla, preferably in white (which would immediately turn gray in the blanket of dust). Even the newest arrival to Kabul noticed that seemingly 90 percent of the cars on the street were Toyota Corollas. The risk of vehicle-borne bombs was very real, and flash updates from the embassy kept us apprised of reported IEDs. The report invariably told us to look out for an older-model white Corolla. After reading the warning, we looked out at the sea of Corollas, each invoking a sense of déjà vu, wondering which one contained our IED.

These State Department warnings, however, didn't account for the quiet dangers lurking in newer Afghan houses. Traditional homes were single-story buildings with sturdy, meter-thick mud walls, reinforced with wood, set behind an equally thick exterior wall, but they

were rarely large enough for an NGO. The more modern houses in
Kabul—the homes of warlords, drug traffickers, and corrupt government officials—were known as "birthday cake" houses—flat-roofed,
multistoried, garish, and poorly made. These birthday cakes would almost certainly collapse the next time a major earthquake hit Kabul.

We wound up in a birthday cake.

Wintertime brought another dilemma: shiver through bone-numbing
cold, or risk carbon monoxide poisoning trying to stay warm. The birthday cake houses' design was cold—both in their forlorn appearance and
their lack of insulation. Afghan houses did not have central heating or
cooling. The traditional houses naturally retained heat through their
thick mud walls. In the winter, we covered our windows with clear
plastic wrap to keep in the heat, but that was not enough. We had
two choices for supplemental heat. We could use the bukhari, a simple
stove heater that runs off sawdust, paraffin, gas, or petrol, or we could
use a Chinese-made, open-flame gas heater. The bukhari, albeit warm,
was a silent killer. Every winter in Kabul brought word of at least one
NGO with staff who suffocated from breathing the carbon monoxide
released by their bukhari.

Our fear of the bukhari suffocating us in our sleep led us to use
the cheap open-flame gas heaters. These had another limitation: their
warmth ended a foot away from the flames, and not only did they not
heat the whole room, but they usually didn't do more than heat the
closest appendage. We wore our puffy down parkas as we worked. To
get the chills out, we would get as close as possible to the fire, which in-
evitably meant a flaming parka at some point during the winter, which
was still a better choice than dying by carbon monoxide. I ultimately
melted two goose-down parkas trying to stay warm in my frozen office.
Beyond being crushed by concrete floors in earthquakes, asphyxiation
by stove, and bursting into flames while trying to keep warm, we faced
another danger in the house. Never mind the Taliban, our bathrooms
were trying to kill us as well.

To supply hot water and make up for the lack of pressure in the
pipes, the hot water tanks both heated water and pressurized it, not

unlike a literal pressure cooker. And much like any badly made pressure cooker, these poorly made units occasionally exploded. When water changes from a liquid to a gas, it expands by 1,600 times. Weaknesses in the metal allowed them to change from a solid tank into flying pieces of shrapnel with no warning—not the best accompaniment to showering or using the toilet. One morning, our heater exploded just after I'd left the bathroom, shattering into numerous pieces of shrapnel.

Despite these challenges, we were relatively lucky, real-estate-wise. A three-story, eight-bedroom house in Shahr-e Naw became our office. Our headquarters was near the main city park and movie theater (we would later use the park for training our field teams) and not far from Kabul's first large modern shopping mall. The Safi Landmark tower was nine stories of green-glass ostentation, fueled by American nation-building dollars. It was full of cappuccino bars and ice cream shops, beauty stores, iPhones, watches, DVD sets of American television shows, and appliances, watched over by aloof security guards who waved everyone through the beeping metal detector.

We also found a beautiful guesthouse in the Qual-e-Fatullah, a quiet corner of Kabul that was home to Afghan families and a few small NGO houses, where children flew kites through the streets. Our simple three-story house boasted a slender, scraggly pomegranate tree that produced bushels of fruit, and a roof patio with brilliant views that allowed you to see the snowy mountains that surrounded Kabul. A lack of diplomatic or military targets kept the area safe; our Afghan neighbors hosted parties in their backyards. The local bakery sold wondrously fresh Afghan naan—warm, two-foot oval sheets of bread cooked in a brick tandoor oven and sprinkled with black caraway seeds. Children would fly kites in the neighborhood. One morning, I got my own kite from a local neighborhood store and climbed to the roof and launched it against the blue Afghan sky. Another kite suddenly appeared and slowly made its way to my kite and then quickly cut the string of my own kite, setting my kite free from its leash. I watched the children chasing after their spoils of victory from a game that I didn't know I was playing. Next door was an NGO that promoted low-cost, solar cookstoves. These stoves were wonderful solutions in a country that had been denuded of its forests, except these particular models didn't seem to work well. Every time we would pass the house, the NGO's guards were looking forlorn as they watched and waited for their teakettle to boil under Kabul's overcast skies.

Overlooking the neighborhood was the fort of Kolola Pushta, which resembled the curled brown woolen hat of the Pashtun people. Also nearby was the British Cemetery, a literal graveyard of empire filled with a small fraction of the dead from the British-Afghan wars. It was a reminder of the two sides of this country: Afghans are friendly and gracious hosts but fierce fighters against those who overstay their welcome.

We had an office to work in, a guesthouse to live in, and a staff for the operations, but we still needed furniture and technical equipment. Chairs and desks were easy enough, but finding specialized technology posed a greater challenge. We already had problems finding a source for legally licensed software; merchants in Afghanistan sold expertly pirated software from Iran that was professionally packaged, fully functional, and a fraction of the cost of regular software. Despite our best efforts, we couldn't find licensed versions of major software packages in Afghanistan.

In particular, we needed a large-format printer to create high-resolution maps. Etienne and Haqiq were setting up a geospatial office that would support us in planning wildlife surveys, analyzing the results of our expeditions, and using that data to develop our conservation programs and delineate the boundaries of the proposed protected areas. The printer was a critical part of the new office. That meant we had to go shopping. We tried store after store until we finally found a merchant who could secure us a new large-format printer. A few days later, he delivered our printer to the office. Haqiq called me in to have a look, sounding concerned.

"I think something is wrong with it. It doesn't look new. It doesn't have any protective materials around it, there aren't any instructions, and it wasn't boxed," he said.

That's when we noticed the rectangular, orange sticker on the printer, which read: TOP SECRET. And below it: U.S. GOVERNMENT PROPERTY.

War and rebuilding brought hordes of American soldiers, development officers, and diplomats to Afghanistan. The Americans brought . . . stuff. Guns, tanks, and all sorts of weaponry, but also snacks, toiletries, and other sundries not usually available on this side of the world. Many of these items quickly found their way to what became known as the Bush Market, a labyrinth of hundreds of stalls, cheekily named after President George W. Bush. Classified laptops and flash drives, commercial containers of cooking oil, A1 steak sauce and Heinz ketchup, jars of protein powder, Colgate toothpaste, Red Bull energy drinks, Pop-Tarts and Clif Bars, and military-issue MREs (meals ready to eat). Even the plastic bags handed out at some stalls bore Army and Air Force Exchange Service labels. According to one study, 1 percent of American military shipments into Afghanistan never make it to their destination. That figure, which probably didn't include pilfering on bases, amounts to 790 truckloads of gear and supplies per year. It was likely that much of those supplies ended up here.

At the Bush Market, we bought Special Forces sleeping bags, still in the package, and MREs by the dozen in boxes stamped with warnings that resale was illegal. The MREs proved useful for field teams in remote locations; they had an incredible number of calories. They also reliably led to constipation, which proved useful when traveling in situations where a bathroom break could be dangerous. The market offered Pringles, a food found in nearly every one of the eighty countries I've visited around the world and whose omnipresence is a testament to the extraordinary global distribution systems of Kellogg's. Odd items also surfaced for sale in the Bush Market—commercial failures from around the world, products that were manufactured in numbers larger than their demand, ended up in a small stall in Afghanistan. In a Bush Market stall, I sampled promotional dirt-, grass-, and grasshopper-flavored Jelly Bellies that were made for the children's animated movie *Antz*. I bought a pack. They tasted remarkably realistic as far as I could tell.

There was a similar market outside the main air base in Bagram, a former Soviet facility. But these sprawling markets weren't new; they were Afghan tradition. During the Soviet invasion, the Bush Market was known as the Brezhnev Market. Where the American version sold lots of candies and consumer goods, the Soviet-era market was mostly military gear.

Our printer most likely came from the Bush Market. I called the seller and told him he was in trouble. The truth was that I minded him lying to us and selling us a *used* printer more than I minded him selling us top-secret government property; since there weren't any flash drives or memory on the printer, it was unlikely to contain any suspect information. Nonetheless, I called up the US embassy's diplomatic security team and asked them to inspect it and clear the purchase. Although I purposely scared the seller by telling him that the US military would soon visit him, I could hardly blame him. He was doing the same thing we had done with the MREs and Special Forces sleeping bags. The bustling black market captured the resourcefulness of Afghans, honed over a long history of invasion, civil war, and strife. It wasn't stealing or trafficking so much as a way to survive.

As WE WERE setting up the office, security was constantly on my mind. The Park Palace had been attacked by an angry crowd after a US military track lost its brakes and killed some Afghan civilians a few weeks before we had arrived. The crash tapped into latent resentment of the US military presence and radiated throughout the city like a pressure wave. As the country director, I was responsible for the lives of everyone that worked with us in Afghanistan, Western and Afghan alike. This included my partner, Kara Stevens. Kara, a kind, beautiful, deeply empathetic, and sweet but fiercely independent woman who had served in the Peace Corps in Nepal and would later do her doctoral work in the remote parts of the Mosquito Coast of Nicaragua, chafed at my attempts to restrict her travel, especially after car bombs. We not only had to consider traditional security risks faced by all organizations working in Afghanistan—kidnappings, IEDs, suicide bombers, mines, exploding water heaters—but we also faced a set of challenges that almost no organization would face, operating in some of the remotest areas in the world. These were areas without roads, where travel would have to be by yak or horse for days and even weeks. We would work in extreme environments at high elevations, where our team would need to learn to take care of themselves until we could get help to them.

To make sure I fully understood the security risks in Afghanistan, I set up a meeting with a staff member of the Afghan NGO Security Office (ANSO) a few weeks after I arrived. ANSO was dedicated to providing security advice for NGOs operating in the country. As a gift, Shafiq and other Afghan staff members had taken me to the tailor's to get a shalwar kameez, the traditional Afghan outfit of a long shirt and loose pants. I had also grown a beard, and as a Persian American, my beard comes in quickly, thick and dark. On the day of my meeting with the ANSO staffer, Khoja drove me, decked out in shalwar kameez and beard, to a café in Kabul and left me there, as he had other errands to run.

I had been e-mailing a German named Christian from ANSO and set the meeting at the café. Christian was going to brief me on some of the places we intended to work—Band-e-Amir, Nuristan, and Wakhan. I walked into the dark café, but there was no sign of Christian or anyone else. Finally, after a half hour of waiting, a white European man quickly peered inside of the café, and, seeing only a bearded man in Afghan garb, closed the door and left. I jumped up from the table and ran after him. He was already some distance down the dusty street when I yelled out his name.

"Christian!"

He briefly looked back but kept walking, perhaps a few steps faster. I quickened my steps to try to overtake him and called to him again.

"Hey, Christian!"

He looked back again with a puzzled and apprehensive look and then doubled his speed to a jog. I started jogging to match his speed. I shouted out again, with extra emphasis.

"*Hey, Christian!*" He looked back again and did not stop, to my annoyance. I wondered, and I yelled as loudly as I could, "*Hey, are you Christian?*"

At this point, the European turned back to me, a mask of fear squeezing his face, and responded in something like anguish, "Yes, I am, but why does it matter?"

I stopped in my tracks. As I watched the man, now in a full sprint, I realized I had just terrified a poor God-loving European who probably thought I wanted to kill him as an infidel because of his religion. I later heard from the real ANSO director, Christian, apologizing that he wasn't able to make our appointment. I wonder if the other European filed a security incident report with ANSO or the UN as the result of our encounter. "Be on the lookout for aggressive Afghans who ask about your religion while chasing you down the street. They probably drive a late-model Toyota Corolla."

Along with the office staff, we hired the security staff from CHF International to get things jump-started; they were already vetted, knew Western procedures, and had worked together as a team. Sabour became our head of security. Sabour was a big, quiet, and gentle man who also looked the part of an enforcer. When we were off work and enjoying ourselves, Sabour danced like a graceful Frankenstein, his arms outstretched straight and rigid, while his shoulders moved up and down in steady jerks while his hands twisted to the melody. He radiated kindness, but it was clear that he had the capacity to do whatever he needed to keep us safe. Another member of our security detail was Karim, a tall, smart, and quiet Hazara. A remnant population descended from Genghis Khan's invading army, the Hazara people mostly live in the Hazarajat Plateau, which punches into the center of Afghanistan, where we hoped to create our first national park. As Ismaili followers of the Aga Khan, the Hazara were heavily persecuted under the Taliban. As many Afghans left the country after the Soviet invasion, including six million that became unwelcome refugees in Pakistan and Iran, such as Qais and Shafiq, I wondered what Karim did under the Taliban since he didn't leave the country and given the Taliban's hatred of the Ismaili.

I asked him once if he'd ever run into any problems.

"I never went outside," he told me. "Under the Taliban, all men were required to grow beards that were two fists long; failure to do so meant staying in prison until you were able to. I couldn't grow facial hair, so I stayed inside. For five years. I wove carpets to keep busy, all day and all night for five years."

Karim's story, while shocking, was not unusual. All Afghans have some kind of story that would seem amazing in the West. For many, hidden below a frequently engaging and optimistic outlook were stories of incredible hardship, courage, tragedy, unfairness, and resilience. This is what made the kindness of the Afghan people so extraordinary; they had every reason not to be hospitable.

Although we didn't have any guns, that didn't mean we wouldn't have strong security systems in place. The office did have extremely high walls—more than fifteen feet high—and a very thick and rein-forced door, a common feature of Afghan houses. The biggest threat was someone coming in intending to hurt us. I decided that everyone coming in and out—men and women, visitors and staff—would be searched with metal detectors, including myself. This was inconvenient, but it also meant there was no excuse for failing to search someone. As a test, we built fake suicide-bomb vests and bought replica pistols. We had the staff members try to sneak them in. One day, we wrapped a fake explosive belt, loaded with Styrofoam C-4, around Qais's waist. The cheerful, upbeat Qais was the last person anyone would suspect as a suicide bomber.

Sabour, Karim, and Dad Ali—a round-faced Hazara guard—weren't fooled. The three of them quickly took off Qais's white suit jacket and threw him against the wall, pinning his arms before jettison-ing the mild-mannered wedding singer onto the dirt outside the office and locking the door behind him. It would be an hour before they let him back in, despite his constant pleas for them to open the door, as he had work to do. I was satisfied that the security team was serious about the work of conservation.

We took other precautions. We lined the floor of our Land Cruis-ers with ballistic blankets to offer some moderate protection against driving over a mine (although the effect of such an attack would be to launch the vehicle into the air). We couldn't weigh down the car with side armor since we would get stuck going into rivers, so we lived with the risk of gunfire penetrating the sides of the vehicles. And we trained all our team members as first responders through an organization called RMSI, run by a cheerful former Australian paramedic named Rob Lamb. While working as a contractor in volatile areas in Iraq, Lamb saw shortfalls in medical services firsthand. That drove him to launch a service for complex and high-risk rescues. We set up communication systems using two types of satellite phones to locate our teams in the field and required them to check in on a daily basis. Within forty-eight hours of a missed check-in, high-altitude helicopters and a team of highly armed sharpshooters would arrive on the scene, although this didn't always happen immediately. Even with these elements in place, the best safety measure was ensuring our teams could rescue themselves.

Rob personally ran a daylong training session at our offices. After an intensive session on CPR and the Heimlich maneuver, Rob feigned choking to test the staff. His performance spurred Shafiq into action. Unfortunately, Shafiq forgot what he had just learned. Instead of clearing Rob's airways, he found a glass of water and threw it into Rob's face.

FINALLY, AS WE sought to get our infrastructure and team into place, we also needed to start engaging our USAID and Afghan counterparts. Two Afghan government organizations played key roles in environmental management—the National Environmental Protection Agency (NEPA) and the Ministry of Agriculture, Irrigation and Livestock (MAIL). NEPA was headed up by the extremely charming grandson of the popular former monarch King Mohammed Zahir Shah, Prince Mostapha Zaher. Prince Zaher would be a critical ally in the push for creating the national parks and, like his grandfather, was Afghanistan's steadiest ally of conservation. The charismatic Prince Zaher was an eloquent speaker and able ambassador for his country. He came of age during the Russian invasion and civil war, which he spent in European exile—stints in Rome, Vienna, London, and finally a degree from

Queen's University in Canada. Handsome, imposing, polished, and eloquent, Zaher looked the part of a prince. Having served as Afghanistan's ambassador extraordinary and plenipotentiary to Italy, Greece, and Cyprus and special presidential envoy to the Balkans, he was also an experienced diplomat. After NEPA came into existence in 2005, Prince Zaher was invited to head it up. He continued in this role until 2017 when he was appointed to the Afghan senate.

Our first meeting with Prince Zaher covered lots of ground: his love for Afghanistan's biodiversity—which came from his grandfather, the last king—and a description of the environmental and political challenges that lay ahead. He highlighted the fact that 80 percent of the people in a largely rural country depended on the environment for their survival. Prince Zaher would make the claim that Afghanistan's new foundational environmental law was one of the most important pieces of legislation in Afghanistan's history. NEPA's mandate would work through three functions—the development of new policies (the behavior and course of action of the government toward conservation), the creation of new laws and regulations on the environment (the system of rules regulating the government and its citizens), and the enforcement of those laws, regulations, and policies.

NEPA had been born from people and resources extracted from the Ministry of Energy and Water and the Ministry of Agriculture and was now therefore a competitor for resources and presidential attention. The scuttlebutt was that the NEPA staffers were personnel the Ministry of Energy and Water wanted to shed. Moreover, like many things in Afghanistan, it was heavily under-resourced for the challenges it faced. Sixty percent of NEPA's meager $640,000 annual budget was earmarked for salaries. The remainder was far too little to make much impact, so donors and technical organizations like WCS and UNEP needed to provide additional resources and capacity.

In Prince Zaher's view, Afghanistan needed to develop a new guard of environmentalists who could shape conservation's future, not duplicate approaches from its past. This was a prescient statement and held true beyond Afghanistan. For many reasons, conservation was not succeeding in meeting the speed and the scale of the challenges that were driving biodiversity loss, so why should Afghanistan adopt failing approaches? This would give us the opportunity to innovate.

We would also need the support of the Ministry of Agriculture in building protected areas. Our counterparts at the ministry included three different personalities. Abdul Ghani Ghurriani was the deputy director general for natural resources management at the Ministry of Agriculture. He looked like a happier, dark-haired version of Lenin, and we took an immediate liking to his enthusiasm. Although he studied at the University of Kabul, he had also trained at the University of Wisconsin and was a thoughtful advocate for conservation in Afghanistan and soon became an advocate for WCS. He would later rise quickly in the ministry, obtaining the rank of deputy minister of agriculture.

Ghani's boss was Eng. Hashim Barakzai. (Eng., for *Engineer*, is a formal title, like Dr., in Afghanistan and the Middle East.) Barakzai was an elegant, tall, fit Afghan with neatly trimmed white hair and impeccable suits and pressed shirts; he lived in London when not in Afghanistan. He worked with us as a forceful and passionate advocate for creating the national parks.

Lastly, Eng. Hazrat Hussain Khaurin—who served as the director general of the Forest and Rangeland Department, which seemed to have completely overlapping competencies with the Natural Resource Management Department—was more difficult. Khaurin's job seemed to be obstruction, while encouraging us to supplement low government salaries with private funding. The UN Environment Programme had adopted the practice of making such payments to encourage highly qualified Afghans to stay in government service, which was understandable, but it put organizations like WCS in a difficult position since the practice seemed too close to structured corruption. We also had to avoid another very tempting practice in any country with low levels of capacity—we couldn't hire highly effective staff away from government positions. Poaching them for our team amounted to undermining our own efforts to build capacity and achieve our goals.

We needed the help of both ministries—the Ministry of Agriculture and NEPA. The solution we hit upon was dispatching Kara to embed herself in the Ministry of Agriculture. This would shrink the gulf between us and a critical partner, but it also forced Kara to take risks on a daily basis by driving through Kabul to the ministry offices. This was the same risk that Afghans took every day, though that fact didn't make me feel less nervous for her safety. We soon learned that the same challenges that affect governments in the US affected governments in Afghanistan—the need for visible political deliverables (in this case, trees planted) and the failure of leadership to bring real change to moribund and insufficiently funded institutions.

For all the stress over collaborating with the Afghan agencies, our biggest challenge proved to be our funder, the US Agency for International Development (USAID). Depending on the political administration in power in Washington, USAID is either seen as part of the State Department or as independent from it. The differences between the two organizations were noticeable. USAID, which was established by President Kennedy over fifty years ago along with the Peace Corps, works in some of the most difficult places in the world and on more technical issues, including food security, global health, energy access, water, education, biodiversity conservation, democracy and governance, and humanitarian response. USAID staff took pride in their fieldwork as much as the State Department took pride in their polished and measured appearances. While the State Department represented the nation itself, USAID represented the nation's generosity.

Although both agencies had their own foreign service, and USAID officials achieving the most senior rank of minister counselor at USAID could go on to become an ambassador, the reality was very different. We could see this in Kabul. USAID officials weren't housed in the beautiful offices and New York–style lofts provided for State Department staffers in the Kabul embassy. USAID's team, rather, lived in a trailer park across the canyon of concrete barriers that bisected the American compound. The walls of barriers spoke to the divide that existed between the Department of State and the aid agency. Although the WCS

Afghanistan Program was funded by USAID, our supporters in Kabul came from the State Department and the Defense Department, who better understood the value of our work and directly benefited from it.

We didn't have that opportunity with USAID. This may have been because while the Afghanistan program was focused on nation-building, this meant more mundane things to them—roads, governance, and food security. The connection with the environment was not immediately clear. In Washington, we had the support of the forestry and biodiversity team, but in Kabul, we seemed to have few friends in the USAID mission. The second issue was that WCS had started the contract late. We had received funding months before my arrival, but the program was just getting under way.

Our first contact at USAID was Dan, a former cowboy, yak herder, and rangeland scientist. He seemed supportive, but he left not long after we arrived. A litany of USAID cognizant technical officers, or CTOs for short, followed, each with different ideas and frequently conflicting directions to us about the program and the country (which they rarely saw beyond Kabul).

Our first official meeting, a month into our start-up, was with Lina, a kind Filipino foreign service national, and our CTO, Al, a rotund man clad in denim overalls who seemed to have walked straight out of a county fair.

In our meeting, I laid out what we had accomplished in the first month. We had set up a base of operations in a safe and affordable facility. We had teams equipped, permissions from authorities secured, and the support of two key government agencies—NEPA and the Ministry of Agriculture. We were training Afghans to work as GIS specialists and conservationists. And within thirty days of our arrival, we had teams in the field doing the first wildlife surveys since the Soviet invasion.

The CTO interrupted me.

"I don't care what you are doing substantively; what I care about is your burn rate. What is your burn rate?"

"My what?" I responded, confused.

"What is your burn rate? How fast are you spending money?"

I was flummoxed. "I'm not sure."

The CTO was incensed and continued. "Why are you trying to save money with a guesthouse when you could be staying at the Serena?" The Serena was a five-star hotel in the center of Kabul. "And why are you training an Afghan as a GIS specialist? Just hire a Westerner who already has the skills. You shouldn't be saving money; you need to be spending it."

Burn rate is development lingo (and ironically, also start-up lingo) for how fast you go through money. In the start-up world (and the common-sense world), you want to minimize your burn rate. But in international development, the burn rate is an indicator of impact that the USAID Mission in Afghanistan can report to Washington. How the money is spent doesn't matter. Just how fast. In wars in Iraq and Afghanistan, frequently the expenditure of money was the easiest proxy of progress for Congress to track. I would later discover that USAID's systems around the world didn't track what USAID's contractors and partners did or where they did it below the country level, only the amounts that were spent.

This was the first of many times I found myself stunned and disillusioned. The world's biggest development agency didn't care about the nature of the work, as long as it gobbled up cash. Their real constituency was Capitol Hill, rather than the people of Afghanistan.

In that moment in Kabul, twisted logic won the day. This was the beginning of a troubled relationship for us. We would develop strong partnerships with the Afghan government, the State Department, the Department of Defense, and the International Security Assistance Force (ISAF) in Afghanistan, and even local tribes. But never with USAID, who had made our role in Afghanistan possible.

CHAPTER 3

AFGHANISTAN'S
BIOLOGICAL SILK ROAD

T HE WAKHAN CORRIDOR, a frigid finger of Afghanistan, squeezes between Tajikistan and Pakistan for hundreds of kilometers, across
the western reaches of the great Himalayan range to the Chinese border. Wakhan is a paradox: it is deeply isolated, hidden by high mountain walls, and located near the "pole of inaccessibility" of the Eurasian
landmass. But it has also been a great crossroads and highway for wildlife and people throughout history. The Afghans also refer to the corridor as Bam-e-Duniya—the roof of the world. From the high peaks that
line Wakhan, a traveler on the Silk Road had a vista onto the succession
of empires that have surrounded Afghanistan.

Fifty million years before any of those empires, a massive, slow-
motion collision of continental plates created Wakhan and the rest of
the Himalayas. What is now India sat 6,400 kilometers south of the
Eurasian plate, with the shallow waters of the second Tethys Sea between them. The Indian plate—containing the Indian subcontinent and
surrounding ocean—rode northward on the hidden convection cur-
rents generated in Earth's inner mantle. As India approached Asia, the
Tethys Sea began to shrink. The collision between the Indian and Eurasian plates crumpled and folded relatively light sedimentary and meta-
morphic rock that makes up both plates, as neither subducted. Some

of the sediments rising from the former Tethys seabed scraped across the newly created mountain range, the majestic Himalayas, sprinkling oceanic fossils among the high alpine peaks.

Amid this corrugated topography is a place deeply remote and hidden, a narrow passageway for men and wildlife through the mountains. The Wakhan Corridor is 220 kilometers long but only 16–64 kilometers wide, cut off from the Afghan heartland and enclosed by the icy ramparts of the Pamir, Kunlun, and Tien Shan ranges, as well as the mighty Hindu Kush. These mountain walls essentially channel the global north–south bird migrations east–west. They served to separate global empires. Wakhan is a place of few roads, fewer people, and freezing temperatures: Over 80 percent of the Afghan Wakhan-Pamir area is about three thousand meters in elevation, and during winter, temperatures can drop to –50°C (–58°F). Coupled with the winds that blow along the corridor, it can get even colder. Marco Polo passed through Wakhan on his travels and complained about its climate, noting in his travelogue from the trip, *The Travels of Marco Polo*, "Because of this great cold, fire does not burn so brightly, nor give out so much heat as usual, nor does it cook food so effectually." This remark holds true even today; Wakhan was a cold, wild, and desolate place, and it took its toll on travelers and vehicles alike. I was surprised one morning in Wakhan to see our Afghan drivers tending a small fire under the gas tank of our vehicle to keep the fuel from freezing.

During the Great Game between Imperial Russia and British India, the Wakhan Corridor served as a natural strategic buffer. Under Secretary Leonid Brezhnev, the Soviets were planning on annexing Wakhan, but Brezhnev's death and the different priorities of his successor, Mikhail Gorbachev, prevented that from occurring. Even today, nestled between Tajikistan to the north, Pakistan and India to the south, and China to the east, this sliver of Afghanistan cuts across conflict and chaos. Geographic remoteness allowed Wakhan's people and wildlife to ignore—and largely be ignored by—the thirty years of strife that have devastated the rest of Afghanistan. In fact, the corridor became something of a desolate refugium from conflict and crisis. But the region has its own problems; opiate addiction has destroyed underlying social systems and economies. Addicts in Wakhan traded their wealth, measured in livestock, for opium. The region, never an easy place to live, is now in decline, but WCS hoped to reverse that.

The massive collision of tectonic plates that pushed Wakhan to the roof of the world had another effect; it created habitat—lots and lots of habitat—that could support many different species at the juncture of the continents. That made Wakhan an important area for our conservation work. Lower Wakhan, in the west, includes the Panj River Valley, which is part of the headwaters for the Amu Darya River, known historically as the Oxus. Before the Soviets attempted unsustainable scales of cotton agriculture and killed the Amu Darya, its waters once replenished the shallow Aral Sea, which has largely disappeared. In the east, Wakhan can be divided into three regions vital for biodiversity conservation—the Great Pamir Mountain Range, the Little Pamir, and the Waghjir Valley. These three areas were at the heart of our conservation efforts in this corner of Afghanistan.

The Great Pamir Range (also known as the Big Pamir) is a vast area extending about 5,500 square kilometers. It is here that a massive block of mountains forms the western end of the Pamir knot, a turbulent frozen sea of granite, snow, and ice in the sky. Here, the highest peaks rise to above 6,000 meters (above 20,000 feet) with the highest peak at 6,900 meters (22,638 feet). At the end of the Great Pamir lies Lake Zorkul, which is part of the headwaters of the Pamir River. Fed by the glaciers that surround it, it is home to spectacular birdlife. Prior to 1968, the Great Pamir was a royal hunting reserve for King Zahir Shah, like many of the current proposed national parks in Afghanistan. Between 1968 and 1977, the Big Pamir Wildlife Reserve was opened up to foreigners who wanted to hunt the legendary Marco Polo sheep (*Ovis ammon polii*), the largest wild sheep in the world. The Big Pamir was designated to become a wildlife park, but the Soviet invasion upended those plans, and, like many of the other protected areas WCS proposed, it was never legally established.

Little Pamir is the extension of the Wakhan Corridor; it is the easternmost end of the corridor and of Afghanistan itself. It is here, roadless and wild, that the Pamir—the rolling valley entrapped by the mountains—is at its widest. In this place, the Wakhi have their summer settlements, and nomadic Kyrgyz set their camps. Marco Polo described the fertility of the river floodplain and the hidden valley and its wildlife in 1273 while crossing what are now the Afghan and Tajik Pamirs on his way to China, fortune, and fame. He noted about the Little Pamir as

> a high place where the traveler finds a plain between the mountains, with a lake from which lowers a fine river. Here is the best pasturage in the world; for a lean beast grows fat in ten days. Wild game of every sort abounds, and there are great quantities of wild sheep of huge size. Their horns grow to as much as six palms in length and are never less than three or four. From these horns the shepherds make bowls from which they feed, and also fences to keep in their flocks. There are also innumerable wolves, which devour many of the wild rams. The horns and bones of the sheep are found in such numbers that men build cairns of them beside the tracks to serve as landmarks to travelers in the snowy season.*

This latter reference to Marco Polo sheep was the first to describe the species that would bear his name.

The third conservation area was the Waghjir Valley. To reach it would take WCS teams a hard week's travel by yak or mule from the closest drop-off point at the town about Sarhad-e-Brogil (China is much closer to Waghjir, but they have been adamant about keeping their border closed). The difficult trek was worth it. Waghjir was largely uninhabited and used by Kyrgyz only for yak grazing in winter. Its very remoteness and lack of human presence made it among the most spectacular places for wildlife in Wakhan and one of the best places to

---

*Rustichello da Pisa and Marco Polo, *The Travels of Marco Polo, the Venetian*, trans. Ronald Latham (New York: Penguin Books, 1958).

find Marco Polo sheep populations. The Waghjir Valley is divided by the Waghjir River, which originates in the glacier that Lord George Curzon, who became the viceroy of India, proclaimed was the source of the Oxus—the Amu Darya River. There were rumors that in the winter, Marco Polo sheep cross the Yuli between China and Afghanistan here, trampling politics with impunity as they freely cross back and forth across the remote border. We also heard stories that anyone approaching the pass would be shot.

Despite (or because of) its bleak isolation, Wakhan's wide, rolling valley floors, supervised by snowy glaciers creeping down the steep ramparts of the western Himalayas, are home to snow leopards, brown bears, and, as mentioned, Marco Polo sheep. WCS sought to learn what had happened to the wildlife of Wakhan over the previous thirty years. In particular, we focused on two apex species as indicators of the ecosystem's health: Marco Polo sheep and the ghostly snow leopards (*Panthera uncia*) that hunt them.

ABOUT A MONTH after our arrival in Afghanistan, we sent teams into the Wakhan Corridor, one of the remotest places on the planet. Our program had already been delayed, and as a result, we faced tremendous pressure from USAID to start spending money and demonstrating visible progress. USAID was under tremendous pressure by Congress to show successes in Afghanistan, to the American people, even as Afghanistan was sliding back into conflict. We didn't even have our own vehicles yet, so we rented some for the trip.

Wildlife Conservation Society teams would be surveying the Marco Polo sheep population. These animals are the most famous residents of the Pamirs and one of the biggest. Marco Polo sheep are nearly twice the size of other wild sheep. They may reach up to 180 kilograms, with horns that can grow to nearly two meters in length following the curve of their impressive spirals. The sheep inhabit high-rolling uplands and broad alpine valleys at elevations up to five thousand meters (seventeen thousand feet) in the Pamirs. The name *Pamir* refers to these wide-open basin valleys at elevation, an ideal landscape for the mountain sheep as well as the nomadic Kyrgyz population. For much of the year, Marco Polo sheep live in large herds, segregated by sex. Females and young form groups of fifty or more animals. As the males mature, they start forming bachelor bands. Eventually, the bachelors join into large groups of adult males. During the rut, which takes place in November and early December, the groups merge, and a great contest takes place. Males fight for supremacy and their choice of ewes (although "sneaky copulators" pursue an alternative strategy to brute strength).

Despite that the West was unaware of the existence of Marco Polo sheep until their namesake's description of them, these mountain monarchs were iconic to local inhabitants for thousands of years. According to work done by the anthropologist John Mock, the people of the Pamirs viewed wild ungulates as "pure" creatures associated with the spiritual world.* The inhabitants of Wakhan inscribed them on petroglyphs predating the birth of Christ. They painted the sheep's image on the walls of their houses, used the horns of the sheep to decorate their houses and shrines, and created giant cairns that served as guideposts to travelers in the deep snows of winter.

In some ways, Wakhan, isolated by the high peaks of the Pamirs, had escaped the worst of the initial Russian invasion. The initial UNEP rapid assessment of the Marco Polo sheep, carried out by FAO (Food and Agriculture Organization) scientist Anthony Fitzherbert, suggested that the Russian occupation was fairly disciplined on maintaining order, and Russian military policy forbade the soldiers from hunting the sheep. Moreover, local hunters, not wanting to get shot by the Red Army as members of the mujahideen, refrained from hunting them as well.

However, the situation changed after the Russian withdrawal. The country was now flooded with the weapons of war that were more readily available for hunting. Moreover, due to the chaos and disorder of the civil war, poorly disciplined and provisioned Afghan troops on both

---

*John Mock, "The Discursive Construction of Reality in the Wakhi Community of Northern Pakistan" (doctoral dissertation, University of California–Berkeley, 1998).

sides of the conflict started shooting the Marco Polo sheep in large numbers for meat. This, coupled with unfettered overgrazing of the rangelands, decimated their numbers.

We therefore not only needed to understand the status of Marco Polo sheep populations but also their potential conflict and competition with domestic livestock. The goals of study were to get an accurate estimate of Marco Polo sheep population numbers, sex ratios, and distribution, which would give us our baselines as to the health of the population. We also wanted to better understand Marco Polo sheep behavior, how they interacted with Kyrgyz and Wakhi herders, their use of the habitat and requirements, and if they behaved differently in Afghanistan than neighboring populations in other countries. Next, we wanted to determine whether Marco Polo sheep populations were part of a larger transboundary population that moved across the borders of the three countries surrounding Wakhan, creating a single genetic population. We also needed to understand the potential threats to the population—this included predation by snow leopards, hunting by humans, food availability and competition with domestic animals, and disease risks. Finally, we wanted to understand the wildlife values in the local communities that interacted with Marco Polo sheep.

This would be a difficult task. Our ability to study the sheep was extremely limited by two factors. First, the Marco Polo sheep were extremely skittish of human presence, which prevented us from getting closer than a quarter mile for direct observation. On several occasions, when disturbed, the sheep sometimes ran for kilometers until they reached the next valley. Given the high elevation, challenging terrain, and extreme weather conditions, it was going to be a difficult study to do directly. Simultaneously, we were limited in our ability to follow the Marco Polo sheep remotely. Commercial drones would not become commonly available until nearly a decade later, and in any case, there wasn't access to power sources to recharge them. Collaring the sheep with satellite collars was also difficult; the skittishness provided one problem, but there was a second issue as well, a strange syndrome called *capture myopathy*, where the sheep would fall over dead when caught.

Capture myopathy hastens death in ungulates (hooved animals, like Marco Polo sheep) during periods of incredible stress. So sensitive were such species that when darted and captured, the animal died while immobilized. Although a number of factors contributed to capture myopathy, the stress of immobility—particularly combined with other factors like body temperature (overheating after being chased) coupled with nutrient and mineral availability in soil—triggered an instant death. One explanation offered for this syndrome was that rather than go through the pain of being eaten while alive by a predator, the animals chose to die on their own terms. However, this behavior seems highly maladaptive; it provides no fitness advantage to a species, nothing to ensure that this behavior would be preferentially passed from generation to generation. In any case, the Marco Polo sheep's skittishness and the difficult terrain, coupled with the risk of capture myopathy, made it nearly impossible for us to dart them and fit them with satellite transmitters for easier monitoring, nor could we easily monitor them directly or even get accurate counts. We needed to find another way to uncover the population structure and size of the species without drones, helicopters, or dart guns. The solution was to collect their dung, carry samples for weeks, and look at their population structure through genetics.

While our surveys of the sheep were important, we equally needed to understand the status of their habitat, particularly the health of rangelands that nourished them. The quality and quantity of available food for the Marco Polo sheep—the grasses of the range—affected the sheep populations in a place where the difference between survival and death in this harsh environment was razor thin for both humans and wildlife. If the locals were overgrazing the grasslands, then the Marco Polo sheep populations would collapse, but potentially, even domestic livestock might end up starving. And when the animals starved, so did the people.

Dr. Don Bedunah led these rangeland surveys. He was a professor of rangeland science at the University of Montana's W. A. Franke College of Forestry and Conservation, one of many people who came to Afghanistan from Big Sky Country. Much as Iraq attracted Texans because of similarities of habitat and climate (not to mention the shared presence of the oil industry and Houston-based Halliburton), Afghanistan's mountains seemed to attract adventurers and conservationists from Montana. Don was a quiet, humble, and rugged professor with a salt-and-pepper beard. His career had taken him to some of the world's remotest grasslands, from Glacier National Park and the Rocky Mountain front to Mongolia's Gobi Desert and the Wild Yak Valley on the northern ramparts of the Tibetan Plateau. However, Afghanistan, with similarities in habitat, wildlife, and culture to these places, would prove far more stressful than all the other places where he worked, even though he had worked in the country previously. This time, the remoteness of our sites in Afghanistan pushed him to his breaking point.

The status of the Marco Polo sheep hadn't been seriously evaluated since the mid-1970s, when legendary WCS biologist Dr. George Schaller surveyed the species in Pakistan, China, and what is now Tajikistan. Schaller returned to Central Asia in 2004 as part of Peter Zahler's initial UN Post-Conflict Assessment Unit rapid assessment and helped guide our teams. Schaller's initial observations suggested that sheep were potentially moving freely across the borders of all four countries and even across mountain passes. If this were the case, it would argue for creating a transboundary peace park that would manage the Marco Polo sheep as a single population. WCS would push for the creation of this transnational park. However, doing so wouldn't be easy; there had been various efforts made to create the peace park since the Russians originally proposed the idea in the 1920s, and we would face challenges on our attempt.

We also considered the possibility of harnessing big game hunting as a way to protect the sheep. The breed's enormous size and horns coupled with the harshness and remoteness of their habitats has given them almost mystical status among hunters. However, hunting is highly controversial, particularly among conservationists. The current debates over permitting big game hunting in Africa highlight the sensitivity to the issue. The argument for hunting is that if we could make Marco Polo sheep too valuable to kill except through a commercial game hunting program, we could not only raise money for their conservation and local development, we tied the communities' well-being to the protection of the population. With the substitution of strictly monitored mortality for rampant shooting, there was greater chance that the population would grow. This had been the case in Tajikistan.

In 1987, the Tajik government, in desperate search for revenue given the impending collapse of the Soviet Union, launched just such a luxury hunting program for the Marco Polo sheep, charging upward of $30,000 for a ten-day trip into the Pamirs and a license to shoot one sheep. The effect was that the Tajik population of Marco Polo sheep grew to several tens of thousands. However, the first hunting program was originally set up by Afghanistan. Afghanistan was the first country to establish commercial big game hunting programs after King Zahir Shah shot an argali in 1967. Afghanistan set up the Afghan Tourism Organization, which ran a hunting program that charged $40,000–$60,000* for the privilege from 1967 to 1979 until the three decades of conflict in Afghanistan decimated the hunting program. However, with the Soviet invasion and the collapse of the Afghan state, tourism in Afghanistan, once the number-two source of revenue for the country, ended, as did the hunting program. The results of the paired experiment between Afghanistan and Tajikistan are worth considering: the population of Marco Polo sheep in Tajikistan is still in the thousands, while the population in the Afghan Pamirs is uncertain but estimated at best by the initial Schaller survey in 2004 to be perhaps in the few hundreds.

A new Afghan hunting program potentially could provide clear incentives to the local population and the government for the protection of the Marco Polo sheep and reduce pressures on the population. Trophy hunting can provide a strong economic incentive to protect wildlife and promote conservation. Such hunting generates a great deal of income for a country at little cost, while the killing of a few animals does not need to adversely affect a large population if the program is

---

*In 2018 dollars.

tightly controlled and scientifically managed in conjunction with wild-life surveys to assess population size and growth rates. WCS reviewed whether reinstating such a program would work in a similar fashion in Afghanistan, given that there wasn't a strong central authority, sub-stantial rule of law, or even data on the species and the health of the population. We also needed to reach out to the Afghan Tourism Or-ganization, if it still existed, and work with NEPA and the Ministry of Agriculture to implement this program.

Beyond ungulates, like the Marco Polo sheep, Afghanistan was also a country that was rich in felid species. At one point, it may have had more cat species than Africa. In addition to snow leopards were tigers (now locally extinct), Persian leopards, Iranian cheetahs (which might still exist—we would go look for them), caracals, leopard cats, Pallas's cats, sand cats, and wild cats. There was a strong possibility that the Asiatic lion, which previously extended from Turkey to India, could have been in southern Afghanistan as well. Iran lost its last Asiatic lion in 1942. A small remnant population of such lions still remains in the Gir Forest in India.

Snow leopards lead solitary lives in the mountains of the Pamirs and travel long distances to prey on montane ungulate species like ibex, urial sheep, markhor, and Marco Polo sheep. They live amid the world's highest peaks in the Himalayas, at elevations ranging from 900 to 5,500 meters. Their physiology has been adapted to the steep, rocky mountainsides they inhabit. In addition to their thick fur, they have two other characteristics that assist their survival. First, enormous paws steady their footing as they race down rock walls chasing their prey, allowing them to waft across the surface of deep snow. The fur on the undersides of their paws provides better traction on steep and unstable surfaces. Snow leopards are also distinguished from regular leopards by the size of their tails: thick and nearly the length of their bodies (regu-lar leopards, by comparison, have thinner tails that are typically a third of body length). A thick, long tail provides a counterweight as snow leopards run down steep hillsides and also serves as a built-in blanket against the severe mountainous weather. Their main predators, as with the Marco Polo sheep, are humans.

Snow leopards are killed for different reasons; retaliatory killing for livestock predation, bored militias looking to use their AK-47s, and local hunters meeting the demand for pelts from Western soldiers and aid workers all threaten the population. As if the human impact were not enough, the leopards are also losing their prey base, as rangeland is heavily overgrazed and humans hunt the ungulates that feed the big cats. Overgrazing became a big issue for both Marco Polo sheep and snow leopards.

Our team also needed to create incentives for the protection of snow leopards, much as we were thinking of doing for Marco Polo sheep. In particular, we needed to step up enforcement of wildlife trade of snow leopard pelts and also prevent retaliatory killing. Snow leopards were frequently shot because farmers believed the cats were preying on livestock. But Afghan livestock weren't dying because of snow leopards, rather succumbing to a variety of causes, usually in combination, including disease, insufficient nutrition, or as a result of winter conditions, usually deep snow combined with extreme cold (plus the occasional avalanche). We needed to collect the data to demonstrate this to the Afghans and offer sufficient incentives to mitigate the harm they already were incurring from snow leopards.

One way was to build predator-proof enclosures to prevent snow leopards from getting into the pens. Another was to pay farmers for the domestic animals that they lost due to snow leopard attacks. WCS would research and design a pilot program to help compensate farmers for the market value of livestock losses that the farmer could demonstrate were due to snow leopards. Farmers would, in exchange for participating in this program, agree to stop killing snow leopards.

The communities would play a major part in providing the governance of the system and to determine level and need for reimbursement from predation losses. If this program worked in Wakhan with snow leopards, we could also extend it to other carnivores, in other parts of Afghanistan.

ON THE EVE before heading to Wakhan, the tension among our team was rising. This was our first expedition. Although Peter Zahler had organized a short survey to Wakhan with the UN in 2004, it was a very different security situation now, and we wouldn't have the resources of the UN behind us. Moreover, this was an untested team in a place where every trip was a game of chance.

Traveling to Wakhan would be challenging. First, we had to get through the mountains that surrounded Kabul (which made the city dangerous to pass in or out of, by land or by air). The trip would grow increasingly dangerous as we approached Kunduz and got farther from the protections of Kabul. After Kunduz, the road turns toward the Himalayas' western end, following the Amu Darya (and farther upstream toward its source in the high Himalayas, the Panj River).

A few miles outside Kunduz, the tarmac road gave way to gravel, and in some cases, to dirt. In the absence of tarmac, riverbeds could serve as a highway. The last big city (relatively large at fifty thousand) on the way to Wakhan is the capital of Badakhshan, Faizabad. The city, dusty and ramshackle like many Afghan cities, was not safe, and despite the beautiful river running through its center, there was little reason to stay there.

After Faizabad, the road would start climbing toward the Himalayas. Once the road entered Wakhan, it became a set of tracks along the long rocky plane of the Pamir Valley, crossing numerous glacier-fed streams and rivers before finally ending at the town of Sarhad-e-Brogil, locally renowned for its single hot spring heating a public bath. What was left of the road ended at the base of a wall of steep mountains.

At this point, the travel went from tough to ridiculous. Once we were past Sarhad-e-Brogil, we were on our own, no vehicles. Even poorly equipped hospitals were two long days away. WCS teams would be on horseback, with no communications outside of satellite phones dependent on solar chargers and batteries. There were two choices for traveling farther into Wakhan. Option one was a narrow footpath that climbed through the mist into the high, snowy peaks of the Pamirs. This path, dotted with two-thousand-year-old petroglyphs and shrines decorated with the corkscrew horns of Marco Polo sheep, was a section of the Silk Road that terminated at the Chinese city of Xi'an, home of the terracotta warriors. From Sarhad-e-Brogil, it was ten days to the Chinese border at the Waghjir Valley. The second option, available in the winter only, involved teams using the frozen surface of the river as their pathway. The frozen rivers would provide a faster and perhaps safer alternative to the dangers faced from weather and altitude of mountain passes.

Overland travel required carrying substantial supplies for weeks at a time, which meant using pack animals—yaks, donkeys, and horses— each with its disadvantages and advantages. Our team could rent animals from the Wakhi and Kyrgyz villages that dotted our path, but it wasn't exactly convenient. They would need to rent yaks in one village, but once they reached the next village, the yaks and their owner were headed home. The expedition team would be left at a disadvantage, packs and supplies on the ground, to negotiate with a new villager for a new set of animals. This was slow going—except in terms of time and money, which they burned through plenty fast.

Back in Kabul, Don was getting more and more distressed as we worked to outfit his expedition in Wakhan. His worry was understandable; he would be on his own with the exception of his Afghan WCS counterpart, Ahmad Jawad. We had set up communications and protocols for staying in contact and contracted an armed emergency relief team to extract someone in the mountains. But the relief team's effectiveness depended entirely on our communications working. If Don were compromised by sickness, kidnapping, or injury, we were limited in our ability to help him. The cultural terrain wasn't much friendlier than the land itself; the Wakhi were Ismailis, a separate sect of Shi'ism that followed the Aga Khan, and the Kyrgyz spoke Turkish, not Farsi; both were deeply insular societies. Even Jawad, who would travel with Don, would be out of his element.

Don asked hesitantly about whether he was secure and what we would do in the case of an emergency. I talked him through the security protocols and procedures in place. I explained that every day, he would need to send us his longitude and latitude via satellite phone. He would have a second phone as a backup and would also carry an emergency beacon that could be activated. If we didn't hear from him in forty-eight hours, we would send in RMSI rescue teams that had secured a high-altitude helicopter for his extraction from Pakistan. What I didn't say out loud was that we had a rescue team ready as long as the helicopter wasn't shot down by a missile when it crossed the border. In any case, he would be responsible for holding himself together until the teams arrived—he and Jawad both had emergency first responder training—and they'd be equipped with medical supplies and drugs in case of an emergency.

His voice started shaking, though I couldn't tell whether it was from fear or anger or both. His eyes glistened with tears. Finally, he asked, "What happens if you can't find me?" I assured him that we would find him; we could track him from his last position.

Don looked at me directly and asked, "What keeps me safe?"

I responded truthfully but tried to reassure him. "Ultimately, you. You will be okay. You have done this before."

The conversation ended there. Don walked away, and we didn't talk again until I saw him off the next day. I was nervous. All I could do was reassure him and myself that he would be fine, despite that he would be traveling at high elevations on challenging terrains, crossing swollen rivers, far away from roads, running water, electricity, or a warm hearth, and in a country that was still a war zone. There would be people who might do him harm before he even got to his destination, which was far away from any roads, with populations who might or might not help him. This reality was bitter and difficult.

Later, as I reflected on this encounter, it occurred to me that I had spent most of my time focusing on strengthening the capacity of the Afghan team members rather than allaying and soothing my US and European colleagues' perfectly legitimate concerns, and even fears, about the danger involved. I was wrong. I assumed my US and European colleagues would be able to take care of themselves and didn't need my attention and care because of the other places they had traveled. But

Afghanistan was a different place, with its own unique challenges that take a toll on both your physical health and also your mental well-being. I should have paid more attention to the toll that our mission in Afghanistan would take on even seasoned professionals, but I had failed to do so.

War zones aren't normal. They force everyone in them, combatants or civilians, to consider their mortality. Everyone who worked for me in Afghanistan was dependent in part on the decisions I made regarding their safety. I wore this burden heavily. If things went bad in Wakhan, there was no real way for me to rescue Don from Kabul in real time; he would ultimately need to depend on his own skills to survive in extremely remote surroundings—and on those satellite phones.

For all our fears, Don's trip was ultimately successful, and he came back from the field with good data on Marco Polo grazing. It was clear that the land was extensively overgrazed, that even in some of the remotest places on Earth, humans have had an impact. We now needed to plan a much more substantial presence in Wakhan, sending up multiple teams to work with communities on the predator reimbursement programs, building tourism infrastructure, starting the scientific surveys of Marco Polo sheep, and continuing the rangeland surveys, among other things. I would travel back with my team to meet with the leadership in Wakhan, but first we needed to finish the setup of our operations in Kabul.

CHAPTER 4

THE ORDINARY EXTRAORDINARY
LIFE IN KABUL

ALTHOUGH MOST OF our work was in the field—Bamiyan Province in the center part of the country where the Buddhas once stood; the Wakhan Corridor nestled between the mighty peaks that make up the Pamir knot; the thick, dark forests of Nuristan; the rolling, verdant hills of Herat in Western Afghanistan—there was considerable work to do in Kabul as well. Some of it was the business of building the WCS program in Afghanistan, from training and hiring Afghan conservationists and staff and building our technical capacities to understanding the status of Afghanistan's biodiversity. It also included collaborations with all our local partners, including the Afghan government, the US government and its institutions, the US and international military, bilateral and multilateral humanitarian and development institutions, other countries (through their embassies), and other NGOs, both international and Afghan. There was also real conservation work to do in Kabul. This included our efforts to stop illegal trading of both timber and wildlife; protect biodiversity hot spots like the wetland at Kol-e-Hashmat Khan; work with conservation institutions like the Kabul Zoo; build the capacity of the Afghan government by working alongside it; and develop legislation, policies, and science capacity within Afghanistan. And while we were in Kabul, we were part of its ecosystem.

Every war zone (as well as places in the midst of radical change) creates unique ephemeral and novel cultures of people and institutions, as well as rituals and events. Russia had its Gagarin rave parties. Afghanistan had its Ultimate Frisbee games. Such places magnetically draw in and populate a unique biota: aid workers, diplomats, soldiers, war correspondents, overpriced World Bank and UN bureaucrats, contractors, war entrepreneurs, Danish Toyota dealers, missionaries and mercenaries, Thai restaurateurs, prostitutes, war addicts, and others, who pop up from Bosnia to Afghanistan, Iraq to Sudan. Afghanistan was no different. Not unlike the backpacking hubs of Thamel in Katmandu or Khao San Road in Bangkok, such places develop service cultures too.

In the early years after the US invasion, before the slow, creeping insurgency turned Afghanistan's embassies and guesthouses into prisons, Afghanistan's service culture proved particularly rich in restaurants and bars—an archipelago of consumption, where expats flush with hardship supplements and per diems indulged in food and drink. There were few places for entertainment or to spend your money. The haunts of the expatriate social scene were frequently off-limits to Afghans, either explicitly or implicitly through attitude and cost, creating an apartheid within Kabul.

Such divisions imposed real costs. While expatriates actually believed they understood the local culture, they created an alternative Arcadia, more familiar and less strange, that didn't represent the culture in which they lived. This bifurcation made it hard for outsiders to understand the dark undercurrents and drivers within society. The Iranian revolution took American diplomats in Iran by surprise, in part, because the diplomats had re-created America as their surrounding medium rather than immersing themselves in Iran.

When we arrived in 2006, the international humanitarian community had largely escaped the scourge of suicide bombings and attacks. There was an assumption that the Taliban weren't interested in soft targets like NGOs (hard targets being the Karzai government, coalition forces, and foreign embassies). The development and humanitarian community had extraordinary freedom in these early days, including

Ultimate Frisbee games, soccer games, golf outings, ski clubs, and dinners with friends in restaurants. Friends in the US embassy and USAID would schedule "meetings" at our headquarters so they would be able to join the Frisbee games or our dinners. The erroneous but seemingly widely held belief was that any humanitarian organizations targeted by the Taliban had done something to "deserve it"—that they were engaged in prostitution or other taboo activities. As a result, while it lasted, Kabul experienced an unlikely culinary and cultural boom.

Given that Afghanistan had just come out of three decades of war, the choices were extraordinary. And there was demand; an entrepreneur could come in and cover his entire investment within a week of operations. There were *two* Texas-themed restaurants, multiple Chinese, Iranian, Indian, and Thai restaurants. There were even imitations of American fast-food restaurants (Afghan Fried Chicken, or AFC) and Afghan restaurants serving dishes designed for the Western palate. There were multiple Lebanese places, but the standout was Taverna du Liban. Kamel, the kind and gracious owner, dished out plates of rich hummus, tabbouleh, baba ganoush, and kabobs. If you were a friend of Kamel's (and nearly everyone was), you might enjoy a decadent slice of chocolate cake on the house. When the city authorities cracked down on alcohol in restaurants, Kamel started pouring red and white wine out of teapots.

Some places capitalized on Afghanistan's notorious history. The Gandamack Lodge bore the name of an infamous British defeat in the First Anglo-Afghan War and had once been the home of a wife of Osama bin Laden. That was before Peter Jouvenal, a former British soldier turned BBC cameraman, opened Kabul's most proper British pub, complete with shepherd's pie and custard. With dual qualifications as a warzone native, Peter understood the needs of his customers—alcohol, food, a sense of history and place, and, if only for a moment, a feeling of safety.

However, the most notorious of Kabul's expat restaurants was L'Atmosphère, a haughty French club. The entrance was on a dark, potholed street lined by the SUVs of UN and NGO drivers. Guards, high walls, and a tunnel shielded the customers from outside attack. Behind the walls was a different world. "L'Atmo" had multiple bars serving cocktails, wine, and beer, and indoor and outdoor dining rooms, where aloof development professionals dined on French cuisine served by Afghan waitstaff who were even more aloof than the clientele. The swimming pool was what really set L'Atmosphère apart. Speedo-clad men and bikini-wearing women lounged around the water, studiously pretending to ignore each other. When night fell, the place turned into an Afghan Ibiza, with DJs spinning for poolside dance parties.

However, L'Atmosphère didn't have a monopoly on pools or decadence. The Serena Hotel, Afghanistan's only five-star luxury hotel, built by the Aga Khan, boasted a pool and a rich brunch that both felt vulgar given the misery experienced outside its walls. There was a jarring disconnect between expats and their appetites and the strict social and cultural norms that prevailed only a few meters of cement stone away. For the Western warzone migrants, the restaurants and hotels were refugia from the daunting patriarchy of their temporary home. During the Taliban years, Afghanistan had moved toward the past. Healing that wound between Afghanistan's modern past and its conservative present was one of the core challenges facing the country. Watching the two parallel societies live in one city reminded me of something from half a world away. In Brazil, the black waters of the Rio Negro collide with the silty coffee-colored flow of the Amazon near Manaus. The two waters run side by side, unmixed, for many miles. What would bring the two societies of Kabul together? The apartheid of the humanitarian community from Afghan society behind the high walls of these places was unlikely to be the answer.

The expats of Kabul ate and drank and danced in part because they wanted to find normalcy within the chaos of war and perhaps forget where they were, even temporarily. I had seen the same phenomenon in other conflict zones. IEDs, mortars, suicide bombers, kidnappings, military choppers overhead, destroyed buildings, and nonstop safety alerts were equal-opportunity sources of stress and anxiety wearing on Afghans and expats alike. For expats, trivia night at the Tex-Mex restaurant or a slice of absurdly rich chocolate cake could provide a quick hallucination of stability.

A strange assortment of types flocks to war zones. Conflict provides an adrenaline rush and a chance to forge a new identity (or forget an old one). This cocktail proved habit-forming. Many of the expats in Kabul were war addicts. They were journalists, humanitarians, aid workers, and members of the military, drawn by the desire to be relevant, to fix a catastrophe, who hopped from conflict zone to disaster. I met people who were in their fifth, sixth, or tenth failed state, humanitarian emergency, or conflict, who had started traveling and had never stopped. For them, such places *were* normal, and they were impatient outsiders in their home countries, unable to return for long. Among those seeking a romantic partner in Kabul, there was a saying: "The odds are good, but the goods are odd." The joke had more than a little truth in it. Everyone was incomplete. Most who came to Afghanistan were searching for meaning or adventure or a story or an experience. Or avoiding some bigger challenge waiting at home. Some were simply searching for enough money to buy a new house or a boat. War zones are a good place to go to forget the past because the past doesn't matter much in war zones. In countries coming out of conflict, the past has been destroyed; it was to be forgotten. Places in the midst of conflict can provide a chance to shape the future and who you are in that future. Or to forget who you are in the present.

For me, Afghanistan was my opium, but it combined that with a sense of home. My experiences in Russia, Madagascar, and Iraq had fueled my love of exotica and adventure. Madagascar, with its rich, unique *Alice in Wonderland* biological diversity and lemurs and equally unique culture that combined Asian and African, was about the pure joy of novelty as my first trip to the developing world as a fledgling adult. Russia in 1992 and postwar Iraq were places in the midst of a tidal change of history. These were places where the influence of individuals, of single humans, could help bring titanic change to the direction of societies. And both Russia and Iraq at first attracted those who wanted to make those changes. Lists of extraordinary people who threw away the mundane certainty of daily life in the West for the extraordinary uncertainty of chaos.

But there was another reason Afghanistan motivated me. It was a more fundamental search for identity. As an Iranian American who had worked as a diplomat for the State Department, I couldn't return to Iran without risk of persecution. I had sought to find the echoes of part of my identity through my work in the Middle East—in Iraq, Central Asia, the Caucasus, and closest of all, in Afghanistan.

Regardless of what motivated the other expats of Kabul, their sanctuaries soon came under attack. Civilian deaths from insurgent attacks skyrocketed in 2006, the year we started our program. This was the deadliest year for civilians in Afghanistan since 2001. The fleeting feeling of normalcy shattered when the insurgency recognized that soft targets were easier to hit than hard ones, sometimes with greater effect on the news media and political decision-making in the West. The war in Afghanistan became asymmetrical, with reprisals for coalition military attacks targeting government workers and schools, diplomats, and civilians. Then, shortly after, came the attacks on the humanitarian community.

BECAUSE OF OUR workload and for security, we ate most of our breakfasts and dinners at the guesthouse, which meant we needed a cook. When an NGO we knew closed up its operations, the staff suggested their cook to us as a possible hire. That's how we met Kaka—a short, obsequious, grizzled, but extremely sweet older man. The NGO brought us over for dinner to showcase Kaka's cooking skills. He served up a magnificent Thanksgiving spread, complete with a whole turkey, sides, and pumpkin pie, and we hired him on the spot. My work has included some dining lowlights; for two years in Madagascar, we ate meals of rice and beans, flavored with small rocks, flecks of dirt, rat poop, and tart crunchy little beetles every day, except breakfast when we just ate rice with sweet powdered milk and cocoa. Kaka would be a three-star Michelin celebrity chef in comparison. He was a bit of a character as well.

Within a few days of being hired, our new cook asked our finance director, Zabih, for a six-month advance on his salary to pay for his wedding. Weddings in South Asia (and North America, if we're being honest) are an important expression of a family's standing in the community. These extravagant celebrations sometimes push those families to bankruptcy. We were a bit hesitant to make such a significant advance payment to Kaka. We had just hired him, and we weren't sure he would stay with our program long enough to repay the advance. But Zabih stressed the importance of the wedding (as did Kaka), and we relented. Two weeks after hiring him, we paid Kaka six months of salary up front. Predictably, it turned out Kaka wasn't quite the master chef that his Thanksgiving feast promised. In fact, sometimes he bordered on abysmal. He wasn't big on presentation either. We gave Kaka's signature dishes nicknames. There was the extra-oniony onion tart with onions. Another favorite was meat shapes (meat of unclear origins ground into patties, some shaped like animals, but not necessarily the animals we were eating). But the worst was Kaka's bloody poop logs (long meat loaves, dripping in a thick, bloodred, oily sauce). That dish in particular drove Kara crazy, but Kaka knew how to endear himself to me. He served pitchers of fresh pomegranate juice, painstakingly squeezed from the fruit of the scrawny but fecund pomegranate tree in our yard. He wasn't bad at spaghetti, either. We encouraged Kaka to cook pasta multiple times a week, partly to avoid some of the other dishes.

The food was hit and miss, but one advantage of hiring Kaka, and providing the advance, was an invitation to his wedding—our first in Afghanistan. We were excited for a chance to witness such an important part of Afghan life. We were also excited to go to a wedding hall. Wedding halls lined the road from the airport. Their glass and flashing lights rivaled those of American carnival rides or casino signs, and like both, they were highly alluring. They hinted at joy and excitement that would await. The halls were often booked months in advance. Weddings were their sole purpose.

The wedding would give us a chance to break out of the segregation that separated the humanitarians from the Afghans. Much like

working hand in hand with the ministries, and living outside the security cordons of the US embassy, participating would help us build
the bonds and give us the insights that would carry our work forward.
I wanted to understand Afghanistan more; I had expected Afghanistan to be exactly like Iran. The language was very similar, they had
common holidays like the Zoroastrian Persian New Year (the first day
of spring), and they shared overlapping histories and empires, but the
more I looked, the more I found greater dissimilarities than similarities. Through the wedding—which, like markets, provided a window
into the soul of any culture or society—I could help understand my
own complex identity as American and Iranian. In Iran, weddings represented the best of the country—the public social restrictions that enveloped the country like a heavy woolen blanket were thrown off—and
they were filled with music, drink, and dance, a paradox to the heavy
Islamic orthodoxy enforced by the clerics and culture police.

On the day of Kaka's wedding, we finally got to see inside one of
these temples to nuptial celebration. Our expectations were easily exceeded. The interior was even more spectacularly ornate than the exterior. The large room was decorated with colorful murals, red Afghan
carpets, chandeliers, and sculpted gold moldings. The space was enormous, almost half the size of a soccer field. We had arrived late, and
hundreds of guests were already sitting at tables. Men and women were
separated in the room by a high partition. This division was typical in
Afghan public life, if not always as literal. Kara and I were split up, and
I waded into an expanse of tables occupied by bearded men wearing
off-white shalwar kameez and the occasional suit jacket over it.

Outside the home or workplace, women almost always wore
burkas—a flowing garment that loosely enveloped the whole of the
body, with a small fabric screen over the eyes for the wearer to see
through. Almost all burkas were made from a royal-blue fabric, which
made their wearers look like Inky, the blue ghost from Pac-Man, darting from stall to stall at the market, although other colors existed as
well. At least the blue was lively in comparison to the always-black
abayas of Saudi Arabia or the chadors of Iran (the latter worn to keep

women and country in perpetual mourning for the martyrdom of Hussein). The blue hue of a burka was uniquely Afghan, reminiscent of Band-e-Amir lakes and the lapis mined from Badakhshan. Our office was designated a burka-free zone where women were not required to wear the burka or even a headscarf but could choose to do so if they wanted, one of the pockets of social freedom in the capital.

The traditional Afghan wedding music heralded the entry of the bride and the groom. The bride looked quite unhappy, but this was to be expected. Afghan tradition requires brides to maintain a stoic, grim decorum or otherwise risk dishonor to her father. We got down to the business of eating. Heaping piles of Kabuli Palau quickly appeared on our tables. This was Afghanistan's national dish and perhaps its most delicious—a Central Asian paella of golden basmati rice filled with fatty cubes of luscious lamb on bone, matchstick-like carrots, almonds, raisins, garlic, pistachios, and onions, and spiced with all the flavors of the Silk Road—cardamom, bay leaves, cumin, cinnamon, cloves, ground peppercorns, saffron, all browned in butter. However, I wasn't prepared for what happened next.

The male guests descended on the Kabuli Palau like lions on a zebra. Seemingly within minutes, the tables were covered with debris: gristle, shards of gnawed lamb bones, and stray rice were all that remained of the wedding banquet, and many of the attendees quickly left after finishing. The cavernous hall was now almost empty except for a smaller group of twenty men who stayed on for the dancing, which started after the meal.

The remaining men gathered in a circle, clapping and cheering on effeminate, beardless young male dancers. These were the bacha bazi, "playboys," who replaced women at parties. They were hired to perform and, it was rumored, sometimes to consort with guests. They moved their thin, lithe bodies sinuously and suggestively to the encouraging cries of the audience. Seeing the dance of the playboys only heightened my sense of cultural dysphoria. The suggestive gyrations of the young men felt like a disturbing substitute for a freer celebration that brought men and women together. I left to find Kara, who was clearly having much more fun on her side of the partition, and asked if she was ready to leave. We found Kaka and his bride and offered congratulations— and left the young dancers and jeering men.

That night, it was really driven home to me that Afghanistan wasn't like Iran. And most likely, modern Iran wouldn't reflect my own images of Iran. For many in the Iranian diaspora, their country, like Afghanistan, had frozen in time after the 1979 revolution. The Iran that was celebrated and remembered in Persian homes in Beverly Hills, Orange County, Great Falls, and Potomac no longer existed. This was a truism of the immigrant experience. The motherland will continue to evolve, but in the minds of immigrants, it does not. It is frozen at the moment of their departure. Nonetheless, I still hoped to find some kinship in Afghanistan as an Iranian.

WITHIN THE FIRST few months of starting the WCS office in Afghanistan, we sought to become part of the two societies we had adopted— our Afghan society and our expatriate one. We were working hard to get the WCS office running, engage with the government, and start putting teams into the field pursuant to our work plan for the country. In those early days, the team worked twelve-plus-hour days six and a half days a week. We only took two full days off during the week after a year. We were so busy with our little start-up that we hadn't seen much of Kabul or its surroundings other than the wedding hall and the restaurants. Shafiq, our office manager, suggested a picnic excursion to the mountains outside Kabul. It was a good suggestion; the team needed a break, and wandering around the mountains sounded like a good antidote to our weariness. So Kara, Shafiq, Qais, Etienne, Khoja, and I got in the Land Cruiser and headed for Paghman, a mountain tea and picnic area where Kabul residents could escape the heat and dust of the city.

En route, we drove by the Kabul Golf Club, a course made out of dirt, with intermittent patches of scrub vegetation. Rather than putting "greens," the Kabul Golf Club had ingeniously built putting "browns," flattened, smooth circles of compacted sand and oil. Hand-painted white stones listed each hole's par and yardage. Golfers were given the option of placing a piece of Astroturf under the ball; others just hit right off the dirt. The course was originally established in 1967, but politics and wars interrupted play. It became a battlefield during both the Russian invasion and the civil war. By the time of the US invasion, the golf course was an active minefield. Muhammad Afzal Abdul, the club pro, working with a former warlord, Ezatullah Atef, cleared mines, abandoned tanks, and mortar shrapnel. The original vegetation, including the trees that lined the fairways, had long ago fallen under fierce mortar and gunfire exchanges. Abdul brought in deminers to sweep the fairways and later invited herders to graze their sheep on the scrub, just in case the deminers had missed anything.

Down the road from the golf club was Qargha Lake. A dam built on the Paghman River in 1933 created this sparkling turquoise lake, one edge of which was the site of a resort where couples covertly met to walk romantically and talk together without fear of attack. Beyond the lake, the road climbed into the mountains and the landscape grew greener and greener, the vegetation sustained by melting snows from the peaks above. We climbed past a string of walled-off holiday villas, refuges for Kabul's elite. Our route took us around a crumbling replica of the Arc de Triomphe. It was built by Afghanistan's King Amanullah, who was inspired by the Paris landmark during a 1927 European tour. He created a slightly downscaled version at Paghman's famous gardens, which now lay in ruins.

After traveling some ways farther, we parked the vehicle and set out on a hike alongside a small, rapid river descending from the peaks of the Hindu Kush. Steep mountain ramparts, crowned with snow and rocks, towered over us, and the waters scampered over smooth boulders down to orchards and gardens below. Simple tea shops—railed wooden decks covered with thick, ornate carpets and cushions—offered tea, fruit, and a place to lounge. Up the hillside was a swimming pool filled by the stream's cold water. Young men joyously splashed in the pool, an escape from the heat and claustrophobia of the city.

Shafiq pointed to a rutted path that vanished into the steep, boulder-filled slopes.

"The mujahideen would come down to attack the Soviet army and then would use this road to disappear back into the mountains."

We looked up at the forbidding peaks. He did not mention that the routes were now being used by the Taliban to attack Westerners.

The steep slopes of Paghman were also the home of Afghanistan's only endemic amphibian, the Paghman stream salamander (*Afghanodon mustersi*). The salamander population is estimated to be between one thousand and two thousand individuals, living in the fast-running crisp meltwater of rock glaciers in the Hindu Kush. The temperature of the water is a limiting factor, as the salamander does not live in water above 14°C. Surveys indicate that the salamanders stay at elevations between 2,440 and 3,750 meters (8,005 and 12,303 feet) and are most likely to be found at the source of the streams in Paghman. This gave the salamander a home range of only ten square kilometers, making it among the most critically endangered species in Afghanistan. Land-use changes, such as irrigation, would decrease the flow of water through the streams, and grazing would remove streamside shade plants that kept the temperature cool enough to support the salamander. But climate change posed the biggest threat. In our lifetimes, we will probably see the extinction of this salamander due to the rising water temperatures. Our friend and real estate agent Richard Scarth had actually gone in search of the Paghman salamander a year earlier and found it. But on our hike and a WCS follow-up visit later on, we struck out and couldn't find them. Before long, Paghman grew too dangerous to continue the surveys.

The high passes used by the mujahideen and then the Taliban were also shared with the Persian leopard (*Panthera pardus saxicolor*). The Persian leopard lives at a lower elevation than the snow leopard; its fur ranges from a pale yellow to a deep gold with more distinct black rosettes, unlike the ivory-colored fur of the snow leopard, and has a shorter tail.

The leopard's current range extends across the Middle East, and its total number might not exceed 1,300 individuals. Most of the cats are found in neighboring Iran (550–850 animals) and especially in that country's northwestern portion, with a few hundred more living in neighboring Armenia and Azerbaijan (160–275). The number of Persian leopards in Afghanistan isn't known with any certainty. There were likely several hundred, but Kabul's rampant leopard fur trade gravely threatened the cats' future.

Our picnic included feasting on fresh black mulberries washed in the cold stream water. Melons, pomegranates, and mulberries all originated in Afghanistan and neighboring countries. Unlike industrially grown grocery-store produce, Afghan fruit is not bred for visual appeal or shelf life—and the natural flavor is spectacular. We gorged on basket after basket of the mulberries until our lips and fingers were stained with dark juices. We headed back to Kabul, refreshed by our outing. On the ride back, though, I noticed the group growing awfully quiet. When we got back to the office, there was a stampede for the toilets. Three days of mass intestinal distress followed. Shafiq loudly cursed Qais for choosing a tea shop that wasn't clean, but the culprit was probably the mulberry overdose, which in the quantities we ate, is a highly effective treatment for constipation.

ON NEARLY EVERY trip in Kabul, we witnessed unexpected scenes, from someone selling bundles of dead pelicans and flamingos on the side of the road, to a man carrying a stuffed leopard. Both NEPA and the Ministry of Agriculture offices were on the Darulaman Road, which ended at the Darul Aman Palace, which was built by Germany and intended to be home to Afghanistan's parliament and the seed for a new capital. It was the first building in Afghanistan to have central heat and running water. Now the neoclassical building was a bombed-out, ruined structure that seemed to symbolize everything Afghanistan had been through in the last thirty years. The road also passed by the derelict and squatter-infested theater and cultural center, relics of the Soviet Union's former presence and power, much like the abandoned troop carriers that littered the landscape.

On one such trip, Khoja, Kara, and I were in the Land Cruiser on a crowded street in the city center. I saw a young child squatting on the side of the street, sobbing, his hands covering his eyes. On the sidewalk before him was a huge overturned tray of eggs, all of them smashed. I could imagine what had happened. He had been sent out to get eggs for his family or for a local shop and had tripped and broken them all. As punishment, he would be lashed or worse. It was a sad scene, but there was nothing I could do, or so I thought. That's when Kara told Khoja to pull over, and she turned to me.

"You have to help him." Kara stared at me directly as if to emphasize that this wasn't actually a request.

This wasn't the first time Kara had sent me on a mission of mercy. At her behest, I had rescued rats in the bottom of trash cans with my bare hands and carried inebriated drunks soaked in their own urine up flights of stairs. Kara liked to help, and I was often conscripted as her reluctant assistant in these endeavors.

This time was a little different. We were in a strange neighborhood in Afghanistan, and I didn't know the boy or what I could do to help him. His situation was sad but not our problem; trying to help could turn into a serious security risk for all of us. When Khoja finally found a place to pull over, we were more than a block away. I got out of the car and dived into the crowded street, feeling exposed. I walked up through the crowds streaming around the boy; tears had cut wet channels through the dust on his face. There were at least two dozen eggs spilled on the ground before him.

I tried to comfort him in my Persian/Dari creole:

"Geryeh nakone. Chese Nimishee." (Don't cry. Nothing will happen.)

The boy cried even harder, his chest heaving in sobs.

"Degee toochamorge meetoony begiree." (You can still get more eggs.)

He whimpered through his tears. *"Man-em mizanam."* (I will be punished.)

And then he wailed even louder. People on the street were now staring at us. The unwanted attention was making me nervous. But the boy's sobs were even more upsetting than my anxiety about safety. I didn't know what awaited the boy at home or at work, to wherever and to whomever he had to deliver the eggs. His cries fired my fears that a brutal punishment was waiting for him. I looked at his tender face lined with tears and considered the tragedy of the broken eggs.

I thought about the war zones and developing countries I'd been in. While they may have differences due to the constraints of place, history, and economics, they also share certain traits, including one: they're all places of cruelty. People cannot afford kindness when they have difficulty seeing to their own needs. It wasn't as easy to show kindness to a child or an animal when you risked your own life—and the value of that life in your society was absurdly low. It made sense to me why the boy was crying.

A sense of guilt washed over me. I started pulling out rolls of afghanis and handed him wads of bills. His crying subsided a bit, and I tried again to comfort him.

"Here, you can buy all the eggs you need to replace the ones you lost. You don't need to cry, just get more eggs. It will be okay."

I picked up the overturned egg cases and handed them to the boy, who was still sniffling. He walked off with his crates and enough money to buy five hundred eggs. I watched him go with a feeling of intense self-satisfaction. I had brought kindness to the bleak desert of despair.

As I walked back to the car, I passed a well-dressed Afghan man. He mumbled something, perhaps to me, or perhaps to no one in particular:

"Every day I walk by here, and every day the kid breaks his eggs."

It was a bucket of ice water on my noblesse oblige. I felt embarrassed and empty. The child had pulled off an Academy Award performance. I had been had.

Back at the office, I recounted the story to Zabih. He told me he had seen the child too, many times, and always gave him money.

"You have given him money more than once?" I asked incredulously.

Zabih responded, "I know it is a fraud, but I give him the money anyway. We all have to survive."

I left Zabih's office feeling somewhat better. *We all have to survive.* Zabih recognized the real challenges that drove the boy to break his eggs on purpose every day.

WILDLIFE AND TIMBER trafficking would quickly become a focal point of our activities. Afghanistan had a serious problem with illegal timber trafficking in its eastern forests. These forests were some of the most dangerous places in Afghanistan, and we were building a program around surveying their wildlife and using remote sensing to better understand the extent and scale of the deforestation. As part of this effort, we hired new Afghan staff, particularly young male students, to help us collect data on the illegal timber trade with Pakistan. By surveying the number of logging trucks going into and out of lumberyards, we could estimate the demand for wood and the scope of the market. That would give us an idea of the deforestation rate.

The influx of young students posed an unexpected challenge. Our computers soon bogged down under an avalanche of viruses, compliments of pornographic websites. The openness of the Internet, combined with the keen curiosity of young men raised in a strict society, had a predictable result. The porn virus epidemic, which started affecting all the office computers, led to an awkward staff meeting where Shafiq, barely keeping a straight face, announced to horrified looks and staff giggles that Sex.com was not a relevant resource for wildlife conservation. Our tech situation was still better than the Afghan air traffic control system, which ran off a single laptop computer. The system went down for a few days, with little explanation, until officials sheepishly approached the FAA official at the American embassy and handed over a laptop paralyzed by X-rated pop-ups and malware.

Illegal trafficking in wildlife was another serious problem that we started addressing. The place to shop for souvenirs in Kabul was Chicken Street, a vast bazaar of antiques, jewelry, and rugs in the heart of the city. Before the decades of war, Afghanistan had a heyday as a backpacking hub. Afghanistan once rivaled Nepal as a favorite stop on the hippie trail, and Chicken Street was Kabul's answer to Thamel in Katmandu.

Countless souvenir and rug shops, punctuated by the occasional hostel or café, lined Chicken Street. The souvenir shops bristled with merchandise: samovars, lapis jewelry, and traditional dresses beaded with turquoise filled every inch of space. Some souvenir shops sold "antiques": Enfield rifles from past British invasions, jewelry and inlaid plates made from semiprecious stones and copper, and Soviet military medals and insignia. The rug shops were dark dens of woolen treasure. The shopkeepers would keep the lights off until a potential customer entered, lighting up the splendor of a thousand looms. The air was heavy with the smells of dust and wool emanating from stack after stack of ochre and deep red rugs bearing frenzied, geometrical patterns of an elephant's foot. Some rugs reflected the reality of Afghanistan's three decades of war. These were war rugs, which featured woven images of tanks, helicopters, Soviet bombers, and jets, as well as the armaments of war—bombs, AK-47s, and grenades. Other stores sold leather goods made from cattle and camel. Chicken Street was also the home of several English bookstores, filled with books long out of print—like tourist guides from before the Soviet invasion, written by the legendary Nancy Dupree.

But hidden among the antiques and rugs in locked compartments under the floor of the shops were the skins of snow leopards, Persian leopards, and leopard cats. The market for furs particularly thrived around military bases established by the US and ISAF, the NATO-led coalition formed after the 9/11 attacks. In fact, the presence of military, contractors, and support staff was driving up the demand for endangered carnivore furs.

Once we saw this, we knew we needed to start work on a campaign against the wildlife trade as part of our mission in Afghanistan. This meant training airport security guards in detecting wildlife, collaborating with military police to shut down markets on bases, and raising awareness of the problem in Kabul. Our fight against the black market in skins had one unintended consequence: nearly setting off an international incident.

I had asked Shafiq to write letters to every embassy in Afghanistan, encouraging them to help clamp down on wildlife trade in late July of that year. Much like soldiers, diplomats could easily bypass customs on their way in and out of the country, which made smuggling easy. Shafiq dutifully complied, sending out letters bearing the WCS logo and, per bureaucratic branding rules, the USAID logo.

A few weeks after the letters went out, I received a phone call. The caller began speaking without identifying himself. Between his curt, authoritative tone, his heavy accent, and the din of the Land Cruiser, I had to ask him to start again and asked who he was.

"This is Bahrami! I received your message."

"Excuse me, could you repeat that?"

"This is Bahrami. I received your letter. I understand your message." This time louder, with growing exasperation.

"I am sorry, who are you?"

"Don't you know who this is? I am *Ambassador Mohammad Reza Bahrami*, and I received your letter! How do you not know who I am after you wrote to me?" the voice on the phone asked irritably.

"I am deeply sorry, Your Excellency. Please forgive me, as the noise was great, and I did not hear you clearly. I am deeply honored by your call."

"I have an important visitor coming to town but will meet you in two weeks at the Serena Hotel, in the lounge area in the back of the hotel. I will call you back after my visitor comes."

"Thank you, Your Excellency. I look forward to meeting you."

The great and mighty Bahrami hung up the phone, leaving me in puzzlement as to whom I had just agreed to meet. The only letters we had sent out were Shafiq's notes to ambassadors about trafficking. We found the letters and looked through them and saw that the mysterious Mr. Bahrami was the Iranian ambassador to Afghanistan. I looked at Shafiq, stunned.

"You wrote to the ambassador of Iran on my behalf?"

"You said that I was supposed to write to all the foreign embassies in Kabul."

I couldn't argue with Shafiq's response; I should have told him to skip the Iranian embassy. Direct communication from a US-funded organization with an official from a government that the US does not have relations with isn't a great idea. And I knew from my previous work with the Secretary of State's policy planning staff that USAID wasn't going to be happy—and they weren't too happy with us to begin with.

Iran, which shares a long border with Afghanistan, had found an unusual common cause with the United States in the fight against the Taliban. There were covert coordinated conversations between Iran and the US about Afghanistan, and during the Afghanistan reconstruction summit, the two countries found themselves on the same side. Iran invested heavily in rebuilding Afghanistan, particularly in Herat. By the time I accidentally wrote to Bahrami, hardliners in both countries had pushed the sides apart.

The next week, President Ahmadinejad of Iran made his first visit to Afghanistan, the first visit in decades by an Iranian president. Ahmadinejad was the ambassador's visitor.

A few days later, after the visit of Ahmadinejad, I got another direct phone call from the Iranian ambassador. "Meet me tomorrow at 2:00 p.m. at the Serena Hotel, as discussed." I didn't tell anyone whom I was meeting except Kara. Meeting with an Iranian official was probably a worse idea than writing a letter to one, but I was curious why Tehran's ambassador to Afghanistan wanted to talk about wildlife trafficking. Perhaps we could start, I naively thought, a transboundary program with Iran around protection of the cheetah—that is, if I wasn't thrown in jail for violating sanctions or the Logan Act, a US federal law enacted in the early days of the United States that allows for the fining or imprisonment of unauthorized citizens who negotiate with foreign governments having a dispute with the United States.

So at the appointed time, I dressed up in a formal suit and headed over to the Serena. I made my way to the lounge, a dark room full of traditional Afghan décor hidden behind decoratively carved doors. Ceiling, walls, and floors were painted dark red. The space reminded me of the hidden meeting rooms in Washington, DC, hotels—designed for comfortable discretion. A very well-dressed man in his midforties walked in.

I greeted him in English. "Are you Ambassador Bahrami?"

He smiled broadly before acknowledging that he was indeed Bahrami. After a warm and polite greeting, he sat down at the table across from me. I handed him my card, which he examined closely with a hint of puzzlement. We continued our conversation in English, not Farsi.

I introduced myself and started talking about the problem of wildlife trafficking in Afghanistan. Within moments of getting into the importance of biodiversity, I noticed that he looked bored and distracted; he glanced around the room as if waiting for someone else, only occasionally turning to me and giving a polite nod. After ten minutes, Bahrami's phone rang, and to my annoyance, he took the call, speaking in Dari. I kept explaining the wildlife trafficking until another man walked up and greeted Bahrami, who promptly turned to me and asked if we could meet some other time. I politely agreed to reschedule, even as I was confused and somewhat annoyed. This diplomat had insisted that we meet today, only to show up and display profound disinterest.

Just as Bahrami ditched me, another man dressed in an equally fine suit approached me.

"I am Ambassador Bahrami. Are you Dr. Alex?"

Two well-dressed men, one an Afghan entrepreneur, the other the Iranian ambassador, both named Bahrami, just happened to show up for meetings at the Serena Hotel in the same alcove at 2:00 p.m. that day. I had just met the wrong Bahrami first.

I explained the strange coincidence to the new Bahrami. He did not see the humor of the situation and was annoyed that I could have confused him, the Iranian ambassador to Afghanistan, with some random Afghan. At least, based on the tone of our earlier phone conversations, I knew I now had the real Bahrami.

I thanked the ambassador for the honor of his presence and gave him my card. He studied the card closely and carefully. Just then, my phone beeped with a text message notification. Not wanting to be rude, I made an officious show of turning off my phone and placing it on the next table over.

Bahrami looked at me seriously. "Ah! Very good idea. I will do the same thing."

He turned off his phone and then, in a highly exaggerated manner, ceremoniously placed it on the next table. Only afterward did I realize he thought I had turned my phone off to prevent digital eavesdropping.

Bahrami leaned forward, looked straight at me, and started speaking. "As you know, the United States and Iran have many interests in common in Afghanistan. The nature of the relationship can be based on cooperation and mutual interest. In fact, during the initial invasion of Afghanistan, the US and Iran worked together closely to ensure the success of the invasion and the overthrow of the Taliban. However, this communication was broken off soon after by your government. This doesn't have to be the case."

I realized I was on the verge of getting into much deeper trouble. I tried to break in.

"Ambassador Bahrami—"

He ignored the interruption. "We have an opportunity to end three decades of mistrust among our countries. The Iranian people are tired of the conflict and isolation. Afghanistan can be the way forward for our nations."

I attempted to interrupt again. "Ambassador, I came to speak to you about wildlife trafficking."

He waved off my objection with an irritated flick of his hand. "There is great opportunity for cooperation on Afghanistan and for rebuilding trust between our countries."

These were amazing statements from an Iranian diplomat about the potential for restored relations, but they were wasted on me and the current administration, and I needed to get that across.

"Ambassador Bahrami, I do not represent the United States; I am not a member of the government."

He again dismissed my comments and continued with his careful invitation to a dialogue between the United States and Iran.

I later learned that Bahrami was the force behind the short-lived co-operation between the two nations early in the invasion and had worked closely with the US ambassador to Afghanistan, Zalmay Khalilzad, who later became the US ambassador to the United Nations. In the tumultuous days after 9/11, the US had secret engagements with Iranian diplomats in Geneva and initial unacknowledged cooperation. The Iranians had almost gone to war with Afghanistan earlier, after a Taliban militia killed eleven Iranian diplomats in 1998. The Taliban saw the Shi'a as apostates. Iran's shared interest in defeating the Taliban and securing and rebuilding Afghanistan brought it close to reconsidering its antipathy toward the United States—at least until President George W. Bush named Iran as part of the "axis of evil" in his 2002 State of the Union address. Iran is a proud country with five thousand years of civilization. Getting lumped in with rogue states abruptly halted the rapprochement until my unwitting summit with Ambassador Bahrami.

I really needed to clear up the misunderstanding. I stopped Bahrami again, this time more forcefully, a bit less politely, interjecting, "Ambassador, you need to listen. I do not represent the United States government."

He refused to believe me. "You have the logo of the United States on your letter. You are representing the United States." He pulled out the letter and pointed to the USAID logo, which demonstrated two clasped hands in front of a red, white, and blue shield. USAID's branding rules required us to print the logo on everything, and I had argued voraciously that placing that logo on our business cards and letterhead, especially as we weren't contractors but were grantees, undermined our security and made us targets. While there were significant strategic reasons for why we wanted the recipients of US foreign assistance to know its origin, the dull-witted application of USAID's corporate branding policy in a war zone had the unwanted effect of generating suspicion that NGOs were an official part of the US government—or perhaps even spies. In most cases, they lacked the security infrastructure that US government entities had. The branding policy had also done a great job of confusing the Iranian ambassador.

"We are a zoo"—and I used the Farsi word, *bogh-eh-havoon-eh-vache*—"and our purpose is to conserve animals. USAID is our funder and requires us to use their logo, but I am not part of the government. I am a biologist. We have nothing to do with the government of the United States other than they gave us a grant. I don't represent them, nor can I."

Bahrami was stunned and sank into his seat.

I took advantage of his depressed silence to finally explain, at great length, why WCS was in Afghanistan, the initiative to curtail wild-life trafficking, and how we hoped the embassies could help. The entire time I spoke, Bahrami never made eye contact and seemed lost in thought. When I finished, he slowly turned to me and said he would ask his embassy to comply.

I felt the need to cheer him up. We talked briefly about his time in Afghanistan, and he noted how much he loved the country, the sincerity of the Afghan people, how this had been his favorite posting ever because of the complexity of the work and the opportunities it presented. He told me that he never wanted this assignment to end. The ambassador asked if there was anything else he could do for me. I did have one more request.

I arrived in Afghanistan hoping to find good Iranian food—given how many Afghans had spent time in Iran during the war years and that the two countries shared a 945-kilometer border—but had been singularly unable to find anything matching the food that I had grown up with, served to me by my grandmother and mother. In particular, I missed one dish. I explained my predicament to the ambassador. "There's just one Iranian restaurant here, and the food is terrible and not even Iranian. They don't even serve ghormeh sabzi. Do you serve any at the embassy?"

Ghormeh sabzi is something like an unofficial national dish of Iran, with a thousand-year history. The English translation of its name, herb stew, can't describe it properly. Morsels of lamb, red kidney beans, Omani lemons, and onions cooked for hours in sautéed herbs—parsley, leeks, spinach, cilantro, coriander, and the all-important dried fenu-greek leaves, served over fragrant basmati long-grained rice, make up the dish. It is my absolute favorite food in the world.

The ambassador looked at me with both a mixture of bemusement, surprise, and deep despair. He had thought he might be reopening relations with the West, but instead he was helping a Persian American find a plate of ghormeh sabzi.

"Fine. You can come to the embassy, eat your ghormeh sabzi, and then go. You have to use the back door and cannot tell anyone that I invited you to the embassy or that I fed you ghormeh sabzi."

I was ecstatic. But the next day, I read that Bahrami had been relieved of his duties and recalled to Tehran. I wondered if Bahrami had mentioned a promising back-channel meeting with an American official to Ahmadinejad and then had to confess that the meeting was about leopard furs and herb stew. I hoped I hadn't accidentally cost him his beloved job. I would never know.

CHAPTER 5

THE FORGOTTEN PEOPLES ON
THE ROOF OF THE WORLD

Lord Curzon, in his search for the source of the Oxus, described its waters as descending from a hidden roof of the world, whispering of a place of forgotten peoples and unknown lands. It was here that we set up our work to census and protect the Marco Polo sheep and snow leopard. During the late summer and fall of 2006, we were ramping up our activities in Wakhan. We sent teams to study the populations of Marco Polo sheep, snow leopards, and birds, as well as the state of the rangelands. We were also laying the groundwork for a park, with plans for a visitor center and other tourism infrastructure, including a potential airstrip. But we needed permission to go further and wanted to engage the region's leadership in the decision-making. There were already tensions between the WCS staff and both Ismaili and Kyrgyz leaders, leading to a request for WCS leadership to formally pay their respects to the local ethnic leaders, the military commanders, and the provincial representatives.

So when an old man, perhaps seventy years of age, walked into our Kabul office and declared himself to be Abdul Rashid Khan, the leader of the Kyrgyz people, and suggested that I visit Wakhan, the timing felt right. Perhaps more extraordinary was that Rashid Khan had spent the last four weeks riding a horse from Wakhan to Kabul to have an audience with President Karzai and others (including WCS), seeking to ask for help for his people. Not only had he traveled through mountain passes, along the edges of minefields, and regions filled with bandits, but at one point, his horse had slipped, and he had fallen off the animal and down the side of the mountain. He suffered broken ribs but still completed the journey. Abdul Rashid seemed to embody the indomitable spirit of the Kyrgyz, and he was inviting me to the roof of the world.

The population of Wakhan is split between two groups, the Wakhi and the Kyrgyz, both with surprising and complex histories—just like the region's wildlife and terrain. The two groups sit on opposite sides of major divides in Central Asia: Persian versus Turkic, farmer versus pastoralist, Shi'a versus Sunni.

The Wakhi, ethnically and linguistically Persian, inhabit the western Pamirs and parts of the corridor. Although basically agriculturalists, growing wheat, potatoes, and other crops, the Wakhi also graze livestock during summer and sometimes winter in the Pamirs. They are Ismaili, one part of the Shi'a branch of Islam (the other major branch are the Sunnis, who make up almost 90 percent of Islam). Other major Shi'a groups include the Twelvers and the Druze. The Twelvers are the largest Shi'a group and predominate in Iraq and Iran. Their name comes from their belief in the coming return of Mahdi, the twelfth imam, who lives hidden from mankind but will reappear to lead Islam to Judgment Day. But the Ismailis are not waiting for the return of the twelfth imam, because their prophet is alive; his name is Prince Karim Aga Khan IV, and he serves as the forty-ninth imam. Although the Aga Khan does not rule any country or geographic territory (although he owns numerous estates, farms, and even a private island, with a net worth estimated at $800 million), he has a kingdom of over fifteen million followers in twenty-five countries. His institutions, operating under the umbrella of the Aga Khan Foundation, are given diplomatic status, much like the Vatican.

The Aga Khan is prince, pope, prophet, CEO, and deity all at once. The Ismailis revere the Aga Khan as a direct lineal descendant of the

Prophet Muhammad, through Muhammad's cousin and son-in-law, Ali, considered the first imam in Shi'a Islam. And the largest population of the Ismailis in the world is in Badakhshan Province of Afghanistan, where we would be working to protect snow leopards and Marco Polo sheep. The Aga Khan's man on the ground there was Shah Ismael. We would need his permission to proceed with creating a series of national parks in Wakhan, including the potential of creating an international peace park among Afghanistan, Tajikistan, Pakistan, and China. He would be key to getting the support of the Wakhi people, much as Rashid Khan was for the Kyrgyz.

The Wakhi occupy the western Big Pamir, a considerable part of which was included in the proposed Big Pamir Wildlife Reserve. They are united by topography, language, and culture but separated by history and politics. They live in China's Xinjiang Province, southeast Tajikistan, and Pakistan, where they predominate in northern Chitral, Ishkoman Valley, and Gojal, Hunza. They speak the Wakhi language, giving vibrant life to an archaic distant dialect of Persian. The Wakhi are mountain farmers and cultivate crops in the spring before following their livestock to the higher pastures in the summer.

In the east of Wakhan, including the eastern half of the Big Pamir, live the Kyrgyz. They speak a Turkic dialect and practice Sunni Islam. The Kyrgyz are Turkic pastoralists who herd goats, yaks, horses, and a few donkeys and Bactrian camels. They shift their animals two or three times a year between summer and winter pastures. Such movements are short, often no more than ten to twenty kilometers. During summer, the Kyrgyz live in round, felt yurts and in winter mostly in stone and mud-brick huts. Their origin is in Central Asia, and they would pass easily into a crowd in Kazakhstan or Mongolia.

The Kyrgyz in Afghanistan are an enclave population, a relict moraine of the global political crisis. Like the Marco Polo sheep and snow leopards, the Kyrgyz exist outside the constraints of political borders. They fled to Afghanistan from Russia in the aftermath of the 1918 Bolshevik Revolution, which sought to suppress non-Russian speakers and identities. Other Kyrgyz came to Wakhan from China after the

cataclysmic 1949 communist takeover and subsequent cultural revolution and collectivization. From the 1950s to the 1970s, Afghanistan
was an island of stability in the midst of what was happening around
it. But another communist takeover, a Russian invasion, and a bloody
civil war, this time in Afghanistan, pushed the Kyrgyz people into crisis
once again.

In 1978, the People's Democratic Party of Afghanistan overthrew
the government. The coup, also known as the Saur Revolution, in-
stalled Nur Muhammad Taraki as the leader of a short-lived communist regime. Taraki, in the style of Afghan politics, was later suffocated
with pillows by three men under orders of his former ally and successor,
Hafizullah Amin, after Taraki tried to assassinate Amin. The Soviets
then assassinated Amin a mere three months later. This turmoil was
too much for Rahman Gul Khan, the leader of the Little Pamir Kyrgyz,
who understood where events were headed. He led some 1,200 of his
people, together with their flocks and herds, over the Waghjir Pass to
Gilgit in Pakistan. Their self-imposed exile was further entrenched by
the December 1979 Soviet invasion of Afghanistan. The Soviets dis-
couraged their return to Afghanistan, fearing that the Kyrgyz might
become a conduit of arms from China to the mujahideen.

Trapped in a hostile country in Gilgit, the Kyrgyz refugees were
compelled to sell their livestock, and the situation grew more desperate
for the migrants. At one point, Ron Petocz, an American biologist
who had done the original surveys of Marco Polo sheep in the 1970s
as a consultant for the FAO (and helped WCS after the US invasion),
argued for transplanting the Kyrgyz and their remaining livestock to
Alaska. However, the United States rejected their visas, human and
animal. In 1983, after much discussion and a visit by the Turkish ambassador who was astonished at the presence of Turkish speakers in
Afghanistan, the Turkish government agreed to give these Kyrgyz refugees a home. Much of the population was airlifted by the United Nations and settled near Lake Van in eastern Turkey.

The remaining Kyrgyz in Afghanistan, like the snow leopard, were
slowly going extinct; their population wasn't healthy physically or cul-

turally. This was the reason for Abdul Rashid Khan's trip down the mountain. We decided to reciprocate with a visit back.

THE TEAM THAT would go back to Wakhan consisted of myself, Kara, Peter Bowles, Ted Callahan, and Inayat Ali, along with Khoja, a second driver, and two members of our security team. Peter Bowles was a South African former military officer who had experience fighting in South West Africa (modern-day Namibia) and would help oversee our security, operations, and logistics. Ted Callahan, a mountain climber and doctoral student, was studying the Kyrgyz and served as our liaison to them. Inayat Ali, an Ismaili from the northern territories of Pakistan, oversaw our community engagement programs. We left Kabul early in the morning in two vehicles, headed for Wakhan. It is impossible to get out of Kabul without passing over steep mountains, through high passes or narrow river gorges. During the winter snows, the capital can become an island. Kabul's isolation in its mountain fortress made life difficult for us, as it had for many previous visitors. During the Soviet occupation, the mujahideen used the mountain passes around Kabul to stage attacks on Russian forces and then disappeared among the peaks. After the US invasion, the mountains became routes for the Taliban in and out of Kabul.

The trip north out of Kabul took us over Salang Pass, which crosses over the Hindu Kush mountains at an elevation of 3,400 meters (11,115 feet) and serves as the gateway to the grand fertile plains of Koh-i-Daman and northern Afghanistan. The Salang Pass tunnel was a marvel of Soviet engineering (in a pre-invasion joint project) when it opened up in 1965 and was the key to the supply route that linked Kabul to the southern Soviet republics. Supply lines have always been the weakness for any occupier of Afghanistan, be it British, Russian, or American. The mujahideen extracted a substantial toll on the Soviets at such bottlenecks. After the Russian pullout, Salang remained a key strategic target during Afghanistan's civil war. In 1997, the tunnel was damaged intentionally by the mujahideen leader Masood to slow the Taliban's advance on his forces in the Panjshir Valley. In December 2001, a team of Russian engineers, working with the British demining NGO HALO Trust, reopened the tunnel. During the repair work, they had to remove more than 6,700 tons of mines and explosives.

We stopped at the top of the pass and looked back down at the road zigzagging up the mountainside, passing in and out of tunnels along the way. Above us sat a massive but empty gun turret, and around us lay the burned shells of fuel tankers and armored personnel carriers. A cargo container was abandoned on the edge of the road. A grim rumor circulated that it had been filled with prisoners of war who were killed when a solider threw a fragmentation grenade into the container. I looked down; the gravel under my feet was filled with empty bullet shells that had been expended in decades of conflict. They were now part of the soil, creating a new geological horizon layer that would chronicle not only Earth's geological history but Afghanistan's turbulent political history. The bullet casings and land mines scattered on Salang's hillsides marked an exceptionally bloody period in Afghanistan's history, but not its first.

I had seen such geological manifestations of political upheavals before. When I was working in the newly created Russian Federation to rewrite the country's environmental law, I traveled to the Moscow countryside to stay with a friend, Ivan, a fellow Russian conservationist, at his dacha—a small, distinctly Russian summer cabin. We spent the weekend drinking beer, cooking shashlik (kabobs) over a fire, and overdosing on berries picked from his garden. One day, as we were walking through the forest, Ivan pointed out some faint undulations in the land among the dachas. These were fading impressions of the frontline trenches that stopped Hitler's advance into Russia during the Great Patriotic War, the bloodiest conflict in Russian history. The trench lines were wounds in the ground, slowly healing but still visible even half a century later. Similarly, traveling in Vietnam in the mid-1990s before the resumption of relations with the US, I noticed that every bridge in the north of the country was surrounded by a cluster of small fish ponds. I later realized these were bomb craters, the result of a US campaign that destroyed nearly every bridge in North Vietnam.

In both cases, these new geologic features were the scars of conflict, and although those memories were being gently eroded and reclaimed by nature, they reminded us of the extraordinary upheaval and pains caused by war, echoes of times past recorded in the landscape.

At the heart of Salang Pass lies the notorious tunnel—a dark, poorly ventilated passage filled with the noxious exhaust of dilapidated British Bedford lorries and Soviet-made Kamaz trucks ferrying goods and passengers from the former Soviet Union and the Afghan hinterland into Kabul and vice versa. As we drove through the narrow tunnel, barely two lanes wide, we were enveloped by its dankness. Many of the lights and fans in the tunnel weren't working, and our Land Cruiser's headlights penetrated just a few feet into the smoky gloom. The 2.6-kilometer tunnel seemed endless, its depressing darkness punctuated with occasional arched openings that looked out at brilliant vistas. When built, this was the highest road tunnel in the world. That elevation offered postwar expats a strange recreational activity: minefield skiing. During the winter, you could jump out the side openings of the tunnel and ski down the steep hillsides, slaloming over mines safely buried under the snow and ice, meeting the highway far below, and then riding up again via a waiting car for another run.

The tunnel wasn't just unpleasant—it had a dark history. On Wednesday, November 3, 1982, two Soviet military convoys traveling in opposite directions collided in the middle of the tunnel, setting off a huge explosion in a fuel tanker. Drivers continued to enter the tunnel after the accident, blocking in trapped troops desperately trying to escape. Soviet troops on the outside, fearing that the explosion was an attack by the mujahideen, closed off both ends with tanks, effectively trapping many inside the tunnel. Fire killed some soldiers directly; others were killed by either smoke inhalation, carbon monoxide escaping from vehicles whose drivers kept their engines idling to stay warm in the freezing cold, or oxygen deprivation fueled by the fire. There were reports even of Russians and allied Afghans firing on each other during the confusion. As many as seven hundred Soviet troops (accounting for nearly 5 percent of all Soviet deaths during their nine-year invasion) and two thousand Afghan soldiers and civilians died that day in the tunnel. As we drove through, I felt their ghosts swirling in the darkness.

Once we passed through the tunnel, the rocky, barren mountain landscape gave way to the brilliant green plains of northern Afghanistan, rolled out before us like a carpet. Here, on the other side of Salang, the Taliban were on the rise; UN security maps showed a dark red stain, previously isolated to the southern half of the country, slowly spreading into the north.

On the road, we passed a caravan of camels, and in the distance, we saw the dark brown tents of the Kuchi, nomads thought to have originated in India. Their lives were made more difficult by mines, increasing insecurity that closed international borders they used to freely cross, and the flood of former refugees returning to Afghanistan, who would forget or ignore the ancient treaties that allowed the Kuchi to move freely across their lands. After driving through miles of irrigated fields, we finally passed through Kunduz, where we spent the night in the house of the GTZ (the German Technical Cooperation Agency) country director, a tremendous courtesy that reflected the harshness of working in Afghanistan and the camaraderie that arises from it among development organizations.

The next day, we departed for Badakhshan, the mountainous province that contained the Wakhan Corridor—our destination. The road between Kunduz and Taluqan had been repaved, elevating our hopes that this would be an enjoyable trip, but we had barely gotten a few miles out of the city of Taluqan when the tarmac quit and we were on boulder- and gravel-strewn roads. We slowed to a crawl and jostled painfully over the rocks. Soon, the road itself merged into the mostly dry bed of a large river that was now a fraction of its old size. We drove along the riverbed for miles. The track was initially hard enough to follow but became much more so when it abruptly multiplied from a single track to multiple tracks. Sometimes the wandering tracks hastily converged back into a single road, only to again splinter into sundry pathways, always obscured by a thin fog of dust.

We had company on the tattered road. Demining crews, clad in cumbersome protective gear, gently prodded the ground in search of anti-tank and antipersonnel mines. This was a routine sight in Afghanistan. Deminers clearing areas adjacent to the runway had greeted me on my first flight into Kabul. After a ten-year occupation from 1979 to 1989 and a subsequent civil war between the Taliban and Northern Alliance from 1996 to 2001, Afghanistan was the third-most heavily mined country in the world. Warring factions often mined the same areas at different times. The decades of conflict have also left the country littered with unexploded ordnance (UXO), bombs that did not explode on contact but remain buried in the ground ready to explode. Over 23,500 people died between 1979 and 2015 due to mines and UXO in Afghanistan, often aggravated by a lack of emergency medical facilities that could potentially save some victims.

The mines weren't just a defensive weapon, as they had been in other countries where they were usually placed along borders; they had become a weapon of terror used against the civilian populations as well. The use of mines in the Soviet conflict was especially insidious. The Soviets made and distributed the brightly colored green butterfly mine known as the PFM-1. These mines could be dispersed from the air, thanks to a set of "wings" that stabilized and slowed the explosive device as it fell. The Soviets dumped PFM-1s indiscriminately out of helicopters, on hillsides, and next to villages. Once the mines were armed, they could not be disarmed. PFM-1s often killed or maimed children who thought they were toys.

Millions of other mines—both anti-tank and antipersonnel mines—were buried across Afghanistan. Bounding fragmentation mines, dubbed Bouncing Bettys during World War II, used trip-wire triggers to spring a shrapnel-laden projectile to chest height before exploding, showering a lethal spray of shrapnel in all directions. This design was meant to ensure that the mines killed enemy soldiers rather than merely taking a leg, preventing the soldiers from returning to the battlefield.

The Soviets, in contravention of international law, failed to keep maps of their minefields—which was impossible to do with mines such as the PFM-1. Over three decades of near continuous warfare, the combatants lost more of their humanity. Civilians, even children, became targets. Military forces mined agricultural farms, grazing areas, residential areas, and roads and footpaths, in both urban and rural areas. Riverbanks and irrigation canals were mined. This last act denied villagers access to water needed for drinking, bathing, animals, and agriculture.

The Soviet army did not clear the mines upon their departure but left them, whether out of spite after an embarrassing defeat that had knocked down a mighty superpower or out of fatigue from a conflict that had killed fifteen thousand Soviet soldiers and maimed another thirty-five thousand. The Red Army was eager to put a bloody conflict behind them, and it faced a crisis at home. Economics and political stagnation, coupled with the costs of the war, would result in the collapse of the Soviet Union a mere two years after the withdrawal from Afghanistan.

After the Soviet departure, Afghanistan was a vacuum. No effective or recognized government or army was left to deal with the problem. Mines cost a few dollars to put down, but they cost hundreds to remove. With over five million Afghan refugees living in Pakistan and another three million in Iran, the UN saw that a potential humanitarian catastrophe would unfold if these refugees suddenly returned home to mine-contaminated villages and fields. The UN Mine Action Program for Afghanistan and a series of Afghan and international NGOs, including HALO Trust, began the work of demining an entire nation. As we drove through the countryside, we saw the results of this work— slender footpaths on a distant hillside were lined with white rocks that signposted the only safe route through the landscape. In some areas, rocks were painted two colors—red on the side facing the minefield, and white on the side that was mine-free.

As we drove along the riverbank on the way to Wakhan, we should have been paying more attention to the mines. Our ride was interrupted by a sharp yell, and suddenly, the deminers closest to us were stumbling away from our lead vehicle, moving as fast as they could manage in their heavy protective gear. Other deminers stared at us in disbelief. I looked down at the road and saw what they had already noticed. The red paint marking the minefield was now facing toward the car rather than pointing away from it. At some point, we had lost the track, and we were now driving through the middle of the minefield. At the same moment, the others in the car saw it as well. We shouted at Khoja to stop. Stopping didn't solve the problem, though. If I ran for safety, I would be safe from anti-tank mines, triggered by weight far greater than a human body, such as our heavy Land Cruiser. However, I would be very much not safe from antipersonnel mines. Staying in the car offered some protection from antipersonnel explosives; our ballistic blankets were made of layers of Kevlar. They wouldn't protect us if the Land Cruiser's bulk set off an anti-tank mine. Neither option was especially appealing.

The dust slowly settled around the vehicle, and when it cleared, we looked back at our tracks and saw where we had entered the minefield. We had driven more than fifty feet into it. The boundary was easy to miss with the dust of passing cars covering the red paint and the multitude of tracks. The only way out was to tortuously reverse out of the field, following our tire tracks as closely as we could. The deminers were now too far away from us to help us keep on our path, and it was unlikely they would come closer.

We went silent as Khoja put the car in reverse and slowly backed up, trying to follow our tracks precisely. We inched out of the minefield in a painfully slow backward creep. After a few agonizing minutes, we crossed back into safety and resumed breathing.

As WE DROVE on toward Wakhan, we passed through the last habitat of the extinct Caspian tiger (*Panthera tigris virgata*). Both Babur and Virgil wrote about the Caspian tiger, as did Shakespeare, who described it as the Hyrcania tiger. They extolled a creature so ferocious that it was remarked to attack elephants. At one point, the Caspian tiger inhabited the largest geographical range of any tiger subspecies, ranging from modern-day Turkey through much of Central Asia to northwestern

China. By the late 1800s, Caspian tigers still inhabited modern-day Afghanistan, Armenia, Azerbaijan, northwest China, Georgia, Iran, Iraq, Kazakhstan, Kyrgyzstan, Tajikistan, Turkey, Turkmenistan, and Uzbekistan. Genetic evidence suggests that the Silk Road served to connect not just merchants but the populations of Caspian tigers in Afghanistan and Iran with the Amur tigers in Siberia, and researchers estimate that the populations were only separated for the last few hundred years before the Caspian subspecies died out, the connection most likely broken by the Soviet colonization of Turkistan, the modernization of Central Asia, and the predator extirpation programs that came with it. The resulting fragmentation had the effect of isolating populations, making each more vulnerable to random effects of extinction.

In Afghanistan, the Caspian tiger inhabited the lower reaches of the Amu Darya and Murghab River basins in the Turgay Woodlands—a boggy riverine ecosystem comprising trees, shrubs, and reed thickets. In this habitat, the big cats fed on Bactrian deer, roe deer, goitered gazelles, and wild boar. However, bounties paid for tiger pelts, destruction of the tiger's habitat for cotton and other agricultural products, and elimination of the prey base guaranteed its demise. The last tracks of the Caspian tiger seen in Afghanistan, perhaps the last seen anywhere, were found on a muddy riverbank in 1967 not far from where we had passed. The freshness of the Caspian tiger's extinction was disturbing; we were so close to being its contemporary. The Caspian tiger wasn't a dinosaur or a dodo; this breed had died out well within living memory. Down the street from our office, an enthusiastic café owner had shown us hide after hide of big-cat skins he had collected of Afghan animals, including that of a tiger. I listened to the wind for echoes of the tiger's roar as we passed. This wouldn't be the only extinction in Afghanistan.

AFTER AN EXHAUSTING drive from Kunduz, we arrived late at night in Faizabad, the capital of Badakhshan Province. The city, perched high over the Kokcha River, was dark and gloomy. We spent a few days meeting with USAID contractors, who spoke about constant threats and occasional attacks, the challenges of poppy cultivation, and the poverty in Badakhshan (this was the poorest province in Afghanistan despite the presence of gold and lapis lazuli). We also sat down with representatives of the National Environmental Protection Agency and the Ministry of Agriculture to brief them on our plans for a national park and to understand the needs of the area.

Soon enough, we were back on the road, headed for Ishkashim—the entrance to the Wakhan Corridor but also one of the only crossings into Tajikistan. As we were leaving Faizabad, a simple wooden kiosk in the market caught my eye. The stand had a hand-painted blue sign with a yellow price tag with the words *Best Buy* carefully printed on it—a recognizable and well-done imitation of the American electronics chain's logo. I was surprised at where this merchant had gotten the inspiration. We stopped to look closer. Although the kiosk, made out of a motley collection of recycled wood, could fit hardly more than a few old and dusty electronic devices on its uneven hand-built shelves, I found something hopeful about the scene. Here the owner had grand aspirations for his future and the future of the country. I had seen the courage and hope reflected in that sign over and over in other places—Iraq, Russia, and Madagascar—also in the midst of titanic change.

Outside Faizabad, we passed showy, newly built birthday cake houses. These small palaces reflected the darker side of Afghanistan. They would have fit right in in Kabul's gaudy Wazir Akbar Khan neighborhood, monuments to Afghan government corruption and war-zone entrepreneurship. But they seemed highly out of place in the outskirts of a small, remote Afghan provincial capital in the Himalayas. But soon, after passing the houses, we drove through miles and miles of brilliant red poppy fields, interspersed with minefields that came right up to the edge of the road. The poppy fields—the source of opium—explained what paid for the extravagant houses in the middle of nowhere. We spent much of that drive facing forward, feigning a lack of interest in the sea of red poppies that lined the road, lest the drug lords think we were surreptitiously surveying this year's crop.

As we rounded a corner on a steep roadside along a river, I looked down at a beach created by an outward bend in the river. Five dead donkeys were sprawled flat on the ground, perfectly arranged outward around a scorched crater in the sand, like petals of a poppy flower. The donkeys were still intact, and their bodies were fresh, with no blood. It was a fleeting but disturbing image. Perhaps had one of the animals stepped on a mine that had washed onto the beach? Within a few seconds, the beach and the donkeys were out of sight as we rounded another bend. But those donkeys lingered with me for years because of the chance callousness of their deaths and the lonely abandonment of their carcasses on the sand.

The road soon started following another river, the Warduj, a tributary of the Kokcha that later met with the Panj River to create the Amu Darya. The road along the Warduj was hewn out of the cliffsides, and we sometimes found our way blocked by sheep and cows being herded to market. We soon came to a flat, tan valley surrounded by high mountains with large, golden and rust-colored colluvial fans that spilled out from the mountain peaks above. Himalayan goji berry bushes lined the road, tinged red with their fruit. The road wound around these rounded fans, with new colors around each bend. The bridges over the river had partially collapsed in the spring floods and were barely held up by a jumble of logs and stone. We got out and walked across and then watched the Toyotas grapple across, hoping they would make it. As we entered into the Wakhan Corridor, Khoja stopped to show us petroglyphs on the other side of a small bridge across a stream, with an expanse of mountains behind the marker. The gray stone was carved with images of ibex and Marco Polo sheep, and it predated Islam's arrival in Afghanistan. We would find such petroglyphs on the footpaths through the mountains, documenting the history of these ancient highways. We were not the first travelers on these roads and would not be the last.

Finally, the road opened up to the broad, wide valley (a *pamir*) of the Wakhan Corridor, and we were soon at the border town of Ishkashim, at the threshold of the corridor, which stretches before it for 220 miles. Via a low bridge over the River Panj, Ishkashim is one of the few crossings into Tajikistan. Every week, a market takes place on a small island in the center of the river that is neither Afghanistan nor

Tajikistan but split between both countries, bringing together Afghan and Tajik buyers and sellers, connecting two similar communities separated by political history. The Aga Khan himself came to Ishkashim (via Tajikistan) to meet with the Afghan Ismailis who met him on the bridge. We met with a representative of the Aga Khan Development Network, who highlighted the extraordinary impact that opium was having on the people of Wakhan.

We had seventy-three miles of rough, boulder-filled road ahead to the village of Qala Panja, but before we could do so, we needed to get the "Wakhan Permission" from the border police commandant, Mir Abdul Wahid Khan, in Ishkashim. Like many Afghan officials, Wahid Khan was a former member of the mujahideen. There was still a large multiple-rocket launcher parked outside his simple office, and new Toyota Hiluxes, perhaps gifts from the United States, parked in front. We went inside to meet with the commander, and I showed him our permissions for entry.

I explained who we were and what we were doing. We would need the commander's help for all our teams. Wahid Khan ignored the substance of my comments and asked me what my name was.

"Alex Dehgan."

"Deh-ghan?"

"*Bah-leh.*" (Yes.)

He was deeply amused at this. Under one interpretation, my surname can mean *landowner*, but by another, it meant *peasant*. This was deeply funny to Wahid. My father, a physician and former medical professor from the Turkish-speaking region in the northeast of Iran, had changed our last name to make it simpler for his Persian-speaking patients to pronounce and so he wouldn't be an outsider within Iranian society with his Azeri last name, *Teleschi*. The thought of an American with an Iranian name was strange to the commandant, but even stranger was the status it assigned me—a peasant from Washington, DC, had traveled to the remote mountains of Afghanistan to talk about snow leopards and Marco Polo sheep. He laughed to himself again and heartily welcomed us to Wakhan with a big smile.

The road from Ishkashim onward was particularly infuriating. Across the river on the Tajik side, we could see a smooth, sealed tarmac road, with telephone wires and satellite dishes decorating the roofs of Tajik houses, suggesting a link to global civilization and its comforts, sometimes only a few hundred feet away, while we bounced along a rocky path on the Afghan side that occasionally seemed to have been made by lining up a series of large boulders. People in Afghan Wakhan gathered livestock dung, which they flattened and pressed against the sides of their houses until dry to use as their sole source of fuel for cooking and heating. The distance across the Panj River covered hundreds of years of human progress.

We arrived at Qala Panja, named after an old shrine and fort of Panja Shah, where Hazrat Ali, a cousin and son-in-law of the Prophet Muhammad, offered prayers. A stone that bears the imprint of his fingers is still revered by the Ismailis. Qala Panja was the capital of the Ismailis in Afghanistan, as well as the widest point of the Wakhan Corridor. Pir Shah Ismael, the leader of the Ismaili people in Wakhan, and his brother came out to greet us. Shah Ismael was dressed in a formal pin-striped suit jacket over a shalwar kameez, with a turban around his head, while his brother wore a military jungle-green camouflage vest and eyes that were deeply bloodshot and distant. We were invited to stay in his guesthouse, he said, a one-story stone-and-clay compound next to a small but beautiful glade of trees, a former orchard whose leaves were turning golden in anticipation of the coming snows. On the other side of the compound was an endless field of golden wheat, and surrounding us were snow- and glacier-covered peaks. It was an enchanting place. A small dilapidated wooden cabin, whose floorboards had started to crack and break, sat within the golden forest. We asked what this had been used for. Shah Ismael noted that we had stumbled upon the former hunting lodge of Afghanistan's last king—His Excellency Zahir Shah. The king was an avid sportsman whose hunting reserves in the Great Pamir, Ajar Valley, and Kol-e-Hashmat Khan were now the basis of many of Afghanistan's protected areas.

We meet with Shah Ismael that afternoon and laid out our vision: a national park that would include a Wakhan museum located at Qala Panja; the research we would undertake to understand the status of Afghanistan's biodiversity, particularly the flagship species of Marco Polo sheep and snow leopards; the potential for restoration of a luxury hunting program for Marco Polo sheep; and our desire to build up tourism again to support the region.

The hunting program was a topic where we needed to tread carefully. There has been growing recognition from the international conservation community that conservation-hunting programs can provide the basis for successful sustainable-use conservation, but these programs have proved controversial when wealthy hunters have legally gone after iconic species, even those past breeding age. The programs have pitted conservationists, managers, animal rights advocates, and social justice advocates against each other. The paired experiment between Afghanistan and Tajikistan, where Tajikistan adopted hunting while Afghanistan abandoned it, proved such programs could work (the Tajik population of Marco Polo sheep was many times that of Afghanistan and much better managed), but success would require transparency, ensuring a significant amount of the funding would return to local communities, good science coupled with accurate monitoring of the populations, and effective governance structures. Afghanistan was still far away from getting there. We didn't want to encourage illegal hunting, but that was happening anyway. At the moment, the sheep were being hunted by the Ismaili leaders, the border patrol on the Afghan and Tajik side, and by the family of Abdul Rashid, khan of the Kyrgyz.

Here we relied on Ted Callahan, our chief liaison to the Kyrgyz people, who was based in Kabul but spent most of his days in the field. Callahan, a tall, taciturn, brilliant, courageous, and sometimes churlish mountain climber, was carrying out his doctoral research at Boston University on the Kyrgyz. Callahan was later instrumental in identifying the incongruities in the Central Asia Institute's school-building projects in Afghanistan. But just then, we needed his help to stop the hunting of Marco Polo sheep with assault rifles. As it turned out, Abdul Rashid, who visited me in Kabul and entreated me to come to Wakhan, was also part of the problem.

The skittishness of the sheep protected them from most common weapons, specifically the "moosh kush" (literally, *mouse killer*), a 1950s-vintage Russian .22-caliber rifle common in Wakhan. The inaccuracy of these dated rifles required proximity to the target, which was difficult given the natural skepticism the sheep displayed about humans. But five of Abdul Rashid's six adult sons had received AK-47s, given to them by the Border Security Force, led by Wahid Khan, whom we had met, which used Abdul Rashid's family as a de facto militia in this border area. These powerful military rifles made hunting much simpler. According to research done by Ted Callahan, the Marco Polo sheep were being decimated by the khan's heavily armed sons, putting us in a difficult place. We needed to remove those weapons from the family whose help and support were indispensable to our conservation efforts and who had been given the weapons by the government. Before we could justify their removal or put a stop to the hunting, there had to be economic alternatives for the Kyrgyz and the Wakhi.

We also addressed the retaliatory killing of snow leopards to prevent the preying on domestic livestock through the compensation scheme and by creating predator-proof enclosures. We would work with other NGOs to improve animal health in the region as well, increasing the survivorship of their livestock. This would generate considerable goodwill by increasing the wealth and food security of the locals and decreasing incentives for poaching of Marco Polo sheep or snow leopards, we hoped.

However, the most effective strategy for the long-term survival and recovery of snow leopard populations was even more fundamental— restoration of Wakhan's rangelands through better management, which would benefit both the region's wildlife and human populations. By restoring the rangelands, we would improve the quality of feed for domestic animals but also help restore the prey base, such as ibex, for snow leopards. And by restoring the prey base, we would ease the pressure on the snow leopards to hunt domestic livestock, which in turn would reduce retaliatory killings. It also had the effect of supporting the Marco Polo sheep populations. But we were stuck in a tragedy of the commons. The overgrazing of the rangelands in the absence of coordination was the more successful short-term strategy but, ultimately, endangered human *and* wildlife survival.

The last topic in our meeting with Shah Ismael was the need to build ecotourism that would benefit both the Wakhi and the Kyrgyz. While ecotourism may at first seem an unlikely economic activity for Afghanistan, before the Soviet invasion, it was Afghanistan's second-largest source of income. Even as one of the remotest regions in the world, Wakhan has enormous potential for a range of tourist activities, driven by the area's natural beauty, high mountain peaks and glaciers, and the unique local culture, similar to trekking culture in other areas in the Himalayas. However, it had something that these other places—Nepal, China, Pakistan, India, Bhutan—did not: it was in Afghanistan.

Tourism in Afghanistan faced many challenges, from security to a lack of infrastructure. Shah Ismael and other Wakhi leaders said they were supportive of the plans because of what it would bring: potential tourism and revenue for Wakhan and infrastructure that would grant improved access to and attention from the rest of Afghanistan. However, while the Wakhi embraced the potential of ecotourism, the Kyrgyz were far less enthusiastic. Ultimately, the WCS was able to work to lower the barriers for ecotourism for both the Kyrgyz and the Wakhi and ensure that we were working with the communities rather than working against them.

To support these initiatives, WCS field teams needed to collect baseline data in Wakhan, the first comprehensive survey in thirty years (and in some cases ever), on such socioeconomic aspects as community structure, political units, needs, wants, and insights, attitudes and perceptions toward wildlife, hunting practices, and other relevant issues; human and livestock land-use patterns; wildlife diversity, distribution, and migration patterns; potential protected-area boundaries; the wildlife-livestock disease interface; and rangeland assessments. We would also need, with

Shah Ismael and Rashid Khan's help, to create conservation committees in each community in Wakhan and work closely with them to develop a functional system for management decision-making.

We also proposed building an interpretative center in Qala Panja, near the proposed Big Pamir Reserve. This could be a center for learning about the cultures and wildlife of Wakhan and facilitate tourism coordination in the region, complementing WCS's efforts to help communities support ecotourism. Specifically, we envisioned the facility as a hub for ecotourists and trekkers to find out about trekking and wildlife-viewing options, a spot for local communities to sell handicrafts, a choke point to collect ticket revenue and issue permits for any proposed protected areas, and as a logistics hub to arrange for horses and guides from the local community. WCS could also use it for their offices and keep proximity to the Wakhi. WCS would need to work with its community conservation committees, governance entities that we would need to create, to ensure that revenue was evenly distributed among the different villages. We also proposed creating a tourism information facility in Ishkashim, as many tourists would come in through Tajikistan.

That night, Shah Ismael organized a dinner party in our honor. We ate and listened to his brother singing as he beat a homemade dayereh, an Afghan drum made from sheepskin pulled tight over a circular frame. The word *dayereh* literally translates as "circle," and as Shah Ismael's brother's voice carried beyond the clay walls of the house, the sound of the dayereh and the simple majesty of his form pushed my thoughts to the other travelers who had passed through this very place, the great Pamir Valley on the rooftop of the world. The frame drum itself originated in the Middle East nearly 5,000 years ago, so it was likely that there had been other such parties just as the one we were having when Marco Polo passed this way 735 years prior.

The simplicity of the exterior of Shah Ismael's house belied the striking beauty of its interior. Rich paintings of Afghan wildlife—images of Marco Polo sheep and ibex standing majestically on a cliff's edge among clouds and meadows—had been painted on its interior walls. This strong identification with nature was everywhere in Wakhan. We had seen doorways decorated with the horns of ibex and cairns made of horns of Marco Polo and ibex sheep at religious sites. Some of the most noteworthy places in Afghanistan were named after wildlife. The Panjshir Valley—home province of Ahmad Shah Masood, the legendary leader of the Northern Alliance, which led the resistance against the Taliban and fought most fiercely against the Russians—literally translated into *the valley of the five lions.*

More than any place I had worked as a conservationist, Afghanistan was notable for the support its people showed to our work. Despite the mines, kidnappings, improvised explosive devices, bombings, dangerous aircraft, lack of infrastructure, and omnipresent military forces, Afghanistan was by far the easiest place I had worked as a conservationist and the most fulfilling. There were two reasons for this. First, with more than 80 percent of Afghans dependent on the natural resources (and which approached 100 percent in Wakhan), the failure of the environment would lead to the failure of the people. Second, for the millions of Afghans who had been refugees in neighboring countries during thirty years of war, the conservation of wildlife was in essence a chance to rebuild the core identity of who they were. Afghanistan's biological Silk Road was as unique as its cultural one. Conservation of Afghanistan's natural heritage resonated with people in every corner of the country, from provincial governors and members of parliament to farmers, because it was protecting the identity that they carried with them when they were living in neighboring Iran, Pakistan, Dubai, and elsewhere. Protecting the wildlife was an easy sell, because I was selling a stake in what it meant to be an Afghan. This wasn't obvious when we started in Afghanistan, and my efforts were only the beginning, but there was an enthusiasm that was not only surprising but imperative to our success.

The next morning, we left Shah Ismael and continued on the road to our final destination, Sarhad-e-Brogil, where the road ended, and the twin pathways—to Kashgar in China or Gilgit in Pakistan—began. From Sarhad-e-Brogil to the Chinese border at Waghjir Pass is only some one hundred kilometers (sixty miles), but the challenges of the terrain make it a multiday journey. One pathway, only crossable in the summer, climbed a high pass on its way to the Little Pamir, Lake Zorkul, and the isolated Waghjir Pass. The other pathway followed the frozen river in the winter.

The road had become noticeably worse past Qala Panja. The sand became pebbles, the pebbles became rocks, and the rocks became boulders. We had to cross swollen streams and small rivers that increased in frequency as we approached Sarhad. In 2007, a major earthquake hit the region, with its epicenter in Wakhan, where a WCS team was traveling. So bad was the jostling from the rough condition of the road, they did not even notice the earthquake when we called to inquire about their status, but had been puzzled at the rockfalls that occurred simultaneously around them.

On the way to Sarhad, we passed a Wakhi shepherd of no more than perhaps fourteen years of age. Behind him was a donkey loaded with grasses that the boy was collecting as fodder to feed his animals. The shepherd and I stared at each other as the car passed. This could have been me in another life, but for the actions of my family to seek education and then move to America. The boy, with his closely cut dark hair, ruddy cheeks, and thick woolen overcoat, looked directly at me, and then put his hand to his chest in a symbol of greeting. That simple, warm gesture was a welcome to Afghanistan and Wakhan. Like the dead donkeys arrayed around the crater, here was another fleeting image with lasting effect. Here was Afghanistan, its danger and kindness coexisting across the beautiful, rugged landscape.

A spectacular mountain wrapped by glaciers came into view. This was Noshaq, Afghanistan's highest mountain, 24,580 feet (7,492 meters) high, the westernmost 7,000-meter peak in the Himalayas. Although land mines were relatively rare in Wakhan, there was an unlikely minefield at 3,000 meters on the way to Noshaq. Masood, the famous Northern Alliance leader, had feared a Taliban invasion from Pakistan through Noshaq and had placed the mines as a preemptive measure. After the fall of the Taliban in 2001, the international climbing community was reinterested in the mountains of Afghanistan, which had been largely off-limits due to decades of conflict. Carlo Alberto Pinelli, director of Mountain Wilderness International, gained permission in 2003 to climb Noshaq; soon, Afghan porters and mountaineers were training, among them, the first female Afghan mountaineers, including the daughter of our Nuristani team leader. Getting across the Noshaq minefield required a dangerous two-day scramble across a flow of fallen rocks (with the help of Wahid Khan, who'd helped lay the mines in the first place). Although an Afghan national was part of the original 2003 expedition, the first Afghan summit of Noshaq didn't happen until July 2009, almost three years after our passing of the mountain, by two Afghans who were the first of their country to summit Afghanistan's highest and most majestic peak.

We stopped at the house of Alex Duncan, a British general practitioner who lived in the tiny village of Kipkut. Duncan lived there with his wife, Eleanor, and their four young children—three blond daughters (Ruth, Libby, and Anna), and their oldest child, Jacob, a brown-haired boy with an infectious smile. Sunflowers populated the garden outside. When we entered into their home, we felt as if we had crossed into a warm and cozy house in the British countryside. In this one twenty-foot-square room, Alex, his wife, and their four children lived, ate, slept, bathed, and did school. Somehow it seemed completely normal.

This was despite that the Duncans lived in one of the world's most challenging environments. In December and January, the nighttime temperature could drop below 25°C (- 13°F) and not even rise above freezing during the day. Alex had arrived in Afghanistan in 2002 to provide care for the people of this harsh region; he was the only doctor in Wakhan. Despite that we had dropped in unannounced and their house was like any house filled with children—chaotic, messy, and energetic—they welcomed us with delightfully fullhearted hospitality. Alex explained his routine with the region's villages and the hacks he'd rigged to be able to stay in touch with the West through a local NGO's satellite e-mail access.

We spoke to them about the significant health challenges in Wakhan. Life in the mountains is difficult and brutish for the Wakhi people in Afghanistan. People age fast in the mountains, and the short growing seasons and harsh conditions created challenges for nutrition and food security as well as other aspects of development. In 2002, the Afghan minister of health reported that Badakhshan had the highest maternal death rate in the world. According to the announcement, 6.5 percent of mothers were dying during childbirth. The children were dying frequently as well. According to one study in 2000, 22 percent of infants did not survive beyond their first year. However, Dr. Duncan found even higher rates in Wakhan. His data from the Afghan Pamir established that child-under-five mortality there was a staggering 520 deaths per 1,000 live births (52 percent mortality), the world's highest rate. It is not unusual for women to lose a child, or two or three, in the merciless environments of Wakhan.

For many, opium is the preferred treatment for dulling the harshness of life. Its effects on the population have been devastating. As herding people become addicted, they slowly surrender their wealth—measured in heads of livestock—to the drug dealers but are still obligated to care for and graze the herds. They become indentured servants to the addictive power of opium, and everything else gives way. Entire communities in Wakhan were addicted to opium, and the habit started early. Afghans were known to put opium on the gums of teething infants to reduce their pain and stop their crying. In Badakhshan, Afghans use opium to treat everything from a headache to cancer, in part because it is the only palliative that is available in such remote regions. The Aga Khan Foundation's Wakhan representative in Ishkashim estimated that 90 percent of the local population uses opium. Even a major demand of their religion—the requirement to do the Haj, the great pilgrimage to Mecca, one of the seven pillars of Islam—was rejected by those addicted because it would mean they would have to abandon their access to opium, even for a few months. They could not bear to part with their narcotic, even if it denied them the chance to meet the fundamental tenets of their faith and potentially gain entry into paradise. For this reason, the drug—both growing it and using it—was forbidden (*haram*) under Islam. Alex and his wife would be awarded the Most Excellent Order of the British Empire in 2010 for their work in documenting opium abuse in Afghanistan and their dedication to improving the health of the people in the region.

It was tough to leave the Duncans' island of happiness, warmth, and cheer, but there was clearly not room for more people in their house. We approached Sarhad in the dusk, and the road grew ever more challenging. The stream crossings were more frequent, and the water seemed to be growing swifter and more powerful.

The darkness gave the crossings an unsettling edge, as we could no longer see how deep or fast the waters were, and the crossings were increasingly obscured. The white, cheerful streams were now dark, roaring, and ominous. The afternoon and early evenings were dangerous times for crossings since the rivers swelled up from the snowmelt during the day. Moreover, identifying the road became harder and harder, as a thick fog had settled in that prevented us from seeing very far ahead or to the sides to orient ourselves. The temperature dropped quickly, and it became very cold. We would drive into one stream, find it too deep, and reverse until we thought we found another crossing, only to find that too deep as well. And now it was almost completely dark, with no twilight remaining. It was September and getting colder, and winter would soon be on its way in the Pamirs. Finally, after multiple backtracking and crossings, we were stuck at the edge of a fast-moving river that seemed too wide and deep for the vehicles to cross. We couldn't stay where we were since it would be too cold once it got dark, and we were unsure what the water levels would do. But we had also lost the road and were unsure whether this was the crossing.

Ted Callahan, our mountaineer, jumped out of the car into the glaring white of the headlights and stepped into the fast-moving freezing water. He struggled against the current and tested the stream in different directions by feeling the bottom with his feet until he located the crossing and found the terminus of the road on the opposite bank. He went back and led the vehicles behind him until we crossed the last river. Ted hopped back into the car, clutching his chilled body and shivering hard. I was concerned that he would get hypothermia. We moved quickly to find a way to warm him. Without Ted's help and courage, we would have been perhaps stuck in the river or would have had to backtrack hours to Qala Panja in the darkness. Soon after the final crossing, we saw the first outbuildings of Sarhad come out of the mist. We had made it, and from here on, the transport would be by horse, mule, yak, and foot for teams going into Wakhan. The guest-house soon appeared. Like other Afghan houses, it was a single open room with a low step for sleeping around a shared common space. It was one of the few guesthouses in Wakhan, and we were happy to have a warm place.

The next morning, we were joined by a Danish army team on patrol. They were clearly far off the path from typical military discipline. Peter Bowles, a former South African military officer, privately grumbled about the Danes' shaggy hair and unkempt beards, but in Wakhan, no one cared. The Danes in turn complained bitterly about the Germans, whom they considered cowards. The Germans, who were in command of their Provisional Reconstruction Team Base, would order the Danes to patrol the most dangerous parts of Badakhshan, while the Germans would stay close to their base, minimizing their risk.

After meeting with the owner of the guesthouse, Kara and I started hiking up the path behind Sarhad to the high pass to Little Pamir. We followed the rocky and narrow path higher and higher into the moun-tains, and more of the Pamirs came into view. A herder and his yaks came down the path, and we made way for the thick, shaggy beasts. Our teams later hired such yaks on their expeditions in search of the Marco Polo sheep populations and snow leopards. Because of the altitude, we were soon out of breath and stopped to rest in a field of boulders. As we sat down, we noticed petroglyphs scratched into some of the stones. A few thousand years ago, someone had etched images of Marco Polo sheep and ibex on the stones. We were walking amid history standing on a tributary of the Silk Road, and these ancient markers illustrated the very animals that we came to Afghanistan to save. It felt like a sign.

That afternoon, after hiking back down from the path, I heard about a bathhouse fed by a hot spring in the middle of the village. I gathered my things and looked forward to my first bath in a week. A man guarding the door told me that Wahid Khan, the border police commander whom we had met earlier, was inside the bath and that I would have to wait. After waiting for him to finish, we gladly climbed into the warm but murky water. It did not look very clean, but it was better than nothing, or so we thought. After a quick wash, and on our way out, our Afghan staff told me that they found out during discussions with the border guard that Wahid Khan had a serious case of dysentery.

After a few days, we started our way back to Kabul. We flew back from Faizabad and had the vehicles meet us in Kabul. When the cars arrived, I noticed one of our security guards removing a birdcage housing an Afghan quail. Such birds were used in bird fights. He had purchased it during the trip, and we had inadvertently trafficked wildlife from Wakhan. I had to spend the next staff meeting reminding our team about our purpose in Afghanistan.

WCS would build a major initiative in Wakhan. We would over the next few years invest heavily into investigating and conserving the Marco Polo sheep and the snow leopards, as well as the many bird species that were found in Wakhan or that used it as a migratory transit point. It in some way would become a refuge for the WCS programs that would find other parts of the country growing increasingly dangerous, restricting our ability to survey them, even with Afghan teams.

However, in the early days of the program, we still had the opportunity to explore. And our first national park would be in Bamiyan, not in Wakhan. And we would build it with the help of a prince.

CHAPTER 6

THE BUDDHAS OF BAND-E-AMIR

NESTLED IN THE Koh-i-Baba mountains to the northwest of Kabul, Bamiyan is not an especially large city by the standards of Afghanistan, but it boasts a history as rich as anywhere in the country. In the first millennium AD, Bamiyan belonged to the Buddhist Kushan Empire, which straddled India and Central Asia. At the height of the Kushan Empire, as Nancy Dupree reminds us, Kushan was the nexus connecting Han Dynasty China to the east, Persia and Rome to the west, and the spices and jewels of India to the south. The city, a crossroads on the ancient Silk Road, hosted merchants, pilgrims, and conquerors and became a center of learning and art, home to the first known use of oil in painting.

Tens of thousands of monks in ochre robes and multitudes of pilgrims from as far away as China came to Bamiyan to study and worship at an enormous multicolored timber monastery carved into the mountain. Numerous other holy sites, monasteries, and stupas (dome-like Buddhist shrines) rose around the valley. The crowning glory of Bamiyan was the giant Buddhas—the largest standing statutes of Buddha in the world. They sat in alcoves that were hewn out of the pebble-filled sandstone mountainside. The western Buddha was 55 meters (180 feet) high, while the eastern one was 38 meters (125 feet) high. Despite their enormous size, they were carved with great care and delicacy, right down to the gently flowing stucco creases of their robes, and then gilded with golden paint.

The two giants gazed down over the valley for 1,600 years, watching overburdened trading caravans stream past. The colossi survived Genghis Khan's cannons, attacks by the zealot Mughal king Aurangzeb, and British invasions. But on February 27, 2001, their death sentence arrived via the radios of the Taliban.

The radio broadcast ordered that all statues representing human forms in Afghanistan were to be destroyed. Initially, the Taliban had deemed the statues as harmless, potential tourist attractions at the best and dead idols at the worst. But that didn't stop the attempts to bring down the giants. Just after occupying Bamiyan in their takeover of the country, Taliban fighters dynamited the head of the smaller Buddha, blowing its face away, and then spitefully fired rockets into its groin, destroying parts of the robes and the intricate frescos that decorated the niches behind the statue. But only after the official order came across the radio did the Taliban get serious about destroying the Buddhas, aiming anti-aircraft guns and artillery at the ancient titans and laying explosives on top of anti-tank mines at their bases.

The Buddhas didn't go down without a fight. When the initial shelling and mines didn't succeed, the Taliban lowered Hazara prisoners down the face of the statues on ropes and tasked them with placing timed charges into the sculptures. Taliban leader Mullah Omar and the head of al-Qaeda, Osama bin Laden, came to watch the final demolition in person. However, even this effort did not completely eliminate them: the blasts failed to destroy the face of one of the Buddhas. Although the Buddhas were too large to entirely erase, the Taliban was successful in mutilating an important part of Afghanistan's cultural identity and patrimony beyond repair. Other Buddhas across the valley met a similar fate. In nearby Kakrak Valley, a 6.5-meter Buddha fell, and many smaller Buddhas and artwork in caves and alcoves were also demolished. Hand-painted ceiling and frescos were burned until darkened.

Bamiyan sits at the heart of Hazarajat, the homeland of the Hazara people. The residents of this plateau descend from the pillaging armies of Genghis Khan. Many Afghans have startlingly fair features, but some Hazara faces are distinguished by broad cheeks and the prominent epicanthic folds of the eyes. Hazaragi, their dialect of Dari, contains some elements of Mongolian vocabulary. Like the Wakhi, Hazaras are Ismailis, followers of the Aga Khan. This makes them Shi'a Muslims and earned them the hatred of the Sunni Taliban. Despite eight hundred years of continuous presence in Afghanistan, the Hazaras are considered outsiders—somehow the Mongol invasion is recounted as recent history. "Hazaras are not Muslims; you can kill them," Taliban commander Maulawi Mohammed Hanif reportedly told fighters after their 1998 capture of Mazar-i-Sharif, which had a sizeable Hazara minority. Within hours of their takeover, Taliban forces acted on their commander's word, launching a killing frenzy. Human Rights Watch documented the subsequent genocide of Hazaras and other minorities. In systematic searches, "scores and perhaps hundreds of Hazara men and boys were summarily executed, apparently to ensure that they would be unable to mount any resistance to the Taliban."

The Taliban regime oversaw countless acts of violence against both the country's cultural heritage and its people. In the chaos that reigned after their fall, we sought to prevent a similar fate for one of Afghanistan's greatest natural treasures.

Just sixty miles from the ruins of the Buddhas sits one of Afghanistan's most unique geological formations. Six lakes, their waters a deep lapis blue, separated by a series of natural travertine dams. At the dams, waterfalls pour from one lake to the next. Rising to elevations of nine thousand feet above the lakes are sheer, magenta-hued cliffs, cutting countless inlets and undulations into the shoreline. Behind it all glisten the fifteen thousand–foot peaks of the Koh-i-Baba, the Father of all Mountains. This is Band-e-Amir, Afghanistan's answer to the Grand Canyon.

The landscape is breathtaking, but it is the travertine dams that make Band-e-Amir a matchless treasure. Travertine is a type of limestone formed by water supersaturated with calcium carbonate. Stalactites and stalagmites are composed of travertine, as is the Roman Colosseum.

Bernini used travertine for the graceful arc of the Colonnade of Saint Peter's Square in Rome, and Michelangelo constructed the ribs of the dome of Saint Peter's Basilica from it.

The travertine of Band-e-Amir forms when snowmelt high in the Hindu Kush percolates slowly through the underlying limestone, dissolving its principal mineral, calcium carbonate. As the water seeps out from cracks in the rocky landscape into the high-elevation air, CO_2 escapes out of the solution. This lowers the pH of the water, which in turn leads to precipitation and accumulation of calcium carbonate. The dams at Band-e-Amir form via deposits of calcium carbonate at the edge of the water, encrusting the edges slowly over centuries, millimeter by millimeter, until translucent-white, porcelain-like dams forty feet high hold back the cold, mineral-rich blue waters. Band-e-Amir is one of the few natural lakes created by travertine systems around the world but was the only one not on the UNESCO World Heritage list.*

Band-e-Amir's significance was cultural as well as natural. At the base of the main lake, Band-e-Haibat ("dam of awe"), sit two important structures. The first is a shrine devoted to Hazrat Ali. The shrine (constructed in 1844) reportedly contains Ali's footprint and the place where he prayed upon the completion of the dams of Band-e-Amir. According to legend, Ali used his great sword, Zulfiqar, to cut off the top of a mountain, creating a rockfall that formed the dams. His feat so astonished Afghans that it helped convert the kingdom to Islam. A few hundred meters west of the shrine, a pair of unfinished standing Buddhas, each about twenty meters tall, preside over the lake from alcoves cut into the overhanging cliffs. Little is known about the Buddhas of Band-e-Amir, how old they are, or why they were abandoned unfinished. This absence of knowledge or awareness about them, coupled with their faint image, may have served to protect them.

Band-e-Amir was not especially rich with wildlife, but we hoped to assess the populations of Persian leopards, urials, and ibex. We would also be working in another protected area—Ajar Valley, which, like

---

* At the time of writing, it is still only on a tentative list for inscription as a World Heritage site.

the Kol-e-Hashmat Khan wetlands and the Big Pamir Reserve, was once a hunting reserve of the last king of Afghanistan. The Ajar Valley is a spectacular long gorge created by the Ajar River and the sheer-sided Jawzari Canyon. It is located many hours north of Band-e-Amir and protected by poor, backbreaking roads. The area around the gorge was once home to robust populations of ibex, urials, Bactrian deer, and more, but years of conflict resulted in a lack of protection for the area. Unsurprisingly, wildlife populations suffered dramatically without conservation; Bactrian deer were believed to be locally extinct, while ibex and urial numbers had likely declined dramatically.

Like many of the sites in which WCS worked in Afghanistan, Band-e-Amir and Ajar had already been identified as places worth protecting. The area was publicly listed as a national park in 1973 and Ajar as a wildlife reserve in 1977, but they were only "paper parks" that hadn't completed the legislative and executive processes for becoming fully fledged protected areas. Christopher Shank and John Larsson, experts from the UN's Food and Agriculture Organization, concluded in a 1977 report that Band-e-Amir was a national park in name only:

Unfortunately, Band-e-Amir National Park is not, in our opinion, functioning as a true national park. Proper jurisdiction and legislation are lacking, tourist facilities are substandard, and ecological degradation by residents and tourists is allowed to proceed unchecked. With proper planning and management, however, the area could be a model of how sound conservation practices can be combined with significant economic benefits.[*]

Thirty years later, all the challenges Shank and Larsson identified remained true, and more had emerged. Band-e-Amir was one of the front lines for fighting between Taliban and resistance forces during much of 2001. The direct road from Bamiyan to Band-e-Amir had

---

[*]Christopher Shank and John Larsson, *A Strategy for the Establishment and Development of Band-e-Amir National Park*, DP/AFG/74/16: Field Report 8 (Kabul, Afghanistan: Food and Agriculture Organization, 1977).

been mined and was the location of a tragic incident in July 2002 in which a passenger bus hit an anti-tank mine, resulting in the loss of thirteen lives. All traffic used a thin dirt track considered safe—but painfully bumpy and slow. The wildlife in the region had likely been decimated, but without surveys, it was impossible to say for certain. Unmanaged tourism and pollution were destroying the fragile geology of the dams. There were also conflicting royal claims to lands in Ajar. Farmers, many refugees returned from Afghanistan's wars, had started cultivation and grazing in the fragile rangelands around Band-e-Amir. To make Band-e-Amir a true national park, WCS and its partners not only had to navigate the challenges of operating as outsiders in Afghanistan but break up a sadistic tangle of bureaucracies to figure out who actually held authority over these natural treasures.

As always, the first step was putting together a team to run the project. Without the support of the community and multiple levels of government, we had no chance of success at Band-e-Amir, so we needed a community liaison officer right off the bat—someone who could provide introductions, explain the concept of a protected area to local leaders, explain the process under the protected area legislation, assess support among locals and get their feedback, develop an understanding of local politics and land and water ownership and community cohesion and feuds, and lay the groundwork for community management. Not exactly the sort of person you can hire off the street.

Fortunately for us, we had a connection to someone who knew the area well. WCS's Peter Zahler had reconnected with Chris Shank, one of the authors of the 1977 report on Band-e-Amir, for an initial UN Post-Conflict Assessment Unit rapid assessment of Afghanistan's biodiversity after the war. It only made sense to bring Chris Shank in to serve as the Hazarajat Plateau Project director. Chris had worked in Wakhan and Nuristan as well, so he knew Afghanistan perhaps better than any Westerner. A slight, sandy-haired American transplant to Canada, Chris was an expert wildlife biologist with deep knowledge of the species we were studying. When he wasn't in Afghanistan, he had carved out a career helping with the management of wildlife in the

Northwest Territories and Nunavut. Chris specialized in conservation in places that tended to be very cold or very mountainous, preferably both. Afghanistan fit that description well.

Notwithstanding his gentle and understated demeanor, Chris was tenacious and tough. He was an avid runner, cross-country skier, cyclist, kayaker, and mountaineer. He had undertaken some of the hardest expeditions in the world, including climbing Everest and Pumori in the Himalayas and scaling the two highest peaks in Canada, Mount Logan and Mount Saint Elias. If climbing mountains wasn't enough, Chris would lead punishing expeditions in Canada's frozen north. He crossed on skis the vast ice sheet that covered Ellesmere Island, located northwest of Greenland, well above the arctic circle. He would even continue his trips between his stints in Afghanistan. We got an e-mail from him noting that he would be out of office and wouldn't be responding to e-mails since he would be canoeing from Athabasca down the Athabasca and Slave Rivers to Yellowknife, Canada, on Great Slave Lake—a distance of 1,800 kilometers. Shank came back and told us stories of being chased by a hungry bear for days on part of the journey, unable to stop on shore and rest for fear of being attacked.

During his first visit to Band-e-Amir in 2006, Chris met Ayub, an Afghan geologist who had studied in Iran but whose family was from Band-e-Amir. Ayub was working for the Asian Development Bank (ADB) at the time of their meeting but soon accepted the crucial position of community liaison. I later traveled to China with Ayub for the Society for Conservation Biology meetings, where he was presenting on his research. Ayub was bright, curious, affable, and, like Chris, an adventurer. After just a few days on the ground in China, Ayub was guiding bewildered Western conservationists through the Beijing bus and metro systems that he had quickly mastered, although neither English nor Chinese was his native language.

Chris and Ayub mounted a survey to determine what had happened to the region's wildlife. They surveyed and camera-trapped both at Band-e-Amir and in Ajar. The surveys of Ajar Valley found the continued presence of low populations of both Siberian ibex and urial and anecdotal sightings of wolves. Camera-trap surveys north of Band-e-Amir National Park confirmed presence of Persian leopard, Himalayan lynx, and Pallas's cat. Most troubling was finding hunters passing by as well. Don Bedunah also surveyed the rangelands, which were threatened by overgrazing, the harvesting of vegetation, and dryland farming on steep hillsides.

The real heart of the project was managing one species in particular: humans. Chris and Ayub laid the groundwork for the creation of the park and the implementation of the recommendations Chris had made in his original 1977 report, which included a local coordinating committee that would work with Bamiyan-based organizations. Ayub played an instrumental role in making local communities aware of the renewed effort for the national park. He visited every village in the Band-e-Amir watershed and helped organize elections in those villages for representatives to the Band-e-Amir Protected Area Committee, the official governance committee for the national park. This body would set the rules and regulations that had been missing or ignored for decades and oversee the operation of the park under Afghanistan's environmental laws.

During our first few months in Afghanistan, we built a strong relationship with the prince and NEPA, thanks in part to Clay Miller, the embassy science fellow who was assigned to NEPA. Bill Taliaferro, the foreign service officer who oversaw environment and science activities in Afghanistan, introduced me to Clay Miller at a lunch at the embassy. Clay had come out of the EPA's Wetlands Regulatory Program and had volunteered to go to Afghanistan to support NEPA and work closely with Prince Zaher's staff. He quickly became my friend and collaborator in fighting the wildlife trade and in the efforts to build up the national parks.

Clay was a charismatic, well-built Californian with surfer-boy good looks and a dirty-blond mop that belied his age. His steady, pensive manner of speech reminded me of a Southern storyteller, and he was generous and loyal to his friends and a terrible adversary to his enemies. He loved to joke and laugh and was eager to make a difference in Afghanistan. He risked his life to do so as one of the few embassy staffers based in an Afghan ministry rather than behind the high walls and armed guards of the US embassy. Clay rode in an armored car from the embassy every day to sit outside the prince's office at NEPA to help build the agency's organizational capacity. He was a critical link to NEPA, and we visited NEPA on multiple occasions (while Kara remained embedded in the Ministry of Agriculture and supported our relationship with the staff there).

Our connection with Prince Zaher was promising, but not every visit to NEPA went smoothly. We usually traveled in one of WCS's Land Cruisers, but on the days they were needed elsewhere, we sometimes would hire Shafiq's ramshackle Toyota Corolla. Because it was nondescript, with civilian plates, and since most of the cars on the streets were also Toyota Corollas, we blended right in, but this also meant we didn't stand out. On one visit, a young security guard, newly hired, blocked our entrance to the NEPA office compound and started barking commands at Khoja, the WCS driver, and me. With surprising hostility, the guard came over to my window and demanded that I lower it—and then stuck his AK-47 into my face through the open window.

The guard's aggression triggered a strong reaction in me, activating deep memories of mortars, rockets, firefights, and IED near misses in Iraq and being drugged and kidnapped in Indonesia. I erupted in anger at the guard's threats. Before I even realized what I was doing, I pulled the weapon out of his hands through the window as I pushed open the door, which knocked him to the ground. I stood over him, pointing the gun at him and screaming in Farsi, "Is this how you treat guests in Afghanistan? Is this how you behave to people who are helping you?" The guard, who couldn't have been more than twenty, cowered on the ground, unsure if he was going to be shot. Khoja and another guard, an older man, pulled me away before anything worse happened. The older guard apologized; the new hire was just a boy, and he didn't know what he was doing. The anger subsided as quickly as it came, but I still dumped out the ammunition from the gun before handing it back to the older guard. And with that, we drove into the NEPA building for yet another meeting with the prince.

During my work in Iraq and Afghanistan, I barreled ever forward, focused on my mission. I tried not to think about the danger. When I did, it was usually when it was going to affect the security of my team. When I was in Iraq, rockets passed overhead, hitting buildings and structures, and the early morning mortars launched at us were close enough that we could hear the sand from exploding sandbags rain down on the roof of our trailer. We felt the pressure waves and sounds of car bombs and rocket attacks shoot viscerally through our bodies. We were once even caught in a firefight that erupted during a traffic jam, when a policeman started shooting into the air, trying to apprehend someone.

In Afghanistan, the threats were subtler until they weren't. The difference was that when I was in Iraq, I always knew when I wasn't safe, and I took precautions. In Afghanistan, I never knew if I was safe or not.

I never thought the threats fazed me, but it was clear later that they did. The ever-present danger in Afghanistan and Iraq manifested itself as a low, nervous buzz in the back of my brain for years, a feeling like drinking too much coffee, which started at the airport in Dubai flying into Afghanistan or Iraq. Every flight into those two countries was accompanied by a sense of dread complicated by excitement. Every flight out was accompanied by trepidation until we were over the Persian Gulf, and then a sigh of relief after leaving the pressure cooker of the war zones.

After my final departure from Iraq, loud noises and even the sound of a car door closing—which sounded remarkably like the sound of a mortar being launched—stopped me cold and sent me into a crouch, shivers shooting up my spine to the back of my head. My first meeting out of Iraq was a stopover in London to brief the British Ministry of Defence. During the meeting, a loud sudden bang made me drop to the floor, which made my British colleagues laugh. I didn't find it very funny. My overreaction at the ministry was automatic in the same way, coming from a place hidden away inside my psyche. I never mentioned the incident to the prince, and I never saw the guard again.

ON THE NATIONAL level, we needed to go beyond just working with NEPA and the Ministry of Agriculture; building the park would require building relationships with other entities, such as the Afghanistan Tourism Organization and the gaggle of international organizations working on the environment in Band-e-Amir, including the United Nations Office for Project Services (UNOPS), the United Nations Environment Programme (UNEP), the Asian Development Bank, and the US government. We would also need to engage the Ministry of Information and Culture.

We were pushing to get Band-e-Amir listed as a UNESCO World Heritage site, which required the support of the ministry. Inclusion on the World Heritage list would allow us to elevate Band-e-Amir's identity by designating Band-e-Amir as a priceless and irreplaceable asset not only for Afghanistan but for humanity as a whole. The World Heritage Convention sought to increase protection for these extraordinary institutions, places, cultural practices, and ecological and geological processes and habitats, given their importance to all nations. The effect of inscription on the World Heritage list would be to draw international attention and prioritization of international funding, make the site eligible for funding from the World Heritage Fund, elevate tourism, and allocate resources to the protection of Band-e-Amir. It would also receive protection under the Geneva Convention against misuse or destruction during wartime. (These conventions, however, would not save the ancient museum city of Aleppo in Syria.)

There were good precedents for Band-e-Amir being listed as a World Heritage site. Every major travertine lake in the world was on the World Heritage list, but due to its geological, biological, historical, and cultural uniqueness, Band-e-Amir arguably had even greater cultural significance than all of them. However, the Ministry of Information and Culture had its hands full, and while the Ministry of Agriculture had gotten the lakes on a tentative list in 2004, the process had stalled. To get things moving again, I met with Omar Sultan, the deputy minister of information and culture, and a liaison to UNESCO. I thought I had a fairly good case, but it didn't go as well as I'd expected.

Sultan received my case for Band-e-Amir coldly. He listed the problems with the potential listing: Afghanistan already had serious challenges maintaining its existing World Heritage sites. The colossi of Bamiyan had fallen at the hands of the Taliban, and other World Heritage sites in Afghanistan were still in peril. Among them was the Minaret of Jam. Once attached to a mosque that was long gone, the single beefy minaret hinted at the original complex's beauty, with intricate brickwork and glazed tile laid out in complex geometric patterns, and elaborate calligraphic inscriptions of Koranic verses. Built in the late twelfth century, and despite being the second-highest structure of its type in the world, it had been forgotten in a remote and inaccessible part of Ghor Province, along a bend of the Hari Rud River. With a lack of adequate funding and support, the minaret was now in serious danger of toppling.

Sultan was extremely pessimistic about the chances for a listing. Given these challenges and the lack of resources, the possibility of getting another site listed would be exceptionally difficult. UNESCO was quite particular about adding to the World Heritage list. The paperwork to list a site was extensive, requiring demonstration of adequate resources. Moreover, UNESCO was in the process for the first time ever of removing two natural sites from its register. One was in Oman, a preserve for the Arabian oryx, which was reduced by 90 percent after the Oman government discovered oil under the reserve. The second was the Dresden Elbe Valley, which was stripped of its title after local authorities had pushed for a highway bridge to be built across the scenic valley. This unprecedented nature of the delisting only increased UNESCO's wariness to Afghanistan's risks.

The conversation with Sultan became more and more difficult, and his responses were becoming shorter and more hostile to the idea and, it seemed, to me. I was getting nowhere with the deputy minister, so I decided to try flattery. His English was impeccable, and I complimented it.

"Where did you learn English? You speak very well."

"I worked and studied in the US."

"What state?"

"North Carolina."

Now, as a graduate of Duke University and avid follower of their celebrated basketball team, I immediately got worried about his alliances. Maybe we weren't clicking because of our natural rivalry, Blue Devils versus Tar Heels.

"Do you like basketball?"

"I love UNC. I am a huge Chapel Hill fan."

Since the meeting wasn't going anywhere, I had nothing to lose. I gave him the only acceptable Duke response to Carolina fans.

"Go to hell, Carolina," I said to the deputy minister of culture in Afghanistan.

He looked initially stunned but then responded in kind. A small shouting match about the failings of each other's basketball team ensued. By the time it ended, a friendship had started. Sultan's attitude toward listing Band-e-Amir with UNESCO turned more positive. He advised me on the preparation of additional materials and agreed to try to push the listing forward.

We still needed to get others to work with us. A multitude of organizations—as many as twenty—claimed some role in managing biodiversity and the environment in Afghanistan. Unsurprisingly with so many stakeholders, they were highly uncoordinated. At official meetings, which were few in number, one organization would complain about the other, but there were few incentives to directly resolve the issues. In reconstruction-era Afghanistan, staggering amounts of money moved through government. A few million dollars was decimal dust when $17 billion was spent on redevelopment. That gave lots of parties real money and little in the way of oversight or controls. Efforts to install an official coordinating body among Afghans or international donors quickly bogged down in politics and bureaucratic dysfunction.

To further complicate things, WCS had to play catch-up. Although WCS through Peter Zahler had been the first on the ground with the UN Post-Conflict Assessment Unit after the invasion, WCS as an institution came relatively late to the game. UNEP, UNOPS, the Aga

Khan Foundation, and the Asian Development Bank had already been working on the environment for a few years in Wakhan and Band-e-Amir. Although these entities didn't do systematic scientific field surveys that were a necessary prerequisite, and some lacked significant conservation experience in building a national park, they did have the status WCS lacked. The backing of USAID gave us important credibility, but we needed to earn more through actions and leadership.

Of course, the huge sums of money spent on redevelopment weren't spent particularly well. International donors contributed massive amounts only to have something like 80 percent of that funding return to the donor nation through contractor profits, security costs, and consultant salaries. Of the 20 percent that stayed in Afghanistan, most was spent in the cities rather than the countryside, where the majority of Afghans lived. By my own rough estimates, less than one dollar in twenty reached those who needed it most.

USAID wasn't the only development actor that was struggling. The US military, increasingly frustrated perhaps by USAID's lack of successes in Afghanistan and flush with resources, started investing more heavily into its own development projects to win the hearts and minds of Afghans on the ground. The Department of Defense gave on-the-ground officers access to something called Commander Emergency Relief Funds—tens of thousands of dollars—for development outlays, frequently with little to no coordination with or input from development professionals. Development and nation-building weren't roles for the Department of Defense historically, and indiscriminate applications of virtually unlimited capital often aggravated the underlying problems, despite good intentions and good people. In Helmand Province, CERF money was used to drill wells that destabilized centuries-old underground water distribution systems, dropping the water table and increasing water take from the Helmand River basin.

This in turn stoked a long-simmering resource conflict with Iran. The Helmand River didn't stop at Afghanistan's borders, but flowed into Iran, specifically into Sistan-e-Baluchistan, Iran's least stable province, which was almost entirely dependent on the Helmand River.

The water supply and flow from the Helmand River had been part of a dispute between Iran and Afghanistan for over a hundred years, and in the 1950s, the US played a major role in setting up an agreement on water take that it was now unknowingly violating. These violations prompted the Iranians to fund the Taliban, their sworn enemy, to attack US infrastructure projects like the Kajaki Dam, a project that was never completed despite hundreds of millions of dollars of spending. In the end, the Afghan farmers got less water and less support, despite millions of dollars of US taxpayer investment.

In the realm of biodiversity conservation, organizations like UNOPS and the Asian Development Bank sometimes worked at cross-purposes to each other and sometimes at cross-purposes to new environmental laws and regulations. All of this was done with the best of intentions. There wasn't by any means a shortage of work to be done on biodiversity conservation in Afghanistan, and the people involved cared deeply for the country. Given the importance of protecting the natural resources that supported nearly three-quarters of the country's population, conservation wasn't a luxury but a human security imperative.

Band-e-Amir alone needed an extraordinary amount of work to help its transformation into a national park. This included building the infrastructure for tourism and management of natural resources, which meant hiring, training, and equipping rangers with uniforms, badges, computers, vehicles, and supplies. The park needed practical infrastructure in the form of signage, bathrooms, waste facilities, a visitor center, hotels, food, and parking. Some entries on the to-do list for creating Band-e-Amir were unique to Afghanistan: "Developing clearly marked and mine-free horse trails around the lake system" was a task claimed by the Asian Development Bank. It would definitely hurt tourism to have visitors blown up by mines.

The rangers would need not only gear but training in environmental laws. The local community also needed an understanding of how ecotourism works. Even simple things like budgeting for insect repellent and visitor logs needed doing. Perhaps most importantly, decisions about how to use the park's revenue needed to be made. That meant coordinating with the government at the village, district, provincial, and national levels, with conflicting visions every step of the way. It wasn't sustainable to have different international organizations following different plans for hotels or signage or revenue distribution, but it was happening regardless. We needed to do something about it.

We decided to feed everyone lunch.

Specifically, we decided to form a donor-coordinating committee for biodiversity. We initially invited everyone and anyone to the table. We wanted to avoid any "official" trappings, so we dubbed our committee "the unofficial, unimportant, informal biodiversity conservation working group." We laid out the rules governing its operation:

- Rule 1: This working group has zero power, status, or importance. If it takes on any official status, we will immediately reject that role. It has no authority under any legislation to do anything or proclaim anything. It seeks to play no formal role.
- Rule 2: Everyone is invited. If you haven't been invited, you are now invited.
- Rule 3: If you come, you will get an unbelievably delicious home-cooked Afghan lunch. (This wasn't hype. We had found a spectacular chef—not Kaka—who made an amazing Kabuli Palau.)
- Rule 4: WCS will report out to attendees on everything it is doing and plans to do, and all participants will receive all new WCS data digitally.
- Rule 5: You are welcome to share what you are doing, but you don't have to. We will, however, go around the table and ask you in front of your peers.

WCS made a monumental effort to fill the void of data on Afghanistan's biodiversity. We had even taken to locating, purchasing, and scanning relevant natural history books from Iran and the former Soviet Union. Scientific papers, consulting reports, historical reports—sometimes dating back one hundred years—were all valuable to anyone working on biodiversity conservation in Afghanistan, as they provided a baseline of what once was. We also provided digital versions of all our current reports, all our biological findings, even (when possible and legal) our satellite imagery and data, such as the high-resolution 3-D digital models of elevation we'd reverse engineered from old Soviet maps of Wakhan. Although it was onerous and extremely expensive to acquire and digitize these materials, we gave it all away at every meeting as an incentive for others to come as well as to encourage transparency and build trust and reciprocity.

As we expected, some initially tried to challenge this organization's authority. Our response was we didn't have any authority, nor were we seeking it. We weren't intending to do anything other than offer information, resources, and free food. People would call up or e-mail, some indignantly demanding to be invited, some cautiously exploring whether they could bring others. Some even complained that we were being exclusionary. Everyone who contacted us was immediately invited to lunch, pursuant to rule 2.

At the first meeting, we prepared gift bags of digital data and laid out a spread. We had nearly thirty attendees. Every one of the thirty-odd attendees received a plate, silverware, a cup, and a DVD—the WCS team even helped with dishing out food from the buffet. WCS gave an intro to all our work, with individual project leaders discussing each project and what we saw as potential challenges to the work—where we were succeeding and where we were failing. We were fully transparent, with no expectation of reciprocity. Of course, we hoped that peer pressure and goodwill might elicit sharing as we went around the table.

We asked guests to introduce themselves, and to describe their role with the environment, and, if they wanted, anything they were doing. Some of the activities we were aware of, but many others were news to us. Attendees started organically asking each other questions, and this back-and-forth resulted in real dialogue. Some of the organizations were unaware of the laws; others were unaware about projects that had been completed, were under way, or were in planning. Some perhaps had purposefully ignored both. But we soon saw the beginnings of collaborations. Our unofficial, unimportant group (soon named the Biodiversity

Conservation Informal Working Group) quickly became one of the most effective donor-coordinating committees in Afghanistan. In one telling example, the Asian Development Bank had been proposing funding a hotel on the water's edge at Band-e-Amir, on the fragile travertine itself, in contravention of the law. Despite the positive effect on tourism, it would have surely damaged the natural environment that made the site so unique. Bringing ADB to the lunch table helped them understand the resistance to the project (and its illegality), and they changed their strategy and abandoned the plans for a hotel at the water's edge.

There were some speed bumps along the way, but we saw steady progress through the first year of work on the national park. Our approach identified two parallel processes for creation of the park. Legal processes for establishing the park under environmental law would be led by UNEP and its smart environmental lawyer, Belinda Bowling, with support from WCS and other agencies. This required legislative action and publications in the official gazette of the Ministry of Justice, followed by a vote in the parliament declaring the national park. This would take anywhere from eighteen months to three years. The second process was developing an official management plan for local, provincial, and national stakeholders, coupled with an ecosystem approach based on a collaborative management agreement. While these two work streams were under way, WCS and the members of the informal biodiversity working group could move toward temporary protected status for the national park via executive decree.

Making a national park, however, wouldn't happen solely through a presidential decree. The central government's power was limited: a joke in frequent circulation was that Afghan president Hamid Karzai was the mayor of Kabul. And in some ways, Karzai's power, and by default that of the executive branch, did end at the city limits. WCS needed to help extend the central government's authority to provincial and local levels and encourage both top-down and bottom-up workflows and close coordination. In Bamiyan Province, that meant working with Governor Habiba Sarābi, Afghanistan's first and only female provincial governor. Prince Zaher from NEPA and leadership from the Ministry of Agriculture would have to come to Bamiyan to help make the case for the national park with Governor Sarābi.

Sarābi's diminutive size belied her power and toughness. She was forceful, pragmatic, and in the style of Afghan political leaders, somewhat autocratic. When the Taliban took over, Sarābi, a Hazara, fled to Pakistan. Trained as a physician and hematologist, Sarābi wanted to create opportunities for Afghan girls. She started a series of dangerous endeavors, starting by teaching girls science in refugee camps, and then, during the Taliban occupation, sneaking back into Afghanistan to set up a secret network of schools for girls. Had she been caught, she would have been executed. Her bravery and dedication led to her being appointed head of the Ministry of Women's Affairs after the fall of the Taliban, and later, governor of Bamiyan Province, her home province. Being in charge of improving the plight of women in Afghanistan wasn't easy, but being the first female provincial governor was even harder. Running Bamiyan after the civil war wasn't going to be easy either.

Sarābi faced serious challenges beyond simple resistance to a woman in power in the highly patriarchal society of Afghanistan. Tourism had been the province's main source of revenue (and the second-most important source of revenue for Afghanistan in 1979), and the war with the Soviet Union and the subsequent civil war disrupted the province's economy, which had been based on travelers for a millennium. Its major attraction, the Bamiyan Buddhas, were rubble, and some of the province's poor were living in caves in the former monastery around the colossi.

Many of the tourism sites in Bamiyan were littered with mines. There was no electricity in the province, nor proper tourism facilities, and even getting to Bamiyan, the capital, from Kabul was a challenge— the 150-mile drive took eight hours. Sarābi also had little reliable help in running her government. She told us that her assessment was that 95 percent of her (all-male) staff were not up to their jobs. She was keen to rebuild tourism in Afghanistan and could be a valuable partner for WCS, but we needed to build the relationship.

We planned the trip for August. Unbeknownst to us, the prince's trip to Bamiyan ended up having additional symbolic importance, since his grandfather, King Zahir Shah, passed away in the compound of the presidential palace in Kabul after a prolonged illness just days earlier. His death was announced on national television by President Karzai, his funeral was held on July 24, and he was buried in the royal mausoleum on Maranjan Hill in eastern Kabul. Zahir Shah was popular with all Afghans, who eyed his reign as a period of stability and progress in Afghanistan, and it was his love of nature that tied him to Bamiyan Province in particular. Despite the fresh loss of his grandfather, the prince was committed to coming to Bamiyan, perhaps to uphold his memory as Afghanistan's first conservationist.

Our traveling party to Bamiyan included the prince, staff from NEPA, Clay Miller from the US embassy, Ghulam Malikyar of Save the Environment Afghanistan, Deputy Minister Mohammad Sharif, and Hashim Barakzai, a senior official from the Ministry of Agriculture. At the end of the short PACTEC flight from Kabul, I eagerly looked for the remnants of the giant Buddhas. As we flew into the valley, I spotted the empty alcoves, whose darkness seemingly lamented the statues' destruction. The small turboprop plane descended toward a broad, gravel-strewn field full of grazing sheep. It looked like a smudge on the landscape created by a giant thumb. The plane circled the field a few times as a herdsman hurriedly urged the sheep to one side of the expanse.

I kept waiting to spot an airfield with a tarmac runway as the plane got lower and lower. I muttered with rising concern to Clay, "We seem to be landing on a field of sheep! Where's the tarmac? Don't we need to land on tarmac?" I was still searching for the runway in disbelief as we abruptly touched down on the bumpy field, creating a cloud of pebbles and dust, no worse for the wear. I hadn't missed any airfield on our approach; there was no terminal, no asphalt, no baggage claim, no gift shop, no Starbucks, no perimeter fencing. Just sheep, a wind sock, and a few Toyotas. But what Bamiyan lacked in airport amenities, it made up for in enthusiasm.

A receiving line of over a hundred men waited for the prince, and Prince Zaher invited me to join him as he made his way through the well-wishers. The greetings were long and formal, with each member of the line offering heartfelt condolences to the prince. The people of Bamiyan, remembering the kind and competent rule of King Zahir Shah, offered their sympathies to the prince about the passing of his grandfather. The former king, even though he had been out of power for thirty-three years, had not been forgotten. It was a moving moment that highlighted the warmth and decorum of the Afghan people, who themselves could have been forgiven for not marking the occasion, given the challenges they experienced during the intervening thirty-three years or the challenges that they had yet to face.

The prince got in a Land Cruiser sent by the governor while the rest of the team threw their gear into the back of waiting Toyota Hiluxes that had been sent by the New Zealand Provincial Reconstruction Team, which kept a base near the airport. I looked for my bag only to realize that it was still on the plane. As I had been with the prince in the receiving line, everyone else had taken their luggage off. I turned to retrieve it, but the plane was ripping down the gravel field, chased by a cloud of dust. It climbed above the cliffs around Bamiyan, into the sky with my luggage. I tapped on Clay's shoulder and pointed to the plane.

"I think my luggage is going back to Kabul," I said.

He looked at my sad and dismayed face and then broke into a hearty laugh that continued through our short drive through the town.

The prince was only visiting for a single day, which meant a whirlwind of discussions awaited. We started with a formal high-level photo op in the lobby of the Roof of Bamiyan Hotel. Governor Sarābi, deputy ministers, the prince, and a host of other officials smiled for the camera before breaking up into private meetings.

In our private sit-down meeting with Sarābi, she was extremely direct about what needed to be done. Sarābi was deeply interested in what she could do for Bamiyan, one of the poorest provinces in Afghanistan, and its people. She wanted help with building guesthouses in people's homes and providing people with energy sources—most were burning plants for fuel. She also spoke about the need for coordination at various levels, not just within the Ministry of Agriculture and the National Environmental Protection Agency but with law enforcement agencies. In particular, she highlighted another potential problem—that the Afghan National Police and the Intelligence Ministry were the "first violators of the law" in Bamiyan and routinely drove their vehicles on the dams and treated the park as their own personal playground. The officials had blocked efforts to eliminate the motorboat that was used to ferry tourists across the main lake, since they enjoyed using it. The boat's wake and fuel leakage were disrupting the growth of the crystalline deposits that produced the spectacular dams, if not worse. Finally, Sarābi insisted there be accountability for equal sharing of revenues collected for the park.

This reinforced the need to provide training and keep pressure from above and below on the management of the park and the implementation of law. A sufficient flow of revenue from the park would be crucial in covering operating expenses and staff salaries. We still had much to do, but progress was under way.

It was time to clock out for the day. We had rented yurts on the top of the Roof of Bamiyan Hotel for ourselves and others in the delegation—a perfect place to watch the sun set on the Buddhas. I sat with deputy ministers and other officials, sipping tea and chatting through the night, with stars shining down through the clear mountain air.

The prince flew back at daybreak. The delegation—Deputy Minister Sharif and Eng. Barakzai from the Ministry of Agriculture; from NEPA, Clay Miller and Sulaiman Shah Sallari, director of the Natural Heritage and Wildlife Division; Governor Sarābi; Ghulam Malikyar; and I—saw Prince Zaher off at the Bamiyan "airport." Missing were the hundreds of well-wishers who had greeted us on our arrival. The same plane arrived, bringing back my suitcase, and quickly turned around and took Prince Zaher back to Kabul. We now had the top cover and authorization to move forward from both the national ministries and the governor, and within a month, we convened the first meeting of the Band-e-Amir Protected Area Committee (BAPAC), tasked with creating the rules for the new national park.

Before we departed for Band-e-Amir proper, a side trip to see the Buddhas was in order. At the foot of the empty alcoves, a temporary wooden structure sheltered the rubble that had been the colossi. Archaeologists believe that there could be a massive (reputedly three hundred meters) hidden reclining Buddha buried here, based on the journal of Xuanzang, a Chinese Buddhist monk who traveled to central Afghanistan around AD 630 on a nineteen-year journey through Central and South Asia. The Afghan archaeologist Zemaryalai Tarzi later discovered a sleeping Buddha in the ruins of an ancient Buddhist temple two miles from the colossi, but the mammoth sleeping Buddha remains hidden.

Dark, steep, and claustrophobic stairs at the base of the smaller Buddha led up to a gallery in the larger alcove. In the inner walls, we could see flecks of color from the destroyed frescos. At the top, we circled around the space that the giant Buddha's head once occupied. The statues were only the most prominent part of a maze of rooms hewn into the red rock. Many of the smaller chambers were burned black where the Taliban had tried to cover up the decorations. Where fire wasn't sufficient, the Taliban had taken off their shoes and covered roof frescoes with white, dusty shoe prints. Their disregard for the Buddhist culture was nothing if not thorough. Everywhere we looked were small recesses that once held small Buddhas, which the Taliban had destroyed. The entire complex spoke to humanity's potential for greatness and as a monument to the hollowness and destruction of war.

We emerged at an opening on the opposite side of the cliffs, looking away from the Buddhas. A steep cliff fell away before us, but there was a small rock shelf of perhaps three meters square where we could take in a dramatic landscape. Just before I stepped onto the small natural balcony I noticed the red-painted rocks that signaled the presence of mines. Explosives had been planted specifically to harm those who stopped to appreciate the view. Even in this modest spot, the evils of war had crept in. No place in Afghanistan was completely safe. We slowly backtracked and explored the other caves before heading for the lakes.

The two-hour drive from Bamiyan city to Band-e-Amir gave us a chance to see everyday life on the Hazarajat Plateau. We saw Afghans harvesting rangeland plants for fuel, a practice that eroded the environment and took away the food sources of the region's wildlife. But it was also key to survival for locals through the cold winters. Abandoned tanks and armored personnel carriers dotted the landscape. This strange terrain was soon interrupted by a glimpse of the deep blue of Band-e-Zulfiqar, followed by the other lakes. No photos could do justice to the brilliant lapis blue of the water and the red and pink alluvial fans of the cliffs. Water flowed from the forty-foot dams of the Band-e-Haibat. This was a place deserving of national park status and every other protection we could provide.

The spectacular natural scenery, however, clashed against the squalid collection of ramshackle teahouses, restaurants, shops, and motor garages, all covered with blue tarps, that crowded the water's edge. Bazaar owners routinely dumped garbage and washed dishes directly in the lake. Six swan-shaped plastic pedal boats, two plastic rowboats, and an 85-horsepower motorboat stood for rent. People diverted the cool lake water into small channels along the footpath used to refrigerate soft drinks, but this also created patches of sticky clay and muddy silt on the path. Ugly, but functional and necessary, concrete bathrooms built by New Zealand Provincial Reconstruction Teams sat next to countless food stalls near the parking lot.

But one structure did offer a glimpse of manmade beauty. The Asian Development Bank was working to create a ranger station and visitor office set back from the shore of Band-e-Haibat. The structure was gorgeous, with rounded horizontal bands of beige-and-tan stone dotted with darkened windows interspersed, topped with a living roof. The architect had sought to match the landscape and employ local materials in the design, aiming to build something that would integrate with rather than distract from the landscape. WCS had already started recruiting rangers for the proposed national park (later this included

Afghanistan's first female park rangers). The new recruits greeted us when we arrived at the ranger station.

We used the facility for another round of meetings—Governor Sarābi, Eng. Barakzai, Deputy Minister Sharif, and Ayub spent the day presenting on stewardship, the environmental regulations and the importance of conservation of the region for generating tourism to local officials, and the obligations to take care of the environment. Later, we retreated to lakeside for meetings with elders and community leaders of Band-e-Amir. The local leaders complained about harassment from and law-breaking by the Afghan National Police and emphasized the need for infrastructure improvements. Some were against any designation of a national park for fear of how it limited their use of the land.

That night, I slept on the living room floor in Ayub's family home. It was a simple house, but warm. We ate a home-cooked meal of lamb and rice together and then all reclined on pillows on the carpet. The house, two hours away from the nearest electrical grid, ran on solar. Panels powered lights and satellite TV that captured content from around the world. Here, at the crossroads of ancient empires, we watched an American sitcom about a group of friends in New York City. At first, I thought Ayub's family was trying to make me feel welcome, but it became apparent that their enthusiasm for the show was genuine. After a few hours of watching American television, we slept on mats in the living room. While the house had satellite TV, the bathrooms weren't quite as modern. They were, however, stunning. A pit toilet outside afforded a view of the starry sky and the sheep pen. Before heading back inside, I took a moment to appreciate the peace of a chilly Afghan night. Stars shone brightly as sheep bleated their displeasure at the cold.

The next day, we surveyed more of Band-e-Amir, visiting the different lakes and valleys before we headed back to Bamiyan. We also stopped by the entrance kiosk, built in the same architectural style of the visitor station. The guard in charge of collecting entrance fees was reticent about where the money went. He told us that all the park revenue was kept by the local regional government, although what it was used for remained unclear.

The valleys and rock outcroppings around Band-e-Amir reminded me of national parks in the American west: Bryce Canyon, Capital Reef, Zion, and Canyonlands, an explosion of a million shades of red and orange that defined the landscape.

After returning to Bamiyan, Ayub and I went to see the City of Screams. Although Bamiyan is best known for the colossi, the valley and environs hold countless archaeological sites and stories. A short distance from Bamiyan's main bazaar stood the remains of a giant citadel. An enormous city once occupied a large conical hill in the center of the valley, replete with towers, mansions, and great walls, all surrounded by a multicolored tapestry of fields. Although this fortress stood up to an initial siege by the armies of Genghis Khan, it was eventually destroyed by a daughter's betrayal of her father.

Ayub and I scaled the ruins of the citadel, and he told me the story behind its destruction as we took in the view. Genghis Khan had sent his grandson to take Bamiyan, and his grandson was killed in the process. The Mongol ruler, infuriated by his grandson's death, traveled with his armies to Bamiyan to exact his revenge. Genghis Khan vowed to kill every man, woman, child, bird, and animal in the Bamiyan Valley. However, the citadel's walls were impenetrable, its stores well stocked, and the weeks-long siege bore no fruit.

Ayub pointed in the distance. There was the Qala-e-Chehel Dukhtaran (house of the forty maidens), he noted. It was here that the daughter of the citadel's king was living in her own castle. According to legend, she had moved out of the citadel before the invasion in protest of her father's decision to remarry. And she still seethed with an anger so great that she was determined to betray her father. Genghis Khan's army provided that opportunity. From the top of the Qala-e-Chehel Dukhtaran, Ayub recounted, the princess shot an arrow bearing a note into the tent of Genghis Khan. The note promised Genghis Khan that she would share the secret of the weakness of the fortress in exchange for marrying her and agreeing to leave her castle alone. The Mongol warlord sent word of his agreement, and the daughter told him of a secret hidden underground source of water that supplied the citadel. If it were blocked, she said, the fortress would fall, and it was accessible at a spot far away from the castle. At once, Genghis Khan's armies found the source and blocked it, and the citadel soon surrendered. Genghis Khan duly fulfilled his vengeful vow; his armies showed no mercy, and not a single soul or animal was left alive. The screaming that accompanied the massacre was so great, Ayub noted, that it could be heard through the valley and gave the hill its eerie name: the City of Screams (Shahr-e Gholghola).

The princess, after betraying her father and subjects, wore her most beautiful dress and waited for her betrothed, oblivious to the slaughter of her subjects. What she met instead was a troop of soldiers ordered by the great warrior to stone her to death. The destruction in the valley was so complete and so terrible that it ended Bamiyan's central role in the Silk Road trade. The citadel has stood in ruins for eight hundred years, never rebuilt, as a monument to the wrath of Khan.

Ayub stayed on for the next month to help organize and support the elections within the villages of the watershed. These elections would determine the representatives for the first meeting of the Band-e-Amir Protected Area Committee (BAPAC). We returned for that summit, this time with a delegation of high-ranking US officials. This would be the first chance to see whether all levels of government—federal, provincial, and local—could work together productively. Kara and I flew into Bamiyan and met up with Khoja and Ayub.

At a morning training session with local representatives before the inaugural convening of the BAPAC, we were shown a Eurasian eagle-owl reportedly shot by Afghan intelligence agency officers, who were illegally camped on the far side of the lakes. It turns out the same intelligence officers had also been behind blocking efforts to remove the swan-shaped pedal boats and the destructive motor ferry. We stood outside the ranger station and saw representatives arriving after hours of travel by foot to attend the training and the BAPAC meeting. The villagers were taking their new responsibilities seriously.

Ayub and members of the Ministry of Agriculture and NEPA spoke to the BAPAC elected representatives for hours on the intricacies of environmental law, the proposed powers of the Band-e-Amir Protected Area Committee, and what a national park designation meant. The attendees weren't hesitant to ask questions. The training proved inspiring; the representatives listened closely, leaning forward in their eagerness to learn about their new roles and responsibilities. After the training, we broke for a lunch of greasy lamb and rice, served off a plastic tablecloth on the ground.

The next day, a large delegation of officials came in from Kabul to observe the inaugural formal meeting of the protected area committee. Representatives from USAID and the US Department of State were present, as were the representatives of the Afghan federal government. Governor Sarābi and the head of the Bamiyan Provincial Council represented the state level, and members of the proposed national park staff sat in as well. Ayub, Kara, and I sat along the side of the room and watched hopefully, but also nervously, as we couldn't guide the process anymore; the outcomes were now totally out of our control. This was WCS's first real test of its effectiveness—developing support for the country's first protected area, creating the management systems, and synching those systems among local, provincial, and national governments. Building such protected areas with broad support was already hard, even in a "normal" biodiversity-rich country; it was even harder to do so in a place that had been through three decades of brutal war, where land mines and a growing insurgency (and, in some cases, outright war) threatened to upend the whole process. And we invited the world to see whether we would be successful without knowing the outcome.

Governor Sarābi and Hashim Barakzai from the Ministry of Agriculture kicked off the meeting, welcoming the participants and noting the gathering's historic nature. The delegates introduced themselves one by one, by name and village. Most had never until the elections spoken publicly in such an open forum. Almost immediately, Said Ahmad Ahmadi from Jarukashan Village stood up and asked to be nominated as temporary secretary, which was approved. Then the voting started in earnest for chairmanship of the committee, deputy chairman, and permanent secretary. According to newly minted regulations, the governor would chair the protected area committee for the first year, so much of the debate concerned the position of deputy committee chair. A number of villagers nominated themselves for the position, but so did members of the national government, including the head of the agriculture department of Bamiyan, whose position wasn't originally intended to be a member of the official committee. Here was the first test.

After a long series of speeches and debate, a community member from Dewarkhana Village won the election, and the governor nominated the Bamiyan NEPA affiliate as secretary, which the assembly agreed upon. A meeting schedule was laid out for twice a month in the summer and once a month in the winter. The agenda for the second meeting was drafted, and it would tackle some of the thorniest issues: review of the management plan, revenue sharing of entrance fees, disbanding the current bazaar shantytown on the edge of the lake, and addressing the garbage problems.

The Westerners didn't participate in the discussion, nor did they need to. We were in awe of what we saw. The community members, made up of farmers and pastoralists, were unafraid to challenge their governor—directly appointed by President Karzai himself—or other high-level officials in the room. They set their own rules, elected their officials, and created their own authority, and they did so with words and thoughtful debate rather than guns or threats. I felt a thrill at watching something historic here in the handsomely designed ranger station. I felt that I was in Afghanistan's version of Independence Hall. Here, in the middle of the cold Hazarajat Plateau, by towering cliffs and crystal blue waters, democracy was working in Afghanistan. We were on the brink of a significant step toward the country's first national park. Most inspiring was the earnestness and dedication of the local people in having a say in the management of their natural resources. They understood their role as guardians of a special place.

After the two-hour meeting, there were congratulations all around and a general euphoria at democracy in action. Then Governor Sarābi pulled me aside.

"Let's just ignore all of this and set our own rules," she said quietly to me.

My joy drained away in an instant. I thought back to the anger she had expressed at the Afghan National Police's and the intelligence agency's conduct in Band-e-Amir. I couldn't help myself from expressing my disappointment, and I turned to her and stated directly and frankly, "If you want to have the authority to stop the Afghan National Police's illegal actions in Band-e-Amir, you have to follow the rule of the law. This is what the rule of law means. You can't expect others to follow the law when you choose to ignore it when it suits you. The laws of this country bind us all, and we only give them power by accepting their jurisdiction." It wasn't just the governor who wanted to circumvent the law; members of the international community did too. Chris Shank wrote to me in September 2006 to point out that the Asian Development Bank's land-use plan for Band-e-Amir specifically proposed circumventing environmental law in the name of expediency. This was both the charm and the challenge of Afghanistan. Anything was possible here, but for the country to build civil society, everything couldn't be possible anymore.

I walked away from the governor, leaving her looking vaguely disappointed and confused. I spoke with foreign service officer David Jea about the comment and asked him to work with the governor, which he promised to do. In September 2008, *Time* magazine would select Governor Sarābi as a hero of the environment, recognized for her work in setting up Band-e-Amir.

A few weeks later, back in Kabul, I met a Westerner in the Serena Hotel gym. He told me that he worked for the National Democratic Institute, an organization whose mission was to support and strengthen democratic institutions worldwide through citizen participation, openness, and accountability in government. As we chatted, he expressed surprise that the US government would fund the Bronx Zoo to do conservation work in Afghanistan. I sought to explain our project—that 80 percent of Afghans depended on natural resources; that the careful management of those resources meant food security, water, and viable health; and that this work also helped rebuild the country's identity. Finally, I told him about the BAPAC's first meeting, the elections, the earnest debate, the participation of all levels of government.

A look of confusion crossed his face before he responded, "You are doing our job." And it was then I realized that we were.

Democracy is a difficult concept in the abstract. For those unfamiliar with democracy, it can seem like a radical and dangerous idea. Empowering regular people in government—rather than the educated, the rich, and the experienced—seems counterintuitive. Even in the US, the Electoral College was created because of the framers' distrust of the common citizen. After my return from Afghanistan, I heard then senator Joe Biden speak at a small lunch of highly accomplished and overeducated Council on Foreign Relations term members. He said something that resonated with me: "The American people's guts are better than your brains." Some countries prefer benevolent autocracy over diplomacy. Some believe that economic development is best achieved through central planning. For them, development, not democracy, represents true freedom. Democracy isn't always successful either; it can support the tyranny of the majority over a minority, it can elect charismatic strongmen (and women) into power who undermine human rights or democracy itself, and it is hard to get right. But in the end, it is a powerful force that can challenge the will of the people toward freedom. This is what I saw in the main room of the visitor center in Afghanistan—hope.

Regardless of the reaction of the man at the gym, we weren't trying to teach democracy. We wanted to help establish a national park. The reality of our mission gave a substance and tangibility to the fuzzy ideas of a social contract. In a way, the park helped make democracy real. We didn't know it when we started, but we wound up teaching more than conservation techniques.

After taking some photos with visitors and local delegates, a few of us broke off to train with local Hazaras for a planned small-mammal survey around the national park. The mammalian diversity of Afghanistan in the collections of the Smithsonian Institution was limited to just seven individual specimens. Not species. *Specimens*. As in, individual animals—skins and skulls. We wanted to change that. Nearly half of mammalian diversity in the world was made up of rats and bats, and while we didn't have mist nets for sampling the bat population, we did have Sherman live traps for catching small rodents. On a visit to Washington, DC, the Smithsonian's mammal department had trained us on preparation techniques for small mammals, and we now passed the training on to our team. We had government permission for the surveys and to ship samples out via diplomatic pouch. We had a problem with one local official who insisted the dead mice were worth millions, but we ultimately got the collections to the Smithsonian.

After we set the field locations for the surveys and placed traps, Kara and I climbed up the talus slopes of the red cliffs above Band-e-Amir. Halfway up, I saw an interesting red rock and picked it up. The feathery lace of a bryozoan was clearly visible. I continued looking and saw that rock after rock held marine fossils of bryozoans, brachiopods, and bivalves. We looked at the broad rock field beneath us, stretching for kilometers. Eons ago, this high plateau had been a shallow sea. I had never heard anyone mention the paleontological riches of Band-e-Amir or anywhere else in the country. We later heard stories of American soldiers uncovering dinosaur bones along the Helmand River. There was always something left to discover in Afghanistan. Despite being in the forefront of the news, it was a forgotten land of forgotten places and people.

Within a year of that first meeting, on Earth Day 2008, Prince Mostapha Zaher signed an executive order on behalf of President Karzai creating Band-e-Amir as a provisional national park. Much work remained, but this was real hope for Afghanistan's wildlife and for the rebuilding of a legacy that the Taliban had tried to destroy.

CHAPTER 7

VAMPIRES IN
THE LAND OF LIGHT

I N THE POPULAR imagination and in most images (including the one on the cover of this book), Afghanistan's landscape is parched, dusty, rocky, and largely barren of vegetation and trees, a legacy of thousands of years of deforestation. But this imagery doesn't represent the whole country; Afghanistan is rich in habitat and colors from the western end of the Himalayas in the northeast, to the rugged mountains of the Hindu Kush and the Hazarajat Plateau, to lush floodplains along the Amu Darya River, to rich wetlands dotted with the fiery pink of flamingos and thousands of birds migrating between Africa and Asia. But it was here, in the country's east, that we found the most unexpected ecosystems that jarred with people's jaundiced expectations of the country's landscape: it was verdant, thick alpine forests drenched by Indian monsoon rains, breaking the summer droughts that limit plant life elsewhere in the country, within the aptly named Eastern Forests Complex of Afghanistan.

This region contains some of Asia's last remaining arid conifer forests. The complex runs from the border of Badakhshan Province in the north to Paktika in the southeast, also touching on the provinces of Kunar, Laghman, Nangarhar, Paktia, and Khost. Here, thick stands of spruce, oak, cedar, pine, and fir mark an interface between Asian and

European fauna. The Eastern Forests are rich in wildlife, including historical populations of many wild cats (large and small), jackals, striped hyenas, yellow-throated martens, bears, ibex, markhor, urial sheep, wild boar, and even Afghanistan's only primates, macaques. There were also reports of a rare, highly valued creature that was thought extinct in Afghanistan: the musk deer, a small mammal with remarkable vampire-like fangs.

Our goal in the Eastern Forests Complex was the bread and butter of conservation—surveying the wildlife that was here before, understanding the threats to the biodiversity, and working to address those threats and underlying drivers. The Eastern Forests were important simply for their diversity, but what made them a priority site for WCS were the risks facing the area and its wildlife. Deforestation posed a major challenge. The region's trees are cut at unsustainable rates, especially in the lower-lying oak forests, to supply both fuel for homes and fodder for domestic animals. High-value timbers such as cedar are also cut to supply Kabul and international markets. Additional demands on wildlife populations came from the heavy hunting levels for food and for the illegal wildlife trade in furs and other animal products.

What made the Eastern Forests different from other parts of Afghanistan was the wildness of the region and its people, the danger of working in one of the world's most treacherous borderlands, and the insurgency against the US occupation that used the illegal trade in timber to obtain revenue to purchase weapons, putting our efforts in conservation on the front lines of conflict. Part of the pressure was that forests in Pakistan were better protected, which increased the demand for poached, poorly guarded timber from Afghanistan. Corruption was rampant, and the efforts to enforce the laws resulted in armed exchanges of gunfire and rocket-propelled grenades.

Of course, the forests of the east don't stop at the border, and neither does wildlife or the people. The Eastern Forests Complex was an important part of the homeland of the Pashtun, a South Asian ethnic group. The other half of the Pashtun reside across the border in Pakistan. The Afghan-Pakistani border—known as the Durand Line—is a notable legacy of nineteenth-century European imperial adventures in Central Asia. The line was established in 1893 by an agreement between Sir Mortimer Durand, a British diplomat, and Abdur Rahman Khan, the Afghan emir. The kingdom of Afghanistan ceded various frontier areas to British India (which at that time included what is now Pakistan), in exchange for the British Raj's withdrawal from Afghanistan. The 1,659-mile border marking their agreed-upon "spheres of influence" remains the border between Afghanistan and Pakistan.

Like many artificial colonial borders, the Durand Line unnaturally carved up contiguous ecosystems and cultures. In addition to the Pashtun, the Ismaili of Wakhan and the Baluch people of the Afghan-Pakistani-Iranian border regions all felt the effects of a border defined by distant, long-dead diplomats. Populations split between two governments heed the control of neither. Tribes in the east of Afghanistan frequently crossed the artificial borders with impunity, creating a porous frontier ideal for smuggling. Timber went from Afghanistan east into Pakistan. By the same route in reverse, jihadist supporters of the Taliban and al-Qaeda flowed west into Afghanistan to combat the West.

The Eastern Forests make up only a part of the long border created by the Durand Line. Our surveys focused not on the whole of the border forests but on one particular area within the region—Nuristan Province, or, as its name translates into English, *the land of the enlightened*. Nuristan stands out among the eastern borderlands, both for its wildlife habitats and for the culture of its human inhabitants.

The province boasts a fairy-tale landscape of steep, craggy cliffs wrapped in carpets of dark cedar and oak and crossed by narrow, perilous trails. The interior of Nuristan is effectively impenetrable, defended by the jagged Hindu Kush mountains. In 1977, Ron Petocz and John Larsson conducted a notable expedition in Nuristan on behalf of the Afghan Tourism Organization to assess ibex and markhor populations for a proposed big-game hunting preserve. They encountered trails so narrow that even pack animals could not traverse them. Steep mountains combined with deep ravines meant that opposing valley walls were as little as fifty meters apart. Furious rivers, bloated with the melt of high mountain snows, carved deep gashes in a landscape ranging from one thousand to six thousand meters in elevation.

Nuristan was not always considered "enlightened." Its people originally fiercely resisted conversion to Islam as they had resisted Buddhism and Hinduism before it—and earned the name of Kafirs (unbelievers). Their home was known as Kafiristan, and they had a well-earned reputation as warriors. From their unreachable villages high above the valley roads, they would launch lightning raids on travelers and neighbors alike, seeking slaves and tribute. Blood feuds between clans in Nuristan were reported to last for decades and, like now, would sometimes draw in the great powers.

The mighty fourteenth-century emperor Tamerlane attempted to conquer the Kafirs at the request of their weary neighbors. In the end, Tamerlane and his mounted warriors were conquered by the landscape, and their horses were unceremoniously hoisted down cliffsides on suspended platforms in a hasty retreat.

According to one legend, the Kafirs were followers of Dionysus and drinkers of wine. This supposedly swayed Alexander the Great not to sack their villages during his conquests, and he is said to have invited some of the Kafirs to join his conquest of India. It wasn't until 1895 that Kafiristan was subdued and its people converted to Islam. Henceforth, the land of the unbelievers became the land of the enlightened.

While the landscape of Nuristan is remarkable, its human terrain is just as distinctive. Many men and women in Nuristan have blue eyes and red or blond hair. The early nineteenth-century British colonialist Mountstuart Elphinstone described the Nuristani people as having the complexion of "an Irish haymaker." Their language occupies its own branch of the Indo-European languages, and their music and clothing were entirely unique and endemic. Whether or not the former Kafirs followed Dionysus, they loved revelry and drinking with vehemence. Traditional dances braided abandon and complexity, detailed hand and arm gestures coupled with the flourishing of battle-axes, all carried by music quick and wild. The women of Kafiristan historically didn't wear veils and, in their villages in the interior of the province, supposedly mingled freely with men, participating in singing and dancing even after the arrival of Islam.

Before submitting to Islam, the Kafirs practiced animism, worshiping multiple gods and local deities, often represented by stone and wooden idols. Their funeral practices included open coffins that were left in the forest, animated celebrations of the deceased filled with oratory and dancing, and effigies placed over graves meant to keep the souls of the departed. They lived in elaborately carved wooden houses piled up precariously on top of each other or propped on stilts, on steep mountainsides, like haphazardly stacked children's blocks. Like other Afghans, Nuristanis wove rugs, but theirs broke from the usual geometric patterns to depict snow leopards attacking ibex, or other animals, or even people. This violated a serious Islamic taboo against aniconism, the depiction of sentient beings. Even the depth and feel of their rugs was unique. The Nuristani, rather than choosing either a flat weave or a thick wool pile, mixed the two styles together in vibrant patterns energized not only by color but by bringing the design to a third dimension rather than to be limited by only two. The channels in the rugs between the mountaintops of piles seemed to recall Nuristan's five river valleys, symbolic of the lives of people perched above the fray of the worlds below.

Although Nuristan is culturally and linguistically distinct from the rest of Afghanistan, it is not homogenous. The mountain chains and deep valleys isolated populations and created considerable diversity among the province's tribes and clans. Different valleys speak different dialects, sometimes mutually unintelligible, so Pashto frequently served as the region's lingua franca. Cultural and geographic fragmentation led to a tradition of independence, self-governance, and isolation.

Nuristan's wildlife, forests, history, and culture gave us plenty of reasons to want to work there, but there were just as many, if not more, reasons *not* to work there. The steep mountains and lack of roads meant that any travel had to happen by foot. We couldn't even use pack animals as we would in the Wakhan Corridor. This was not merely an inconvenience; slow-moving teams were exposed to greater risks. The

Eastern Forests Complex was among the most dangerous parts of Afghanistan.

Nuristan offered the first sustained resistance against the communist government backed by the Soviets. There is no zealot like a convert, as the saying goes, and Nuristanis embraced Islam passionately. Afraid that the Russian invasion would mean the imposition of the anti-theist ideology within communism as well as a loss of self-governance, Nuristan fought ferociously. In fact, during the jihad against the Soviet occupation of northeastern Nuristan, many embraced conservative Wahhabism. Nuristan was critical to the mujahideen in providing a pass-through for armaments coming from Pakistan, and some of the heaviest guerilla fighting during the Soviet war took place in Nuristan.

Nuristan's resistance did not end with the departure of the Russians. As part of the "N2KL" area (Nuristan, Nangarhar, Kunar, and Laghman Provinces), the eastern borderlands have proven deadly for US and NATO soldiers as well. Forward-operating bases in Kunar's Korengal Valley and Nuristan's Waygal District saw some of the fiercest attacks on US forces. The US military resorted to firing missiles at the snow-covered mountaintops to trigger the release of suffocating avalanches to bury high mountain passes and combat the trafficking of illicit goods, including natural resources, across them.

The province was not an especially safe place for any outsider, and it was particularly unsafe for Western civilians, but to assess the Eastern Forests Complex's unique flora and fauna, we needed to be there. We decided to open an office in a mountain village, high above the roads traveled by insurgent jihadists and hammered by American bombs but not high enough to feel entirely secure.

The WCS program in Nuristan would focus on three elements. First, we would launch the first biological surveys within eastern Afghanistan in over thirty years (including the region's first-ever winter survey). Second, we would begin satellite analysis of forest cover to better understand forest decline and identify particular areas of interest for biodiversity research. Third, we would assess the timber trade to better understand the demand for timber in Kabul by surveying lumberyards

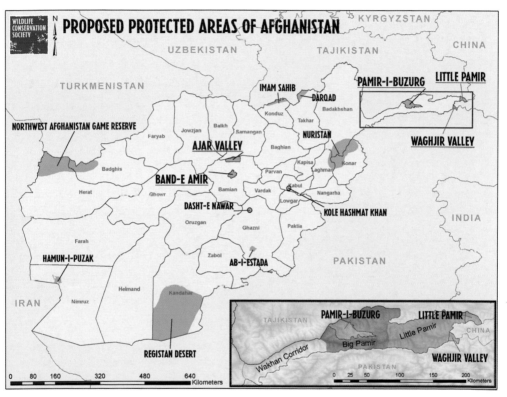

The initial map of WCS's proposed protected areas in Afghanistan. Many of these were originally hunting preserves of Zahir Shah, the last king of Afghanistan, and were proposed to be protected areas in 1979, but that effort was interrupted by the Soviet invasion.
Credit: Wildlife Conservation Society

The mausoleum of King Mohammad Nadir Shah (king of Afghanistan from 1925 to 1933) on Tepe Maranjan overlooks Kabul. The war's battering of the tomb reflects the suffering and injury endured by the whole of the country, its people, and its wildlife.
Credit: Alex Dehgan

When I first got to Kabul, some neighborhoods and buildings still reflected the wounds of war. As reconstruction monies poured into Afghanistan, shiny new buildings rose in the capital, replacing the ruins, but the memories of the war still persisted.
Credit: Alex Dehgan

This pile of buses, four levels high, peeked above a high wall in Kabul. Dozens of similarly wrecked buses, relicts of the civil war, were in this compound. I was always torn between my curiosity and desire to explore such detritus of war and my reservation about reawakening the nightmare that Afghanistan endured.
Credit: Alex Dehgan

WCS Afghanistan's garish "birthday cake" headquarters in Shahr-e Naw District of Kabul. We added the bamboo on the roof deck so we could minimize the security risk of being observed from the street. The extensive windows on the building were single paned, and the building was freezing in the winter. They also posed a liability because they would shatter in a car bombing into lethal flying daggers.
Credit: Alex Dehgan

Shafiq and Qais picnicking in an open-air tea house during an office outing to Paghman. We would all get sick afterward from overeating mulberries.
Credit: Alex Dehgan

Tank Henge, on the road north from Kabul to Kunduz.
Credit: Alex Dehgan

Demining along the road in Badakhshan Province.
Credit: Alex Dehgan

Ancient petroglyphs, thousands of years old, depicting ibex, at the gateway to the Wakhan Corridor. These petroglyphs lined the footpath into the Big and Little Pamirs.
Credit: Alex Dehgan

Shah Ismael and his brother.
Credit: Alex Dehgan

Ibex painted on the walls inside Shah Ismael's house, as a singer serenaded us.
Credit: Alex Dehgan

A welcome from a Wakhi shepherd. This photo for me reflected the generosity and welcome I experienced even in the harshest environments and with the least fortunate in Afghanistan.
Credit: Alex Dehgan

The challenges of travel in Wakhan.
Credit: Inayat Ali

The skull of a Marco Polo sheep in Wakhan.
Credit: Don Bedunah/WCS

An alpine meadow in Wakhan, with multiple glaciers running down the sides of the mountains.
Credit: Don Bedunah/WCS

A WCS camera-trap photo of a snow leopard in lower Badakhshan Province.
Credit: Wildlife Conservation Society

Prince Mostapha Zaher, executive director, Afghanistan's National Environmental
Protection Agency (in formal Afghan shalwar kameez with a suit jacket) standing
at the Bamiyan airport with Dr. Habiba Sarābi, governor of Bamiyan, on one side,
and Mohammad Sharif, the deputy minister of agriculture, on the other. I am next
to Governor Sarābi. Also pictured are Clay Miller, embassy science fellow, and other
government officials. The plane in the background had returned my suitcase, with
which it had previously absconded.
Credit: Alex Dehgan

An alcove for the large Buddha in Bamiyan. The white sheets covered the pieces of the colossi that had been destroyed.
Credit: Alex Deligan

Band-e-Haibat, the Lake of the Grandiose, in Band-e-Amir National Park, Bamiyan Province. The shrine (the buildings) and the alcove for a never-completed Buddha can be seen at the edge of the lake, which was created by the formation of dams due to the accrual of supersaturated calcium carbonate in the water.
Credit: Alex Dehgan

The elected village representatives voting on the rules for organizing the Band-e-Amir Protected Area Committee, which would oversee the proposed national park at Band-e-Amir.
Credit: Alex Dehgan

WCS's low-key regional office located high in the mountains of Nuristan.
Credit: Wildlife Conservation Society

Nuristan's impossible mountains, which have been legendary for stopping invasions and enabling the independence of these fierce people.
Credit: Wildlife Conservation Society

WCS staff with a cheetah skin.
Credit: Alex Dehgan

A man carrying a stuffed Persian leopard walks down the street in Kabul.
Credit: Lisa Yook/WCS

Persian cheetah and tiger skins in a fur market in Kabul.
Credit: Wildlife Conservation Society

Military police training at the US airbase in Bagram.
Credit: Alex Dehgan

and counting the trucks that came from the east loaded with wood. This would allow us to assess the toll that harvesting the timber took on the environment.

The region's forests and fauna were important not only in Afghanistan but globally. They contained the most significant populations of species like the markhor and also provided habitat for other vulnerable species, like Asiatic black bears, Persian leopards, snow leopards, leopard cats, and many other important species of mammals and birds.

For the wildlife surveys, we would need to build and train a team to lead the surveys. The team members would need to learn the fairly complicated basics of fieldwork: identification of animal scats and tracks, mark-recapture sampling, fecal DNA analysis, and the use of camera-trap technology. WCS needed to learn some basics as well— how to work safely in Nuristan, or at least as safely as possible. Outside the US military, practically no foreign organizations worked there. There was one notable exception: Madera, an enigmatic French NGO. I decided to travel to their office in Jalalabad to meet with them.

Jalalabad is 150 kilometers from Kabul, but the highway is hardly a straight shot. The road follows the Kabul River, which transitions from a languid, shallow, and bounded waterway inside the city into a rampaging current as it enters the Kabul River Gorge. Fed by mountain snow, the river crashes over boulders and plunges through ravines in a descent of 1,200 meters, and the highway does its best to chase the river through hairpin turns along steep chasms. Carcasses of wrecked cars and trucks line the road like mileage markers and document the insufficient patience and caution of reckless Afghan drivers trying to overtake slow commercial trucks. Although the road had been newly reconstructed, spring floods had already taken large bites out of the new tarmac, leaving little more than a single lane in places, with no warning signage or barrier to protect unaware drivers. The cutouts resembled a mutant layer cake: different colored and textured horizons of sediment and gravel, frosted here and there with dark asphalt.

As we wound our way to Jalalabad, I considered the history of this route. This was the Grand Trunk Road, stretching from Kabul all the

way to Kolkata on the eastern coast of India. It ran through the famous
Khyber Pass, crossing the frontiers of empires bound by forbidding
mountains. The road had carried goods, ideas, insurgents, and invaders for centuries. It has been burdened by the misery of millions of
refugees fleeing the death and destruction of war and the billions of
dollars of military equipment and the goods and supplies necessary for
nation-building.

Much of the route was jammed with heavy trucks bringing in commerce and material for the coalition forces, everything from frozen piz-
zas and DVDs to jet fuel. Eighty percent of supplies for American and
coalition forces traveled across Khyber Pass. As it had for centuries, the
pass became a choke point. The Taliban and other insurgents attacked
trucks and executed drivers with frequency.

It had also carried Afghanistan's own identity *back* into the country.
Wars have the effect of wiping out the collective memory of a country,
of fragmenting its cultural icons far and wide and shattering the core
identity of a people until nothing is left except broken buildings, detritus of the armaments of war, fading bitter remembrances of better
times, and the tyranny of misery from lives lost or destroyed.

Nancy Dupree—an engaging, quixotic, and delightful woman
whose diminutive size belied the forcefulness of her will—brought the
energy of a nuclear-powered aircraft carrier and became a one-woman
dam against this slow effacing of Afghanistan's identity. She was a
colleague and comrade in the battle to protect Afghanistan's identity.
While WCS focused on protecting Afghanistan's biological identity,
she had led the battle for the preservation of the country's culture
and history (along with the Turquoise Mountain Foundation, which
sought to restore traditional arts in Afghanistan, led by the peculiar but
strangely charismatic Rory Stuart, who was Kara's erstwhile Ultimate
Frisbee teammate).

Nancy Dupree had first arrived in Afghanistan as the wife of an
American diplomat, with a degree in Chinese art and having spent
her childhood in India. Her husband, Louis Dupree, was a former
paratrooper and adventuresome Harvard-trained ethnographer and

archaeologist of Afghanistan. After a torrid love affair (when they first met, both were married), they spent much of the next decades studying and describing Afghanistan's virtues to the rest of the world, including writing its first travel guides, still sold in Kabul's markets today, still the best and most comprehensive guides to the country. However, their most important work was ultimately creating the institutions to preserve its cultural identity lost in the Soviet invasion and civil war that followed it. After the defeat of the Taliban in 2001, Nancy brought sixty thousand documents and books over Khyber Pass by donkey caravan—collected at great pains from refugees in Peshawar, Pakistan, a wartime magnet for Afghan refugees, intellectuals, and insurgents— to help rebuild Afghanistan's culture and remember its history and create the Afghanistan Center at Kabul University.

As we approached Jalalabad, the Kabul River's temperament changed again back from angry to serene as it poured into an enormous shallow wetland filled with waterfowl, a result of the Soviet-built Darunta Dam, which provided the city's electricity. We pulled off the highway to identify and note the species—hundreds of black-headed gulls, egrets, and herons populated the waters.

Jalalabad, at lower elevation and within the shadow of the Indian monsoons, had the feel of the tropics; the air felt more humid, warmer, and heavier compared to Kabul. The city had a long history of serving as a royal winter capital and was known for its orange blossoms in the spring that scented the air in the town. A short distance from Jalalabad was Hadda, one of the most sacred spots in the Buddhist world, which included one thousand stupas and enormous monastery complexes. Thousands of sculptures, mixing elements of Buddhism and Hellenism, were excavated from the site. According to Nancy Dupree's guidebook, even the Buddha himself had visited the area, and one of the shrines supposedly contained a fragment of the Buddha's gilded and bejeweled skull. The stupas were destroyed by Soviet bombing, and the caves and monasteries were used by the mujahideen and later the Taliban. Sadly, we didn't have time to search for the stupas; we were there for Madera.

Madera's offices were in a low-key traditional Afghan house, away from the center of the city. This French organization had been working in eastern Afghanistan since 1988, somehow operating during Afghanistan's introverted days of Taliban rule. They knew what it took to work in Nuristan and could provide us with some much-needed advice. Madera's mission was renewal of the people, of the land, of opportunity for the people of Afghanistan. In the aftermath of the Soviet Union's vindictive scorched-earth tactics, they worked to help restore land and farming, to allow for the sustainable return of refugees and revival of village economies.

Inside the offices, the décor matched the architecture of the house; there were cushions on the ground on carpets in the place of Western-style fixtures, as well as a few pieces of carved Nuristani furniture. Large windows looked out on the landscape—if not for the natural light, the place might have felt a bit like an opium den. The feeling of this office, and meeting with a staff garbed in traditional Afghan dress (even the Westerners), was surreal. This was the complete opposite of the USAID contractors we typically worked with.

The Madera offices felt organic, mysterious, almost clandestine—and, perhaps, more likely to succeed in its mission. Pascal Arthaud, Madera's Afghanistan country director, kindly agreed to lend us his expertise. Over tea and sweets, we spoke (mostly in French) about the eastern region's environmental problems, illegal timber harvesting, and wildlife. The advice from Madera was straightforward and perhaps obvious: Nuristan was exceptionally dangerous. Use locals. Avoid entering the region yourself for any reason. Keep a low profile. But they had one interesting insight; they suggested we should appeal to the independence of the community to promote self-governance and better management of natural resources. Rather than seeing their autonomy as a barrier, we could harness it to our advantage.

In Jalalabad, we also met with Dr. Halim, dean of the faculty and professor of veterinary medicine at Nangarhar University, whom Kara had found. This wiry, white-haired, and cheerful professor shared a deep enthusiasm about our efforts in conservation; he had even reached out to us long before the trip to the east, introducing himself with his nickname of "Dr. Tiger," although we never quite learned why. We discussed getting some of his best veterinary students to work with us in Nuristan, and he happily introduced us to three of them. The first was Dr. Farid, a compact and somewhat morose Afghan who spoke English fluently. Dr. Esmael, quiet, tall, and balding, wore a long beard and traditional Afghan clothes. His English was weaker, but conversations in Farsi revealed his good nature. Dr. Bahadur Khan was kind and quiet, with a rugged, square face—a bit of an old soul. Although all were from the east borderlands, none were from Nuristan. They help lead the forest survey teams.

After returning to Kabul, Kara went to NEPA to get recommendations for additional team members for Nuristan. One member of the NEPA staff actually hailed from Nuristan, the appropriately named Abdullah Mayar Nuristani. Nuristani was enthusiastic and had deep community connections, and a sense of adventure ran in his family (his daughter became Afghanistan's first female high-altitude mountaineering guide). He put together a local team of Ministry of Agriculture natural resource managers and community leaders recognized for their knowledge of the region's fauna and flora to assist with the surveys. The local team assembled by Nuristani joined our veterinarians to make up the Nuristan survey team.

Our GIS officer, Haqiq, conducted satellite analysis of the landscape for the surveys, including building a three-dimensional model of the region from radar topographic data created by space shuttle missions, combined with Russian topographic maps that we turned into three-dimensional digital reliefs based on their contour lines. We planned our physical survey using Haqiq's maps. With the help of the WCS India Program and the world-famous tiger researcher Ullas Karanth, we brought in Devcharan Jathanna and Srinivas Vaidyanathan, who helped us design survey methodologies. Luke Hunter, WCS's big-cat biologist, helped us get camera traps that we set up to complement our survey work. WCS in partnership with the American Museum of Natural History analyzed scats we would send back to verify the presence of carnivores.

As with other places in Afghanistan, we knew little about the condition of Nuristan's wildlife and forests. The United Nations Environment Programme, using satellite imagery, found evidence of deforestation in the eastern provinces between 1977 and 2002, with decreases in forest cover of 53 percent in Nuristan, 71 percent in Nangarhar, and 29 percent in Kunar. However, there wasn't new information on wildlife distribution and abundance since the work of Petocz and Larsson under the FAO in the 1970s.

In addition to documenting the status of the forests, we were especially interested in a few key species that were globally threatened and were reported in Nuristan before the 1979 invasion. These included the snow leopard (*Panthera uncia*), the Persian leopard (*Panthera pardus saxicolor*), the markhor (*Capra falconeri falconeri*), the Afghan urial (*Ovis vignei cycloceros*), and the Asiatic black bear (*Ursus thibetanus*).

Among these species, the markhor, a mountain goat that lives on vertical cliff walls of the Hindu Kush, was the most unusual. It boasts two fantastical unicorn-like spiral horns that give it its English name—the screw-horned goat. In Farsi, *markhor* means something else entirely—"snake-eater," and supposedly after dispatching with a snake, the markhor drools out the poison, which is collected by locals. We also looked for the urial, a large sheep with proud circular horns. It is smaller and less impressive than the Marco Polo but still a favorite of international big-game hunters.

The Asiatic black bear, sometimes known as the moon bear because of a crescent-shaped white spot on its chest, is broadly distributed across multiple subspecies in Asia. These bears are in decline due to an insatiable medicinal trade in bear by-products, including bile, that has increased as China's wealth has grown.

The mention of Asian black bear bile in Chinese traditional medicine dates back three thousand years to the Ming Dynasty. According to the International Union for Conservation of Nature, traditional medicine in eastern Asia has used bear bile for millennia to treat fever, inflammation, liver toxicity, poor eyesight, and gallstones. The demand is high in part because bear bile actually does have healing properties.

The active ingredient in this ursine bodily fluid—ursodeoxycholic acid (UDCA)—has been approved to treat liver diseases, prevent against retinal degeneration, protect against type 1 diabetes, and fight a series of other neurodegenerative diseases. UDCA helps prevent cell death and may have evolved to protect bears during hibernation. But even so, there is no reason to kill the bears to extract the bile.

Synthetic versions of UDCA exist, are just as effective, and are in widespread use; however, traditional medicine practitioners prefer using natural bear bile, particularly from wild populations. The bile is sold in a panoply of forms: whole gallbladders, raw bile, pills, powders, flakes, and ointments. Perhaps most disturbing is the rise of bear bile farming. These farms extract bile from captive bears with a catheter or drainage tube or through regular puncturing of the gallbladder and collection of bile. The technique was developed originally in North Korea. The bears are kept in cages so small that they can't sit, stand, or turn around, and the direct portal inside the body is a pathway for infections. Worse, there is significant evidence that such farms may be fronts for wildlife trafficking, where most bears are captured as cubs in the wild, smuggled into the farms, and represented as having been born there. In Vietnam, small-scale bile farms hold hundreds of cubs removed from the wild.* In China, one estimate suggests there are still as many as sixty-seven farms, extracting bile from over ten thousand live bears. These farms haven't been sufficient to meet the demand for wild bear bile but may have actually increased it. According to the IUCN, the availability of farmed bile may have enticed more users into the market, some of whom were willing to pay considerably more for the wild product.

Beyond snow leopards and Persian leopards, the mountain sheep and goats, and the Asiatic black bear, we were on the lookout for another more mysterious species. The 1977 Petocz and Larsson survey included reports from locals about a goat-size quadruped known as the *rhombozai* in Pashto and the *rutswaming* in Nuristani, with hind legs

---

*Vietnam would agree to end the practice in 2017.

longer than its front legs, no horns, and large ears, with particularly delicious meat. Petocz and Larsson identified this animal as the endangered Kashmir musk deer (*Moschus cupreus*). These animals have an additional identifying characteristic that neither the surveyors nor the locals mentioned: the presence of saber-like tusks, more colloquially referred to as fangs.

The musk deer's curved, vampire-like fangs extend two to three inches from the animal's upper lip. During mating season, the fangs are used to seduce females and fend off rivals. There had not been a sighting of the musk deer in Afghanistan since 1948. Despite occasional reports, like Petocz and Larsson's from 1977, there weren't any confirmations, which made its persistence doubtful.

The lack of sightings might result from the difficulty of actually finding a deer. They aren't large animals. Musk deer are small-bodied, ranging between seventeen and twenty-seven pounds and standing roughly two feet high. They are timid, solitary animals that spend the day hiding in dense undergrowth (their nocturnal lifestyle, plus their fangs, have led to the unofficial English name of "vampire deer"). Moreover, they live in challenging environments to access. The bodies of the Kashmir musk deer are adapted for climbing Nuristan's steep mountainsides. In the summers, they stay at higher altitudes, between 3,000 and 3,500 feet, and traverse twenty-degree slopes, which makes them both difficult to find and difficult to reach. The musk deer's scarcity could also result from the fact that it has been hunted nearly out of existence because of a market for the gland that gives the deer its name.

The male musk deer marks his territory by dropping grain-size secretions onto shrubs. These secretions are produced from an odiferous and highly valued gland housed in the deer's abdominal pouch. Each mating season, a male may produce twenty to twenty-five grams of waxy secretions containing a rich pheromone called *muscone*. These secretions have an earthy fragrance that some liken to freshly cut wood. The name *musk* originates from the Persian word *moshk*, meaning "deer's navel."

Musk has been used in perfumes, incense, medicine, food, and even as an aphrodisiac since ancient times. It is mentioned in the Talmud, dating to the fifth-century AD. The tenth-century Egyptian physician al-Tamimi described a method for preparation of a scent called *ma jun al-misk* and a perfume mixture known as *nadd* made from musk and ambergris. In India, it was valued as a cure for pulmonary diseases, and in Europe, it found favor as an ingredient in baked goods, beverages, candies, ice creams, molasses, and puddings. In religious contexts, the fragrance was associated with immortality and purity, as noted by the Prophet Muhammad himself, and even mixed into the mortar of mosques.

As with UDCA, synthetic musk has long been available, but there is still a heavy demand for the real article. In the 1970s, Petocz and Larsson recorded Afghan traders paying from ten to thirty dollars for a single gland. The current market is now driven by musk's use in Asian medicine. Current estimates of musk's value on the global wildlife trade market range as high as $70,000 per kilogram. It takes thirty to fifty sexually mature bucks to gather a kilogram. Although musk can be sustainably collected by gathering the grains after a deer marks its territory, the demand for musk is so high that hunters often kill the deer to get the entire gland in one go. Given the deterioration of habitat, the chaos of war and absence of government, and the skyrocketing price, it was possible that the musk deer had long since disappeared from Afghanistan.

We had our objectives laid out. Now we needed to train our three teams in a host of techniques. In the middle of the summer, we brought the teams to Kabul for six weeks of training. That entailed instruction in setting up of camera traps; conducting transects (a systematic and scientific way of recording wildlife observations along a specified path); reading topographic maps; using GPS units, compasses, cameras, range finders, satellite phones, and binoculars; and measuring transects using hip chains (gossamer biodegradable threads that measure the path walked). Down in our office's basement, Dev and Srinivas took the three teams, made up of our veterinarians, the Ministry of Agriculture staff, Mr. Nuristani from NEPA, and the community members from Nuristan, through complicated discussions of capture-recapture and occupancy theory via endless slide presentations.

To help turn the slides into actual techniques that our teams could use in the field, we took the teams out into the wilds of Kabul. We had them use the GPS units to record the latitude, longitude, and elevation and take compass bearings of some favorite spots around town: the WCS office, the Nomad Carpet Store, Afghan Fried Chicken, the Hanzalah Mosque, and more. We practiced GPS navigation through the city, simulating the grids they would survey in Nuristan. We drove up to Paghman, above Qargha Lake, to test their ability to follow way-points using GPS. This was critical, as we needed to ensure that the surveys covered all areas equally and didn't bias the data by following existing paths around human habitation. They also needed to be able to read topographic maps and understand the landscape. For some team members, this meant learning to read roman script. Despite all the challenges, the team, eager to learn, caught on quickly.

Srinivas and Dev also took the teams to the Kabul Zoo, where they could practice identifying scat and tracks from animals that they might encounter on the survey. The scats provided us with a wealth of information: through the scats, not only could we confirm the presence or absence of a species, but with enough samples, we could also get insights into the population size and gene flow. Gene flow is the quantity of genetic material regularly exchanged with other populations; the more gene flow, the more likely a population (and a species) has sufficient resilience in the face of stresses because it can maintain its genetic diversity as well as replenish its population. This is the kind of improvisation required when you can't necessarily see the animals.

Our next test was training them on conducting transects for the occupancy surveys. We decided to use Shahr-e Naw Park. This was Kabul's Central Park, although much more modest, and was not far from our office. The park held Kabul's only working movie theater, the Park Cinema—a grungy, run-down building where Afghan men went to escape everyday reality of postwar Afghanistan by watching Pakistani movies and Bollywood hits. The park was lined with shir-e-yach shops—the sweet Afghan ice cream. It was a green, leafy oasis within Kabul and was the perfect place to put into practice the training of the Nuristani teams.

We broke the group into teams, similar to what they would do in Nuristan. Each of the teams had four members. Three of the four roamed the park, while a fourth remained at the "camp." In each threesome, the lead person took the role of wildlife spotter, hunting for direct observations or signs of wildlife, including scats, tracks, calls, scrapes or territorial markings, or even carcasses of the animal itself or its prey. The second person recorded the observations on data sheets and, using the GPS units to navigate, marked their locations. They also ensured that the survey was within the boundaries of the grid being surveyed that day. Finally, the third person measured the distance walked using the hip chain and also recorded location, elevation, and habitat type on the transect log every two hundred meters. The hip chains attached one end of a line to a tree or other object and then unspooled as the researcher walked away, allowing him to measure the area being surveyed in meters.

To test our teams, we hid stuffed animals throughout the park among the trees and shrubs. The whole undertaking took on a comic air: the teams, dressed in traditional Pashtu clothing from Nuristan, lumbered under the weight of their equipment. They wandered slowly through the park, using high-powered binoculars and laser range finders to hunt for plush toys. When they made a "sighting," they took photographs and conferred among themselves studiously over data sheets. Not suspicious at all.

Passersby watched with a combination of concern and confusion at the strange cluster of men from the Pashtun eastern borderlands, toting fancy expedition equipment in a downtown park, documenting stuffed animals in the trees and acting like silkworms. Eventually, we realized it might have looked like we were planning an attack on the movie theater or ice cream shops or something comparably insidious. Kabul was a relatively modern metropolis, so the group stood out. As the training went on, I grew increasingly nervous that the Afghan National Army or coalition forces might show up with guns drawn. Thankfully, there was no military response to our stuffed animal survey (a fact that was in its own way disconcerting). The teams passed the training without a hitch.

We needed to stock up on equipment for deployment. Off we went to the George W. Bush Market, where we found US-issue heavy-duty mountain sleeping bags and tents. The full complement of equipment included GPS units, compasses, camera traps, headlamps and flashlights, binoculars, cameras, detailed maps, data sheets, identification guides (translated into Dari and Pashto, of course), satellite phones, medical supplies, food, and more.

One of the more critical pieces of equipment was a letter of introduction—for their protection. The teams faced danger from multiple directions. Because they were Afghans carrying heaps of technical gear, they risked potential misidentification as hostiles by the US military, which could lead to a drone attack or trouble at checkpoints. But their connection to a Western organization could lead to attacks from locals, foreign fighters, or the Taliban. That only covered the danger from fellow humans; there was also the steep terrain and remoteness of the sites.

We contacted the Nuristan Provincial Reconstruction Team and the International Security Assistance Force for Afghanistan to let them know our teams would be there, but we weren't sure if that was enough. Groups of specialized US forces and intelligence, not directly in communication with reconstruction teams or ISAF, roamed the mountains. Our teams would look suspicious to anyone who didn't know what they were doing, particularly from a helicopter or a drone. It would be the stuffed animal hunt all over again, but much more dangerous. Fieldwork is never completely safe. Even looking for lemurs in Madagascar, hardly a war zone, I was once asked by a local why I was there to "drink our blood and break our bones." Misunderstandings happen, and in war zones, they are deadly. In Nuristan, our concerns about safety would prove justified.

We had broken up the survey area in Nuristan into twenty-seven grids of fifty square kilometers each, with each grid broken up into sixteen sub-cells. Then we selected a random sub-cell as the starting point for each of the surveys. From that sub-cell, teams would utilize stream courses, animal trails, and footpaths as survey transects.

Although our survey teams would cover a lot of ground, they might not be there at the right moment to encounter wildlife. To supplement their observations, we set up camera traps to spot animals more active at night or shy of human presence. During the initial survey, teams placed the camera traps in areas suggested by community members and along animal pathways that showed signs of activity (scats, tracks, etc.). We later evened out the distribution of the traps across the grids with the greatest apparent animal abundance and forest cover. Camera traps, when scientifically set up, allow you to answer progressively rigorous questions about the presence, distribution, and abundance of wildlife. While live survey work could detect the presence of wildlife in a defined area and even start to map distribution, occupancy of the landscape, and hot spots, it would be difficult to get good measures of abundance and density or track change in those numbers without camera traps and the underlying population genetics revealed by the scat surveys.

Surveying also has a human element. The teams conducted interviews with locals and recorded possible sightings of our target species and otherwise undetected wildlife. Talking to the people on the ground also let us assess whether any of the predators (like the leopards or wolves) were taking livestock and assess the level of hunting in the fifty villages across the region.

Our teams were well trained and enthusiastic. The survey's methods were clearly defined and tested, thanks in part to the hunt for teddy bears in Shahr-e Naw Park. But all the prep work still needed to translate into the steep, daunting terrain of Nuristan in December.

The first set of surveys didn't go well. Meters of snow made movement very difficult, as demonstrated clearly by scores of photos sent back to Kabul showing team members buried in the snow up to their chests. But winter was an important time for such surveys since the animals moved down from the mountain peaks to lower elevations in the winter and were more likely to be seen. For some species, winter was the main hunting season. Working in deep snow is hard enough, but slopes of 30 percent grades and higher made transects limited and difficult. Even with all these challenges, the teams were able to start verifying species in the country and start collecting information from the local communities.

The camera trapping also had its difficulties. One camera trap collected thirty consecutive shots of a young man, clearly fascinated and aware of the camera, in a host of different poses, but never smiling, that would burn through the film on the cameras. There were more serious problems as well. Dr. Farid, one of our vets and a highly capable scientist, grew increasingly concerned about the security situation and asked repeatedly to be assigned to another region where WCS worked. This was someone *from* the east of Afghanistan, which spoke to how hard it is for outsiders in Nuristan. Security was a constant and serious worry.

We monitored security reports for news of anti-government insurgency forces in neighboring valleys. Teams constantly adjusted the survey schedule to avoid running into fighting, which was sometimes just a valley away. The risks only grew as time passed. While the team drew stares practicing in the Kabul park, the attention was far more serious in Nuristan. Villagers demanded to know why the team was surrounding their lands with white string: some accused the teams of surveying the mountain for sale to foreigners, while others accused the teams of using the hip chains to signal bombing locations for coalition forces. The camera traps also came under suspicion. Locals claimed that we were actually looking for potential mujahideen. Given the frequency of bombing in the area, such seemingly illogical suspicions could make sense, and correlation turned into causation. One morning, I got a call on my cell from one of the teams checking their camera traps. They noted that the US was actively bombing one of the trap sites and asked if I minded if they waited until the bombing stopped. I graciously agreed to their modest request.

In the end, the surveys proved more successful than we could have hoped. Over two years, the teams traveled more than 370 kilometers across twenty-five of the twenty-seven grids by foot, carefully surveying a difficult landscape. The combination of camera traps, genetic analysis of scats, and direct observation identified the presence of many species, including some of the key species we sought out—the markhor and the Asiatic black bear. The teams also encountered a leopard during their survey (although they were never able to ascertain whether it was a snow leopard or Persian leopard since it quickly disappeared and Persian leopard coloration can vary toward the lighter side) and found evidence of the leopard cat, gray wolf, golden jackal, red fox, rhesus macaque, crested porcupine, the common palm civet, and yellow-throated marten.

The village interviews suggested that Persian leopards, snow leopards, lynx, Pallas's cats, jungle cats, urials, ibex, and brown bears were also present. Villagers also reported hunting the markhor, whose horns held important symbolism in the Kafir religion and were stylized in elaborate wood carvings to signify wealth and prowess of hunters. Conversations with the residents also suggested the presence of another species—the musk deer—and that it was still being hunted to serve perfume markets. More than sixty years after its last sighting, we now had the chance to find it.

Dr. Stephane Ostrowski, the WCS Afghanistan veterinarian and leader of the EcoHealth team, and his research assistants Jan Mohammad and Rita Ali started the search for the musk deer. Jan and Rita conducted a community mapping exercise carried out through 249 interviews with local communities—twenty-six villages in all—to pinpoint where the musk deer were most likely to be found—only 14 percent of the interviews recognized that the musk deer were still present. Jan and Rita then conducted nearly forty hours of transects on the regions that the interviews suggested would be most likely to have such populations. During the transects, they looked for a number of different signs of potential presence—sightings, feces, latrines, bedding sites, and tracks. This was extremely rugged and steep terrain and was hard going. However, the terrain worked to their advantage; the inaccessibility of the cliffs meant that any bedding sites or tracks they found among them would most certainly be a markhor or a musk deer rather than a domestic animal.

And then, on their transects, Jan and Rita saw the deer not just once but five separate sightings of one or two deer. They also later came across a female musk deer that had been freshly hunted. This carcass would be the key for confirmation. Jan and Rita collected hairs from the carcass, since the female deer lacked tusks (had it been a male, the tusks would have been sufficient). Because of a worsening security situation in Afghanistan, it took another three years to get the hairs out of the country for review by a taxonomic expert. Under the microscopes of experts, the unique scale patterns on the surface of the hair confirmed the hairs as coming from a musk deer. This was proof, not just conjecture. After sixty years, they had verified the continued presence of Afghanistan's vampire deer in the land of light. Despite bombs, insurgency, deforestation, hunting, and war, they had survived.

Despite this success, WCS ultimately had to withdraw from Nuristan as the security situation in Afghanistan continued to degrade. This meant abandoning other elements of our conservation program in Nuristan before they could even start, including household economic surveys and assessments of the carbon potential of Nuristan forests as a way to value and protect them. Although we were willing to take on the remoteness, the deep snow, and the impossibly steep terrain, in the end, we couldn't take the risk created by our own species. Nuristan, the land of light, became once again dark, shrouded behind dark forests and craggy mountain peaks, its secrets hidden.

CHAPTER 8

THE SEARCH FOR THE LAST
AFGHAN CHEETAH

THE ASIATIC (OR Persian) cheetah (*Acinonyx jubatus venaticus*) is a distinctly different subspecies from the African cheetah, branching off tens of thousands of years ago from the African cheetah lineage. Asiatic cheetahs are smaller and lighter than their sub-Saharan African counterparts and once ranged from across the Indian subcontinent through Afghanistan, southern Kazakhstan, Turkmenistan, and Iran all the way to the Arabian Peninsula and the Levant. In ancient Egypt, Sumer, and Assyria, as far back as 4,300 years ago, the cheetah was a hunting companion, used to run down game, much like falcons are used today in the Arab world. Hunting with cheetahs started in Egypt, and it is believed that the practice then spread to Mesopotamia and from there to Iran, India, and Central Asia. Cheetah hunting featured in the Iranian national epic, the *Shāhnāmah*. In Mughal India, cheetahs were considered fully fledged members of the royal court. They had their own tents in the royal hunting encampments and were sometimes carried in a litter with a canopy for shade. Akbar (Abu'l-Fath Jalal-ud-din Muhammad Akbar), the great Mughal ruler, was reported to keep one thousand cheetahs, which sported decorated collars and leashes and gold-brocaded saddlecloths and consumed four thousand pounds of meat per day.

But today, the Asiatic cheetah is potentially the most endangered member of the big cats, competing with the Amur leopard for this unhappy distinction. The subspecies has declined due to herder persecution, poaching, and road collisions, as well as prey and habitat loss. There may be fewer than forty Asiatic cheetahs left in the world, and as far as the global carnivore conservation community believed, the Islamic Republic of Iran hosts the entire remaining population. The cheetahs' once sweeping range has decreased by 98 percent. We suspected, however, that the cheetahs still survived in Afghanistan, and we were going to find them. The problem was that this wasn't part of WCS's cooperative agreement with USAID.

When a species population shrinks to dangerously low levels, it falls into an "extinction vortex." As the name suggests, an extinction vortex works like a giant whirlpool around a drain. The forces that drive a species toward oblivion result from a combination of random chance and constant predictable threats. This whirlpool of extinction only gets stronger and faster as a population gets smaller.

Threats to wildlife can roughly be sorted into two categories: random and deterministic. No matter how large a population, a species is always vulnerable to random chance events: car accidents, disease outbreaks, harsh weather, or even more practical matters, such as the ability to find a mate, birth and death rates in a given year, or variations in sex ratio (imagine within a single year, the possibility that all the newborns are male). Deterministic factors are sustained and consistent pressures on a population. They stem from known causes rather than random chance. Examples include steady loss or degradation of habitat or overhunting of the species itself or its prey base. Deterministic factors also include genetic factors, such as inbreeding depression. As populations shrink, recessive genes, some of which may be deleterious, are more likely to express, depressing the fitness of the population or species.

At a certain point, an extinction vortex becomes nearly irreversible. Geneticist Ian Robert Franklin has theorized that once an idealized animal population sinks below five hundred individuals, its evolutionary potential to adapt to environmental change erodes. Once a population falls below fifty individuals, factors like inbreeding depression kick in, essentially putting the animal on an irreversible trajectory toward extinction. In a healthy population, the frequency of genes (in the absence of migration, selection, or mutation) maintains an equilibrium. But as a population dwindles, the random sampling of members of a population can bias the subset of genes that are passed on.

You can visualize the impact of inbreeding depression or erosion of adaptability using a jar of jelly beans. Imagine each flavor of jelly bean represents a gene. When you grab a handful of jelly beans, you're randomly selecting genes. Imagine that handful represents the selection that occurs when a population is subdivided or reduced. The larger the handful, the more flavors you have. More flavors (i.e., greater genetic diversity within a population) means more potential to adapt to a wider variety of threats. A smaller handful means less diversity and less adaptability. As individuals die and take their traits with them, the diversity of the handful shrinks more. Moreover, your handful may not reflect the makeup of the population well because some flavors may be overrepresented in the subsample as compared. Perhaps your handful includes a lot of flavors you don't like, in a greater proportion than their distribution within the whole jar. This is how inbreeding depression works. When a subdivided population contains a greater proportion of genes that lower the fitness of individual animals (measured by an organism's ability to survive and reproduce, which determines the size of its genetic contribution to the next generation), expression of those "bad" genes becomes more likely.

And determining the size of a population isn't as simple as a head count (not that gathering cheetahs for a census would be simple). The fifty-individual break point refers not to the absolute size of a population but to its "effective population size"—the number of individuals in an idealized population who contribute to the next generation (i.e., reproduce). While the Asiatic cheetah's population was estimated around forty individuals (the census population), its effective population size could be much smaller, as not all individuals are located together in a single area with gene flow (subpopulations may be fragmented and iso-lated). Some of those forty theoretical cheetahs may not be healthy, at breeding age, or even able to get a mate. According to some estimates, for every five to ten individuals counted in a census population, on av-erage, there may be only one individual that is passing on its genes to the next generation.

With an estimated census population so low, the Asiatic chee-tah was in profound danger, but that risk was compounded with the cheetah's tendency to spread out. Cheetahs in general are one of the most wide-ranging carnivore species, with home ranges documented in excess of three thousand square kilometers and movements of trans-located animals sometimes exceeding one thousand kilometers. As a result, cheetah densities seldom exceed one cheetah every twenty square kilometers. In marginal habitat, that may decline to one cat in every 250 square kilometers. This was the case with the Asiatic cheetah.

Unlike the African cheetahs, which live in prey-rich savannahs, the Asiatic cheetahs mainly live in hilly terrains, foothills, and rocky val-leys. Asiatic cheetah lives were lonely and difficult. Asiatic cheetahs patrolled some of the largest ranges ever recorded for the species. In Iran, one female had a home range of 3,629 square kilometers, and her sons ranged across multiple reserves, covering an estimated 4,862 square kilometers in their first three years. Such patterns of movement make cheetahs susceptible to getting hit by cars or ranging into un-protected land where they may be killed by herders protecting their stock. This extreme ranging behavior also suggested another possible problem: a sparse prey base. In areas with a high abundance and di-versity of prey, cheetah densities are higher, and their ranges are much smaller. However, where food is scarcer, cheetahs need to range over a much wider range. Low-density and wide-ranging distribution make the cheetah more susceptible to the chance and deterministic pressures of the extinction vortex.

Finding Asiatic cheetahs in Afghanistan would give cheetah con-servation efforts an additional source population as a bulwark against extinction—a separate library of genes and a separate population both

geographically distant and perhaps not subject to the same chance factors affecting the populations in Iran. Afghanistan has fewer roads and
cars than Iran and offers greater chance of survival for the species, as
long as hunting of both cheetah and its prey can be controlled.

The cheetah once ranged through much of west and northwest Afghanistan, particularly around the basins of the Helmand, Farah, Hari
Rud, and Murghab Rivers, living at elevations under one thousand meters, particularly within sandy and clay soiled deserts and open areas.
In 1965, the Field Museum mounted a massive four-month survey in
Afghanistan, creating one of the greatest collections of the country's
mammals anywhere. But the Field Museum's expedition never saw an
Asiatic cheetah. Jerry Hassinger, then a graduate student who accompanied the expedition and wrote up the survey's results, noted that "if
Cheetahs exist anywhere in Afghanistan, it is probably in these [river]
basins." That's where the WCS teams would look.

This area also encompassed a protected area we had proposed—the
Northwest Afghanistan Game Reserve, an extensive grassland and pistachio savannah in Afghanistan's northwest corner, next to Iran and
Turkmenistan. Earlier expeditions had described the area as full of lush
pastures that supported an abundance of wildlife, from herds of onager
(a wild donkey that roams the grasslands of Asia) to goitered gazelles.
Like our other proposed protected areas, this preserve had a royal prec-
edent; in the 1970s, King Zahir Shah designated the region as a game
reserve, and as with Afghanistan's other proposed parks, it never was
legally established. Efforts to create and "gazette" the park—inscribe
it formally as a protected area—were interrupted by three decades of
war. And like elsewhere in Afghanistan, we needed to understand the
impact of war on the region's wildlife, especially so in the case of the
Asiatic cheetah.

Recent years have seen a global effort to study and conserve the
Asiatic cheetah in Iran, but there has been little evidence of the Asiatic cheetah's presence in Afghanistan; the last visual sightings in the
country dated from the 1950s. There was also a single sighting by Iranian conservationists around the Sistan wetlands on the border with

Afghanistan in the 1970s. In 1971, a conservationist photographed a cheetah skin in the Herat fur market. The only Asiatic cheetah pelt known to be from Afghanistan within global natural history museum collections was purchased in Farah Province in 1948 by the Third Danish Expedition to Central Asia. So why would we even try to find the cheetah in Afghanistan?

Chance would favor the search for the cheetah. WCS discovered new evidence suggesting that the Asiatic cheetah was in Afghanistan, but the evidence wasn't in Afghanistan's northwest; it was right in Kabul. One day, Shafiq and Zabih went to lunch at a restaurant near our office called Baba Amir. Nailed to the dusty whitewashed walls were the pelts of endangered cats, including a tiger, snow leopards, Persian leopards, caracals—and one cheetah pelt. Once again in Afghanistan, serendipity would lead us to a breakthrough.

Shafiq and Zabih spoke to the owner about the work of WCS and asked whether they could borrow the cheetah pelt to show it to me. Despite the restaurant owner's clear predilection for decoration with pelts of large endangered cats, he quickly became enthusiastic about WCS's conservation work in Afghanistan. He later lent Shafiq and Zabih the entire pelt collection, literally pulling out the nails from walls, for use in wildlife-trade training sessions.

Asiatic cheetahs can be distinguished from African and Saharan forms by a short mane on their shoulders, left from the mantle coloration they had as cubs. It appeared that this one had such a mantle. After I examined the pelt, I invited the owner over for lunch to thank him for sharing it with us, but more importantly to learn about how a cheetah hide came to decorate his business. The owner claimed that the cheetah pelt was hunted within the last two years in Afghanistan. He insisted it did not come from Iran or alternatively trafficked from Africa. The pelt didn't seem especially old, and if his story were true, it would put the cheetah in present-day Afghanistan or at least suggested a population that crossed the border from Iran.

A few weeks later, we gained a second piece of evidence for a cheetah presence in Afghanistan. We had just started surveying the fur

markets, trying to estimate the demand for endangered wildlife products, when we found a jacket that appeared to be made out of cheetah
fur. The jacket came from a fur factory catering almost exclusively to
the foreign presence spread at bases around Kabul. Unbeknownst to
us, at almost the same time, an Afghan biologist completing a doc-
torate on the wildlife trade in leopards at the University of Cologne
discovered another cheetah skin for sale in a market in the northern city
of Mazar-i-Sharif and published the finding in *Cat News*. Taken together, these two pelts and a jacket represented more certain evidence
of the cheetah's persistence in Afghanistan than had been accumulated
in the previous seventy years.

There was a catch, however. These skins could also have been
poached from Iran (which was worrying in any case, given the low
population numbers), or from Africa (which would suggest a wide-
ranging trafficking network). We conferred about our findings around
the cheetah with WCS headquarters at the Bronx Zoo and with WCS
field biologist George Schaller, a tall, lanky, focused, and indefatigable
German-born biologist who did pioneering work on everything from
mountain gorillas (preceding Dian Fossey) to Serengeti lions, snow
leopards in the Himalayas, jaguars in Brazil, and giant pandas in China.
Schaller had already traveled to Afghanistan to survey Marco Polo
sheep during Peter Zahler's initial rapid assessment, and WCS was
already quietly working with the authorities across the border in Iran
regarding the Asiatic cheetah. If there proved to be a cheetah population in Afghanistan, our work represented a chance to build on WCS's
established efforts in Iran and manage a transboundary population of
cheetahs in one of the most complex foreign-policy minefields in the
world—along a border region that included plenty of actual minefields
and even worse threats.

My team hadn't worked in western Afghanistan before and weren't
sure what to expect. I decided to travel to the region in advance of the
longer expedition with Schaller to scout out some locations, understand the security situation, and secure permissions and support for the
expedition. Specifically, I wanted to meet with the governor of Herat

Province, local *shurras*, district representatives, the head of USAID's local efforts, officers of the Ministry of Agriculture and National Environmental Protection Agency, and anyone else who could provide advance intelligence for the longer cheetah expedition. I also wanted to do some surveys for the cheetah myself.

We also met local military and police chiefs to plan a security detail for the expedition and better understand the risks in the region. While Herat was the safest region in Afghanistan (outside remote Wakhan), regions to the south and east were quickly turning crimson on the security maps. We were receiving reports of more and more incidents, from IEDs to outright attacks on NGO facilities. Our survey work took us north along the Turkmenistan border, west near the Iranian border, and to the southern edge of Herat Province. When I came on as the director of the Afghanistan program, Peter Zahler sent me regular security reports. As those reports got less and less encouraging, Zahler scribbled on one missive, "I think if you just black out all provinces from Nuristan to Herat that border another country, you're good to go." Luckily for me, all the places with interesting wildlife happened to be in those zones he just told me to black out.

On our advance trip, after securing permissions and sorting out logistics, we would do some initial scouting of potential survey sites. Traveling to Herat by road wouldn't be safe even for Afghan staff, so we decided to fly. Qais had arranged for Abdul Razaq, one of our security guards, to travel ahead by plane and arrange a car and driver and then meet us at the airport. This trip would be my first with Inayatollah, one of my favorite members of the WCS team. He was a logistics expert, a kind man with Hazara features and a stellar command of English. Soon enough, we were on a plane to Herat, and we met up with Razaq and our middle-aged Herati driver at the airport.

Nancy Dupree wrote that the city of Herat "reflects the cultures of Iran, Central Asia, and Afghanistan for it is the pivot around which these areas spin." If Afghanistan was the crossroads of the world in ancient times, Herat was the crossroads of the crossroads, a brilliant hub, one where kings and queens from ancient Iraq to China would pay homage. Long ago, Herat was a capital of the Timurid Empire, and Alexander the Great spent time there as well. The city has endured attacks by the Mongols, Russians, and the Taliban, but many of its ancient minarets and battlements stand, fiercely defiant in their frayed beauty.

Herat, greened by the waters of the Hari Rud River, is an oasis not only among the desiccated and rocky hills that surround it but also a figurative oasis within Afghanistan. It is among the most beautiful and civil of the Afghan cities. Its wide avenues are tree-lined and clean, and roads are well paved and signed. Herat was the only city in Afghanistan where power worked around the clock. Residents drank clean water, the sewers were covered, the roads were well maintained, and a robust economy thrived on not just agriculture but industry. Factories that fueled the regional economy built by Iranian investors after the war dotted the outskirts of the airport.

In the eyes of many residents, Ismail Khan, the charismatic former provincial governor, deserved much of the credit for Herat's wealth, cleanliness, and beauty. Khan rose to power as a fierce resistance fighter during the Soviet invasion, taking on Russian tanks, helicopters, and MiGs on horseback. He had actually served as a captain in the army of the Taraki regime, but after government forces bloodily suppressed demonstrations in 1979, killing up to twenty-five thousand people in Herat, Khan convinced his troops to switch sides. Brutal violence and reprisals followed, setting off a chain of uprisings that eventually led to the Soviet invasion in December 1979. Ismail Khan led much of the resistance against the Soviets in the west and became known as the "Lion of Herat," the supreme commander of thirteen thousand fighters. After an ally betrayed him, Khan spent more than two years imprisoned by the Taliban in Kandahar, manacled in a *zawlana*, an iron device that hitched his neck to his wrists and ankles. Eventually, he escaped through the desert to Iran, only to come back and fight alongside the Americans in the 2001 invasion.

After the fall of the Taliban, Ismail Khan built an extensive trading relationship with Iran, where he and his militia had taken refuge when the Taliban overtook Herat. The ties to Iran proved a source of exceptional customs revenue, which he used to rebuild and beautify a city that had been pulverized by decades of war. There was a great deal to rebuild.

The extraordinary British adventurer Nick Danziger entered Herat from Iran in 1979 at the beginning of the Soviet invasion with the mujahideen. He encountered profound destruction:

> The Western part of the city was devastated. It was far worse than any pictures I had seen of Dresden or London: It called the total wreck of Nagasaki to mind. . . . Twisted timber beams jutted from collapsed walls like arms reaching out for help from a buried body. Embedded in walls were rockets, still unexploded, their fuses clearly visible in their tail sections. Everywhere was the litter of modern warfare, and across it ranged the mujahideen, scavenging for reusable weaponry.[*]

Ismail Khan's heroic status came from his military exploits, but his efforts to rebuild Herat won him the unwavering support of the local people. He restored infrastructure, schools, parks, and museums; paid government workers on time; and provided public services. Khan's Iranian friends built modern highways connecting Herat to the east of Iran, replete with modern rest stops and modern signage. But how Khan went about restoring Herat brought him into disfavor with the Afghan Transitional Administration in Kabul. Ruling during peace was fundamentally different from leading during war.

Ismail Khan turned Herat Province into a fully fledged emirate, holding weekly audiences where the poor and needy beseeched him with requests for aid or advice. He also started holding back customs tax revenue from trade with Iran and Turkmenistan. Rather than transferring the funds to the central government, where it was very likely to be misappropriated, Khan kept the revenue and reinvested it in Herat. This approach generated tremendous goodwill within the province and

---

[*] Nick Danziger, *Danziger's Travels* (Boulder, CO: Paladin Press, 1987).

led to Herat's accelerated recovery from the war, but it also earned him powerful enemies. The Afghan president Hamid Karzai, seeking to limit Khan's power and defuse a standoff with other warlords in the region, appointed the fierce fighter Khan as the Minister of Energy and Water in 2005—a way of kicking him upstairs.

On our first day in Herat, Inayatollah and I visited the dusty provincial offices and made the case to various officials about the importance of our search for the Afghan cheetah. The officials listened to us, bemused by their first pitch from American conservationists. Despite, or because of, the novelty of our request, they approved our search effort and pledged their support. We also arranged for a trip to travel to the regions south of Herat, accompanied by members of the Afghan police and Afghan National Army, along with the police chief, as these were some of the most dangerous areas in the region.

At a subsequent meeting at the local NEPA office, we received another approval and more indications of a possible cheetah presence. Another cheetah skin had reportedly been sold in the bazaar in Herat within the last week. We quickly secured needed permissions from the relevant ministries (Interior, NEPA, Agriculture, Rural Development) without any difficulty but rather with actual enthusiasm.

We also paid a visit to the ISAF Provincial Reconstruction Team, or PRT for short. The concept of a PRT aimed to scale foreign assistance effectively on the local level, with different teams spread across the country. PRTs were usually led by military officers but also employed diplomats, development officers, and reconstruction subject matter experts, all working together to support post-war humanitarian efforts. In my experience, PRTs in Afghanistan (and Iraq) in more unstable areas became de facto prisons for development workers, who could only travel to take meetings and review projects under military escort or with similarly heavy security. The PRT in Herat, like the one in Bamiyan, was the exception, and as such, it was a highly desired appointment. The relative stability of Herat and Bamiyan and low security threats to Westerners permitted PRT staff to leave their compounds and actually engage the populace without a full military convoy. This was a significant advantage over posts in higher-risk PRTs in the east or south. Moreover, the Herat PRT was run by the Italians, who were rumored to wear tailored battle-dress fatigues and serve terrific food.

The PRT and government officials both provided positive reports regarding security. Mines were in low frequency in Herat Province, but their numbers increased exponentially as one got closer to the Iranian border. To the south and east, the threat level from the insurgency was rising. The biggest threat, however, surprisingly enough wasn't the Taliban but came from another source: drug runners. The opium smugglers who illegally crossed the desert border into Iran outgunned even the Iranian army. They had nothing to lose and would perceive any encounter with foreigners as a risk. The smugglers were crossing the border in remote regions that were the very areas where we thought we would find Afghan cheetahs.

That evening, Inayatollah and I did some sightseeing around the city. We climbed up to the old citadel, which was being restored. From afar, the citadel resembles a giant sandcastle, with heavy, rounded fairy-tale turrets interrupting the thick walls. According to legend, the fortress dated all the way back to 330 BC, when Alexander the Great and his army conquered ancient Herat. However old it was, the sloping mud-brick walls of the citadel had seen countless empires come and go. It had been attacked by Mongol warriors twice, as well as British and Persian armies. It had been captured and conquered but seemingly always rebounded, much like Afghanistan itself.

We walked up to a guard post, hoping we might get access to the citadel's interior despite the ongoing restoration work. The guard kindly let us in when we told him we'd traveled from Kabul. Architects were rebuilding the walls and battlements with sand-colored bricks, filling in countless bullet and RPG holes from decades of conflict. Nearly every pre-conflict building in Afghanistan bore similar pockmarks, but as time passed, these wounds healed. Inayatollah and I stood upon the ramparts and saw the city's stupendous mosques and distant minarets laid out before us as the setting sun bathed everything in the last golden light of the day.

We then walked to the Musalla Complex, a fifteenth-century religious center and school marked by five enormous minarets. The legendary British travel writer Robert Byron saw Musalla in the 1930s and described it as "the most beautiful example in color in architecture ever devised by man to the glory of his God and himself" in *The Road to Oxiana*. But by the time I arrived, nearly all the tiles that once covered the buildings and the minarets were gone. All that remained were brilliant diamond-shaped flakes of blue that hinted of a glory that had once been. Four noticeably askew minarets stood together in a square north of the mausoleum of a long-dead queen, marking the corners of a now long-gone madrassa. A fifth minaret leaned dangerously, supported by wires, scarred by an enormous hole about three-quarters of the way up—a memento of a hit from a tank shell. The stump of a nearly completely destroyed sixth minaret stood nearby. These minarets had long attracted the attention of Afghanistan's invaders. British soldiers destroyed the original musalla in 1885 to clear a sight line for their guns to fend off a Russian attack that never materialized. The Soviets used the minarets for target practice during their occupation. Despite the degradation, here they stood, even while the mighty Soviet and British empires had disappeared into dust on the Afghan plains.

The next day, we went into the old bazaar, an ancient marketplace of the Silk Road. The day prior, Herat's NEPA staff had reported the sale of a cheetah pelt in the bazaar. We wanted to search fur shops to see if there were any others still available or if we could uncover other information about the status of the cheetah. Herat's ancient bazaar had been one of the last covered markets in Afghanistan, but like so many other landmarks, it was damaged during years of war. The arched roof was now gone, but the bazaar was still an intriguing warren of side streets, hidden shops, and secret squares. Although our search for cheetah pelts proved fruitless, we found other skins for sale, including wolf, jackal, and fox. The shops around Herat's magnificent Friday Mosque and its gardens also proved fruitful. Inayatollah and I found a hunting and gun shop proudly displaying two mounted and stuffed goitered gazelles—a critical prey species for the cheetah. The store owners noted during the

Taliban's rule, they heard reports of cheetahs near a large wetland near the town of Kuhestan, close by the Iranian border, and much farther to the north than the Sistan wetlands, the site of a previous sighting.

As we interviewed more government officials over the next few days, we heard the same stories over and over. The deputy head of agriculture for Herat told us that thirty years ago, cheetahs and leopards had been present, but they were missing today. He noted that people reported the onager was still present but significantly in decline. The region reportedly still had wild cats, caracals, wolf, fox, jackals, wild boar, urials, and gazelles, particularly at higher elevations.

We repeatedly heard about possible habitats for our elusive cheetah. Terrains as varied as mountains and salty wetlands had been the sites of rumored cheetah encounters. Officials also repeatedly encouraged us to focus our survey efforts on the flanks of mountains, particularly near the border. Perhaps the mines and drug runners in the border regions ironically had helped preserve the cheetah, but they would be threats to our teams.

The stories we heard in Herat also reinforced the expert opinion we had received from an Iranian biologist, Mohammad Farhadinia, who ran an NGO dedicated to the conservation of the Asiatic cheetah in Iran—the aptly named Iranian Cheetah Society (ICS). Farhadinia's research showed that in Iran, the Asiatic cheetah had been forced to become an opportunistic forager because of the decline of its traditional prey base. Traditionally, Asiatic cheetahs lived in plains and pursued gazelles as their main prey species. However, a drastic decline in the gazelles in Iran may have led the cheetahs to shift to mountain ungulates (wild sheep and goats) as prey, along with other species. In our correspondence, Farhadinia told us that some cheetahs in Iran survived on small mammals, particularly hares. His work showed that hares weren't a sufficient food source for the cats to thrive and grow their numbers, but it could be enough to help maintain low densities. He also gave us a pep talk to persist in our search. Many Iranians had told him cheetahs were vanishing and dissuaded him from working on cheetahs when he first started, but his work showed that the carnivores had an uncanny ability to avoid human notice. "They are like ghosts," he wrote in an e-mail. "I am sure that [Afghanistan has] cheetahs, but [you need] some time to find them." We would need to find our Afghan ghosts.

During our interviews, we heard accounts about a trade in wild-caught falcons and the hunting of another vulnerable species, the houbara bustard. One official told us of a recent hunting party of 120 tents, guarded by the Taliban, that included the defense minister of the UAE. There were also reports of Pakistanis traveling into Afghanistan's west to trap falcons. Before long, we found ourselves in the midst of this trade, but for now, cheetahs were our priority.

The next day, Inayatollah, Razaq, and I decided to travel north of Herat toward the Turkmenistan border and swing by the village of Koshk-e Kohneh to survey the landscape; there was a large mountain near Koshk-e Kohneh that looked potentially promising. We interviewed some of the local elders who said that during the war, everyone had guns, and there had been no control over the game reserve. Unsurprisingly, they acknowledged many animals disappeared, although there were still gazelles and urials in the mountains, along with reports of wolves, jackals, hyenas, and wild boar. There were also large numbers of long-clawed squirrels, another potential prey source. However, there were no reports of leopards or cheetahs. When I asked the elders if they thought the cheetah might be found in the border region between Turkmenistan, Iran, and Afghanistan, they responded with one word: "Nothing."

On the back way to Herat, I had the driver stop when I saw what looked like a large group of eagles and buzzards. The birds were preying on some unlucky ground squirrels. One bird had captured a squirrel and had begun dismembering it. I leaped out of the car trying to make an identification and document what I was seeing with my telephoto lens. Everything in Afghanistan was new data from a conservation perspective, and any chance to document was valuable. Inayatollah ran out with me. We stumbled over hundreds of meters of rough terrain to get closer to the birds and take photos—there was a large steppe eagle, a greater spotted eagle, and a long-legged buzzard. As I snapped away, I noticed a faint natural undulation in the terrain, almost like waves. A few pictures later, I stopped to consider the undulations more carefully. They were shallow, U-shaped, about a meter wide, and ran for one hundred meters with side branches running perpendicular to them. They were too neat and even to be natural. A realization sank in: we had run out into what had once been defensive positions, perhaps the site of the Northern Alliance's last stand against the Taliban at the end of the civil war prior to the US invasion. These ruts were trenches, and we were on a battlefield, which meant we might be in or near a minefield.

There's a handy acronym to remember if you find yourself in a mined area. We worked it into all our security briefings.

IF YOU ARE IN A MINEFIELD—USE THE MINED STRATEGY
M—MOVEMENT. *Stop all movement.*
I—INFORM. *Warn people around you.*
N—NOTE. *Note the area. What can you see?*
E—EVALUATE. *Evaluate the course of action. Take control.*
D—DO NOT MOVE. *If there is no safe area, wait for help to survive. Do not step on unknown ground.*

I looked at all the myriad domestic animal tracks that covered the ground and didn't see any indication of whether the region had been previously mined. There were no craters or red-and-white warning rocks, although around a former battlefield or front line, laying defensive mines was a common tactic. I warned Inayatollah not to come any closer. We then started retracing our footprints in the dust back to the car. I had failed my basic mine training by rushing out onto the field after the birds of prey without knowing if this had been a former battleground or the specific mine risk.

On the next and final day of our scouting trip, we traveled with the police chief, whom we referred to as *the commander* given his role in the mujahideen, to the southwest of Herat. He was a jovial, powerful, nimble man, a veteran of the Northern Alliance's fight against the Taliban. He accompanied us, dressed in traditional garb, in a separate car full of military officers. One officer rode in our car. As we rumbled over bumpy terrain, I could feel the barrel of the officer's AK-47 jutting into the back of my seat. In my politest language, I gently asked him to point his assault rifle away from his fellow passengers.

We stopped at various villages on our way south. Residents recalled hunting cheetah near a saline lake named Kol-e-Namaksar on the Afghan-Iranian border, including hazy accounts of shooting two cheetahs in a single day, thirty years ago. The steppe areas south of the border town of Islām Qala around Kol-e-Namaksar also had lots of grass and supported gazelle and urial populations, which sounded promising. The elders were able to accurately distinguish between cheetahs and the light-colored Persian leopard and snow leopards when we quizzed their expertise and knowledge with photos. They also spoke of a place farther south—Kuh-e-Shak, an isolated mountain chain rising out of the steppe. Local residents described a "large cat—a *palang*" residing around the base of these solitary mountains, which also had a gazelle population. This matched the habitats of the Asiatic cheetah in Iran, but *palang* was also the word for *leopard*. Either way, we had some mountains and marshes to investigate.

We started climbing some of the peaks with the commander to get a better vantage point of the landscape. He didn't have any trouble climbing the hills and cliffs. In fact, I had trouble keeping up with him. We spent the next few hours scaling the steep, undulating landscape. We didn't see any traces of wildlife as we scampered across the hillsides. We scrambled down and headed back to his mostly empty headquarters, where he offered us tea. It looked like we were not going to find our cheetah today. We thanked the regional chief for his help and for joining us on our search.

He locked eyes with me. "We want you to help us. We need the West in Afghanistan to rebuild the country. We have struggled a lot for our freedom."

I responded with the truth. "We are here to help, and I will do my best."

The commander kept looking at me directly. After a pause, he slowly said, "We have paid a great price and cannot go back." With those words, he lifted up his loose-fitting shalwar. Both of his legs from his calves down were missing, but instead there were two prosthetics, one for each foot. I was stunned. We had spent the day navigating extremely steep terrain, terrain that I'd had difficulty with, and he never appeared to be limited by them in any way.

I mumbled, with a touch of embarrassment, "You climb better than I do!"

To my astonishment, he burst out laughing. "Yes, I do."

"How did you lose both of your legs?" I asked, my curiosity overcoming my manners. "Were you born like this?"

"When I was fighting with the Northern Alliance against the Russians, we crossed a minefield, and I stepped on a mine and it exploded, taking my leg. When I got better, I returned to fight more. Once again, I had to cross another minefield, and a mine took my other leg. This is the price we have paid. This is why you cannot give up on us."

The next day, as I watched swallows chase each other inside Herat's airport, I couldn't get the words and bravery of the Afghan police chief out of my mind. Although I didn't find any direct evidence of the cheetah, it fueled my conviction that there was a chance for the cheetah to exist, particularly in the regions to the south and west of Herat. If we were able to find the places with prey, we would have a chance to find the last Afghan cheetahs.

I was looking forward to coming back for a longer expedition with Schaller. I had spent nearly three years living in a tent in the southeast forests of Madagascar on a long-term expedition to understand the behavior of extinction in twelve species of Madagascar and was trained in tropical biology in Costa Rica and Panama, but my job in Afghanistan trapped me in reams of bureaucracy with USAID and the management of a country program. My passion was for the adventure of the field.

A few weeks later, George Schaller came out to Afghanistan, bringing with him Beth Wald, a remarkable *National Geographic* photographer with whom he had worked previously on his surveys of Marco Polo sheep in Wakhan. Zalmai, a recent graduate of Kabul University, who had been recommended to us by one of the few Afghan conservation scientists and a professor at the university, would accompany Dr. Schaller on the trip. We had been training Zalmai in survey techniques for snow leopard populations and other species, including Persian leopards, brown bears, urials, markhor, ibex, and Bactrian deer, including paying for him to get his master's in India. He was smart, eager to learn, and on his way to becoming one of Afghanistan's top conservationists. Yama, a smart Afghan who spoke fluent English and whom I had met on my first plane ride out to Herat, also joined the survey to help with logistics and translation. Yama came from a well-known family in Herat who could help build relationships for the expedition. Abdul Razaq returned to Herat to handle additional logistics and security. I was eager to resume our work from the initial trip.

As we were pulling together the team and supplies for the second expedition, an e-mail from USAID arrived. It expressly barred me from joining the expedition or WCS from spending any USAID money on it. Although WCS worked under a cooperative agreement—a managed grant—we were effectively treated as contractors, or worse. As all my salary was paid by USAID, the WCS headquarters limited my participation since they didn't want to further undermine relations with the agency. I wouldn't be able to return with Schaller, who would use outside funding to cover his costs. This was a disappointment for me—a lost chance to work alongside a legendary conservationist to search for an elusive and very endangered species that was tied to my own heritage and to score a significant conservation win and potential science diplomacy opportunity with Iran.

Schaller and Zalmai surveyed the provinces of Herat and Badghis by foot and by car for twenty-one days, driving 1,800 kilometers, ultimately covering 10,000 square kilometers, including much of the former Northwest Afghanistan Game Reserve. Interviews with villagers and local herdsmen supported the idea that small cheetah populations may still remain. Southwest of Dau Shakh, in a desert badlands called Sarta Khat Ka Kari, herdsmen identified the cheetah from photographs and drawings (and distinguished it from the leopard). A local guide showed the WCS team where two *"palangs"* had been seen fighting six months prior. When the field team talked to the man who had observed the squabble, he was emphatic that the animals were cheetahs. He described long legs and rather doglike tracks and identified the correct species from the pictures.

At another village in the far northwest, villagers reported that a *palang* had clawed a man forty-five days earlier. The villagers showed the team the site of the attack in a canyon of conglomerate rock, but WCS found no spoor of a large cat in spite of considerable searching. They later met the young man who had been attacked. Schaller described the encounter in his report back to the Afghanistan program:

> Later we met the young man named Fadah who had been attacked. He told us that he suddenly came upon the 'palang' which reared up and clawed him on the right shoulder and bit the right side of his head. He pushed the cat away and it fled when he and his companions yelled. He showed us a fresh scar about 2.5 cm long on his shoulder, and one small scar on his head. Shown pictures of cheetah and leopard the village crowd that had gathered all agreed that only cheetah occur here. An attack by a cheetah on a human is atypical but the slight injuries do not reflect the power of a leopard.

Ultimately, security issues limited the expedition. The expedition team could not travel to the salt lake of Kol-e-Namaksar near the Iran border or the surrounding deserts, one of the most promising areas according to local residents. Local military commanders were nervous about encountering the heavily armed drug smugglers, particularly to the south of Herat. In Ghurian District, site of several promising potential habitats, fifteen armed soldiers guarded the WCS team for a one-day trip. The local commander also insisted on accompanying them in his own vehicle, despite assuring them that everything was fine.

The surveys also were disappointing because of the paucity of other wildlife in the Northwest Afghanistan Game Reserve. In 1889, a British military officer named Aitchison saw over one thousand onager in the Gulami-Maidan area of the Hari Rud valley in Herat Province.

Neither Schaller's nor my expedition saw a single one of these endangered wild equids. Locals told researchers that a few onager occasionally crossed into Afghanistan from Turkmenistan in the central part of the game reserve but that the Soviets had built a razor-wire fence during their occupation that limited transboundary movement. Schaller's survey made clear that in the 1970s, the reserve had been filled with urials, goitered gazelles, and onager.

But thirty years of war and neglect had broken down the fabric of Afghan society, including laws protecting the land and limiting hunting and grazing. Even iconic Kuchi nomads played a part in the erosion of the country's wildlife. In the late spring, some onager often find their way into Afghanistan and stop to drink at a river. The WCS expedition was told, "If the nomadic herders [Kuchi] hear of a wild animal, they jump on their motorcycles and hunt it down." The rolling grasslands that make up much of the game reserve provide few hiding places for wildlife. The species that survived—wolves, foxes, wild pigs, and the like—were at low numbers. Schaller and the rest of WCS quickly moved on to other priority sites and other expeditions, but my mind rested with the potential that Afghanistan still harbored the cheetah. The multiple skins reported from Afghan markets and the ability of the locals to correctly distinguish the cheetah from a leopard were compelling to me; I felt they were out there.

For all this disappointment, the work in Herat suggested that a more in-depth survey, using camera traps, might find evidence of the Asiatic cheetah. Most work on the Asiatic cheetah focused on Iran, a safer and simpler place to do conservation work. The deserts, steppes, and mountains of the northwest may still be home to the last cheetah in Afghanistan.

CHAPTER 9

ADVENTURES IN CONSERVATION DIPLOMACY

ONE OF THE projects we had planned was a nature reserve that straddled the borders of Afghanistan, Pakistan, Tajikistan, and China. As part of our work to save the Marco Polo sheep and snow leopards, we wanted to turn these beautiful, daunting landscapes into a transboundary preserve where the wildlife and the ecosystem could be managed not on the basis of political boundaries and interests but driven by scientific fact and conservation goals. We were trying to build a peace park among the four countries, but when peace itself was in short supply, there would be serious challenges ahead of us.

The proposed preserve was to cover the mountainous territories where Afghanistan, Pakistan, China, and Tajikistan came together. This land was some of the remotest and most pristine in the world—one of the planet's last remaining wild places. The notion of a transboundary park here dated to the 1930s. The long-disputed borders between Pakistan and China, Pakistan and India, and Afghanistan and Pakistan led to an innovative idea: making these remote mountains into a multilaterally governed conservation area could work to defuse the international tension. And if the four countries engaged each other on science issues, like how to protect a snow leopard that crosses from country to country, they might engage on other matters. Scientific cooperation could build trust, resolve tensions, and build the scaffolding for a deeper relationship. The Wildlife Conservation Society, through its Afghanistan program, had taken up the challenge of creating the peace park, and we made a plan for three international meetings to lay out the groundwork. Although the concept of the park was simple, getting everyone on board proved the opposite. Further, although USAID required us to create the park and had approved our work plan to do so, we paradoxically were not allowed to spend money in other countries outside Afghanistan to make it happen.

This was a spectacular place, from the perspective of a snow leopard, to host a peace park. The peace park would be in the heart of Asia, where many of the world's greatest mountain ranges come together. The Hindu Kush, Tien Shan, Himalayan, Karakoram, and Kunlun rise around the land that would become the park, creating a thrillingly complex terrain, providing thousands of square kilometers of vital, high-altitude habitat filled with cracked glaciers weighing down the earth as they slid into the valleys and angry, cascading rivers, powered, drop by drop, by melting snows, cutting deep, narrow valleys among silent, gray cathedrals of sharp-edged stone, with slopes littered with rocks. These mountain cathedrals, much like their human counterparts, inspired silence and awe.

However, it was the political topography rather than the physical one that was a barrier. There are few places where the four countries bordering each other could seem so different. Afghanistan was an Islamic republic reeling from multiple invasions, a protracted civil war, and the fanatical Taliban theocracy. It had achieved a temporary stability, but the risk of collapse remained, especially because Pakistan, its neighbor, was encouraging an insurgency funded by the opium trade. Pakistan itself was grappling with an instability fueled by competing tribal interests, vast economic disparity between rich and poor, and a never-ending nuclear standoff with India. Tajikistan was a former Soviet Socialist Republic, still seeking its place in the post-Soviet world after more than a decade, weighed down by a history of collectivization, a bloody civil war and undercurrent of Islamic fundamentalism, ongoing authoritarian rule, and a persistent Soviet mind-set. China, the authoritarian heavyweight of the group, was making a claim as the world's next superpower behind a supercharged economy, but a Muslim uprising simmered in the remote, desolate, far-west Xinjiang Province, precisely the part of China the park would occupy. Each of the four neighbors speaks a different language, or multiple languages, with their own scripts and tones. The greatest difference in time zones across any international border is the three-and-a-half-hour difference at the Afghan-Chinese border within the transboundary peace park— the difference between the hour in Beijing and Kabul, the locations to which each country's singular time zone was set. The enormous time difference was mostly an irritant, but it carried symbolic heft as well. In many ways, it represented the gulf that we needed to cross to bring the four countries together.

Countless empires have jostled for control of these frontiers, and they are one of the planet's great crossroads. The great mountain ranges were created by a slow-motion fender bender between two tectonic plates that brought together three of the planet's eight major ecozones here: the Afrotropic, the Indomalayan, and the Paleoarctic. Brown bears, hyenas, and snow leopards shared the habitats within the peace park along with the famed Marco Polo sheep and the fantastically horned markhor. The snow leopards that live on the sheer mountain walls preyed on the markhor, hunting across borders.

The need for a transboundary park had its roots in the simple fact that only one species had established and respected the artifact of international boundaries: humans. The flora and fauna didn't care what country they were in. Effective conservation practically required international cooperation in the form of a preserve that spanned the borders. Fencing, poaching, and policy differed between the neighbors, and the WCS worked to standardize and coordinate conservation efforts, such as protecting the transboundary migrations of the iconic Marco Polo sheep.

To launch the process of creating this critical preserve, we brought envoys from the four countries together in Ürümqi, the capital of the

Xinjiang Uyghur Autonomous Region of the People's Republic of China in fall 2006, a few months after WCS Afghanistan was up and running. This was the first of the three meetings we saw as necessary to create the national park. We had three objectives for the Ürümqi meeting. First, we wanted the countries to send senior officials who were sufficiently empowered to sign a framework agreement that would allow for the negotiations to continue and increase cooperation among nations for the joint management of natural resources and promotion of ecotourism. Second, we wanted to develop the political coordinating structures—initially informal, but with gaining authority through its action—that could help carry forward the work under the framework agreement. We needed to develop a Pamirs transboundary protected area commission and, under it, working groups for wildlife management, community development, protected area management, and legislation and policy, each that would be chaired by one of the four countries. Third, we wanted to bring high-profile, multilateral and bilateral donors, such as the Asian Development Bank, the World Bank, the Global Environment Fund, the European Union, the Aga Khan Foundation, and USAID, that could help fund the peace park. We had high ambitions.

Ürümqi is remote but not small. The ancient Silk Road outpost has a population of over three million people and the distinction of being the world's most landlocked major city, more than 1,400 miles from any sea. It's also the closest significant city to a geographic footnote called the Eurasian Pole of Inaccessibility, the location most lacking in features that might permit access—like navigable water, for instance—but is generally determined by distance to a coastline. The landscapes around Ürümqi illustrate its isolation. The city is separated from Beijing by inhospitable terrain: towering mountains, vast steppes and plateaus, and the dangerous expanses of the Taklimakan (one hundred thousand square miles) and Gobi (five hundred thousand square miles) Deserts. Han Chinese dominate Ürümqi politically, but the region is mostly populated by minority ethnic groups: Uyghurs, Kazakhs, Tartars, Uzbeks, Tajiks, Wakhis, Hui, Mongols, Russians, Xibes, and Manchus, most of whom had tense relationships with Beijing. One guide to the Xinjiang Uyghur Autonomous Region describes nineteen major ethnic groups residing in the parts of the expansive province fit for human settlement. Enormous tracts of land around Ürümqi are classified as "uninhabited." In other words, these are great places to find and conserve wildlife and to get into serious trouble.

Four countries would be hard enough to convene in Ürümqi, but early on, it was suggested we needed a fifth. In the planning for the peace park, I met with representatives of the Afghan government and multilateral agencies in Afghanistan to build support for it. I noted, as I had in my presentations, that we planned to convene the three other countries that bordered Wakhan—China, Pakistan, and Tajikistan. My visitor, a member of the Afghan government, asked a strange question: "What about India?"

"India doesn't touch Afghanistan," I replied smugly at his ignorance of world geography.

"I believe you are mistaken," he responded.

"I have traveled to the region; we plan expeditions there all the time. I am fairly confident of this," I replied more confidently.

"Yes, it does. Look at your map."

At that moment, we both looked to the map of Afghanistan on my wall. I had bought it a month earlier at an Afghan bookstore in downtown Kabul. In it, Wakhan bordered four countries, not three. India did indeed border Afghanistan, according to my own map, which I had purchased and had hung on my own wall. The Afghans, in constructing the map and detesting the undermining influence of Pakistan on the country, had taken the tribal regions that were split evenly along the Durand Line and had through the magic of cartography awarded the entire disputed province of Kashmir to India. Pakistan was now a slender sliver of land, while Afghanistan looked pregnant on its eastern borders.

I paused, trying to figure out my response.

"This map is not accurate; India doesn't touch Afghanistan," I stammered.

"So why did you put up a map if you knew it was wrong? It is your map."

He had a point.

I sat silently, embarrassed at my inability to explain that the map, printed and sold in a Kabul bookstore and mounted as a sign of credibility on my wall, was not what it seemed on its face. So much of working in Afghanistan reminded me of the map.

What was even more ironic was that India could be potentially part of the peace park in the future. It would be a natural continuum to turn the conflict flash point of the Siachen Glacier, the world's highest battlefield, into an opportunity for conservation.

Even if we ignored India, which we had to do since including them too early would have created an international incident with the Pakistanis, just getting delegates from four different countries to Ürümqi posed a challenge. While the Afghan officials were happy to fly Ariana Afghan Airlines—the national carrier—from Kabul to Ürümqi, they refused to fly Ariana back from China, even though it was the same route and the same plane. In fact, the only way back if you didn't take Ariana directly was to fly across China to Beijing, then from Beijing to Dubai, before finally returning from Dubai to Kabul, three long flights that would take two days, instead of a direct two-hour flight. I was perplexed why anyone would want to do this.

There was reason for some concern; Ariana didn't have a great safety record. Although their performance most likely improved after US forces destroyed most of its fleet of decrepit Antonovs during the 2001 invasion, the EU transport minister had called Ariana planes "flying coffins" and banned their flights from landing in Europe for safety reasons. However, this still wouldn't explain why they were willing to take the flight in one direction but not in reverse. Afghans take a lot of risks and survived nearly thirty years of war. They were fine with replacing one helicopter engine with an engine from a different manufacturer and flying it, but this return flight was of more concern to them. I wasn't going to dismiss the seeming illogic so easily, so we dug deeper.

It was only after talking to a member of the Afghan Ministry of Foreign Affairs who was traveling with the delegation that I understood the Afghans' reasoning. While the planes flying to China were largely empty, they were overloaded with tons of cheap Chinese goods for sale for the Afghan market. Moreover, the wide-scale bribery permitted the merchants to bring in heavier loads than were officially registered for the flight, thereby distorting the basis for fuel and flight calculations. As the planes had to fly over the "roof of the world," the colloquial name for the Pamir mountains, they felt that the heavier loads, incorrect fuel calculations, poor weather, high altitudes, and mountainous terrain would result in the plane crashing into a remote part of the mountains somewhere along its route. In the end, the Afghan delegation took the very long way home. Afghans are acclimated to risks, but they are not foolish. Given most of these travelers had made it through thirty years of war, I took their advice and took the scenic route with them.

Ürümqi also hinted at the political sensitivities of bringing these four countries together. The problems started with the invitation list itself. The Chinese hosts tried to downplay the significance of the gathering and, as a result, didn't want high-level officials from other countries in attendance. As we later found out, the head of the WCS China program, a member of the Chinese Academy of Science, did not have official permission for such a high-level meeting, nor was, as it turned out, WCS even registered in China. Adding more complications was that the Chinese government had a long-running conflict with the Uyghurs, ethnic Turkic Muslims predominant in Xinjiang Uyghur Autonomous Region, the largest and perhaps wildest of China's administrative regions, which would contain the Chinese side of the peace park. This was perhaps China's most unstable province and a geopolitical sensitivity. The Chinese government has tried to dilute the Uyghur influence by flooding the province with Han Chinese, who now make up 40 percent of its population, declaring a war on terror on the Uyghurs and preventing the Uyghur government workers from practicing their religion, such as fasting during Ramadan. The result has been a steady escalation of violence, with its focus in Ürümqi. The last thing they wanted was ungoverned borders coupled with international attention on their treatment of the Uyghurs.

Despite the protestations of the WCS China program, the Afghan delegation sent Prince Mostapha Zaher as its leader. In meeting documents, Prince Zaher's title was mysteriously shortened to "conservationist." The Tajiks and Pakistanis sent comparably high-level delegates, whose titles were also somehow relabeled. Given the high level of three delegations, the Chinese officials ignored diplomatic protocols. No one from the Chinese government was there to greet the officials at the Ürümqi airport. The airport was almost devoid of people when we landed, and the Afghan delegation passed through pedestrian security checks with a solitary immigration officer and had to find a taxi. Prince Zaher seemed confused by the subtle protocol snub. The Chinese themselves sent lower-level delegations from Xinjiang Province and the deputy director for wildlife conservation and natural reserve management, but not the Ministry of Foreign Affairs or any party officials. This was the beginning of the problems we faced.

The meeting started with opening statements, chaired by Peter Zahler, with greetings from the highest members of the delegations, followed by a review of the basic premise by George Schaller. The run of the day was to review current conservation efforts among the four countries, shared challenges with wildlife protection, and briefings on how to create a transboundary park, followed by formal discussion on a ten-year action plan, the creation of the protected area commission and working groups, the signing of a framework agreement, and a final negotiated statement being issued by the conference. Finally, the event would end with a celebration banquet.

It was soon clear that WCS was too ambitious in its goals for the meeting and had failed to realize the one rule of such events: finish the negotiations before the meeting, not during it. The Chinese protested and blocked every attempt to move the discussions forward. Even the seemingly innocuous name of the proposed park as *Peace Park* raised worries for politically risk-averse Chinese officials. Specifically, they didn't like the word *peace*, despite its historical use in transfrontier parks.

The first peace park in the world connected Glacier National Park in the United States and Waterton Lakes National Park in Canada as the Waterton-Glacier International Peace Park in 1932. The purpose of such transfrontier parks was not only to better manage wildlife and its threats across political boundaries but also to help build the foundation for cooperation between countries.

The Chinese representatives noted cynically that the four countries were "at peace," and therefore, the park didn't need to be called a peace park—logic that blithely looked past the historical and intensifying conflict between Afghanistan and Pakistan, the frozen border war between Pakistan and China, or even internal conflicts between Beijing and the Uyghurs.

The same representatives also claimed that China had no problems with wildlife trade. In any setting, this claim would be tough to swallow; a huge amount of the global illegal wildlife trade serves Chinese markets. But in this case, it was especially absurd. The conference was held a few blocks from a major market where the pelts and taxidermic mounts of endangered species could be found, including even Marco Polo sheep heads, a species at the heart of the purpose for the park. Apparently, no one had told the merchants that China didn't participate in wildlife trade.

At the end of the meeting, the Chinese officials refused all the goals of the meeting. They said no to the commission and working groups, the framework agreement, even to a simple closing statement where any text approaching substance had been scrubbed away in compromises and the vaguest generality in support of wildlife was going too far for the hosts.

Despite the failure to sign any sort of declaration, a spectacular post-meeting dinner redeemed Ürümqi a bit. I tried not to mind that the large mammal roasting on a spit looked suspiciously like a juvenile Marco Polo sheep. The Chinese hosts repeatedly urged alcohol on the Afghan guests, not realizing that they didn't drink (at least not in public). After dinner, young contortionists hopped around with their heads between their ankles while spinning plates on poles with their toes. Chinese nightclub singers screeched a soundtrack as dazzling Uyghur dancers took inspiration from the dervishes of Cairo and Iran. This multicultural chaos set an appropriate tone for the next stage of creating the park, where we would swap one former (current) communist country for another. We would try again, which would lead me to the problem at the Sher Khan crossing.

CHAPTER 10

BACK IN THE CCCP

D ESPITE THE FAILURE of the first meeting, we started planning for the second peace park conference in Dushanbe, the quiet, leafy capital of Tajikistan. On the surface, holding the second meeting in Dushanbe didn't seem like a very good idea. Tajikistan remains among the poorest of the former Soviet Republics, marred by a legacy of Soviet-era dysfunction and post-Soviet decay. Air connections into Tajikistan were less frequent and perhaps more dangerous than Ürümqi. The hospitality resources were almost nonexistent for a larger international meeting. Tajikistan was also still an authoritarian state with a high level of bureaucracy. And beneath the seemingly calm surface of the country were the lingering remainders of a brutal Afghan-style civil war between Islamic radicals and the government, which was still smoldering like a turf fire, hidden from view, unmentioned, but still present and dangerous.

Despite these problems, it was currently our best choice. Pakistan was entering the throes of parliamentary elections and a looming potential presidential change. Even greater instability was just around the corner. We didn't want the Chinese to block further progress on the peace park, so we couldn't go back to Ürümqi. No one wanted to come to Afghanistan, for fear of being shot, kidnapped, or blown up. Holding the meeting in Dubai or some other outside location would suggest a lack of support for the peace park in the four host countries. This left us with one choice: Tajikistan.

In June 2007, the small capital only had one hotel large enough to support the international delegations, a tired and cheerless Soviet monster named the Hotel Avesto. This drab relic had hosted the US embassy in Dushanbe after the fall of the Soviet Union. Its long, dingy hallways were still populated by rotund babushkas, and the dated rooms were probably still infected with Cold War–era listening devices left over from when it was occupied by US diplomats. But finding conference rooms was just the beginning of the logistical worries. We needed simultaneous translation between a mélange of languages: English to Mandarin, Mandarin to Tajik/Dari, Dari/Tajik to Mandarin, Tajik to Urdu, Mandarin to English, Urdu to Mandarin. There were no hotel restaurants that could hold all the participants or were willing to feed them all.

I planned an initial reconnaissance mission to Tajikistan to secure the support of the government. WCS had not been in contact with the Tajiks since the original meeting in Ürümqi. It was already high summer, and we wanted to hold the meeting in the middle of December to ensure adequate preparation (and to avoid Pakistan's parliamentary elections). December is not exactly Tajikistan's tourist high season. Whatever the date, mounting any significant undertaking in Tajikistan required government approval at high levels, and anything involving foreign matters actually required the personal approval of President Emomali Rahmon, an unparalleled level of micromanagement by the country's leader. As in many former Soviet states, setting up something in Tajikistan didn't happen via e-mail or phone; face-to-face conversation was required.

When I worked in Moscow in the turbulent early 1990s, I had developed the "three things" rule: never try to do three things in a day, or run the risk of getting nothing done. Doing one thing was achievable, doing two was possible but pushing your luck. Attempting to do three things almost always resulted in catastrophic failure of all the goals. For my scouting trip, we had multiple needs: I needed (1) the president's permission to hold the meeting, (2) an on-the-ground point person for WCS and a contact at the government, and (3) dates and venues to hold the meeting. Time would tell whether I was pushing my luck or worse.

There was only one flight to Dushanbe per week, and I had a busy WCS travel schedule coming up. I was required to be in Indonesia and Florida with WCS leadership in the days immediately before the trip to Tajikistan, and I could only spend three days in Dushanbe before heading to Port Elizabeth, South Africa, for the presentation at the Society for Conservation Biology conference—our first exposure of the Afghanistan program before the international conservation and scientific community. It would be our coming-out party for the Afghanistan program. Moreover, the once-weekly flight to Dushanbe was aboard an Ariana Antonov An-24, a Soviet-built prop plane that dated to the late 1950s. Of the approximately 1,100 An-24s ever built, 142 experienced "hull-loss occurrences," an ominous euphemism for crashing, exploding, or getting blown up on the ground. On the positive side, 87 percent of the An-24s hadn't crashed.

In theory, driving to Dushanbe was simple. The Afghan roads had been reconstructed all the way to Tajikistan, so the drive to the border crossing at Sher Khan Bandar would take six to eight hours. At the port, a ferry would take the vehicle across the Amu Darya. Once we crossed into Tajikistan, Dushanbe was just two hours more. I would have a good team with me: Qais as a translator and fixer and Ghulam as our driver. Qais, who served as the logistics manager in Kabul, was a genius with visas and travel arrangements even in the face of extreme bureaucratic intransigence. His fluent English would help with translation in Tajikistan, and he would oversee the details of getting in and out of the country, including visas and permits. Ghulam, large, silent, and bearded, had spent time in Tajikistan working with the Northern Alliance. I would find out on our trip that Ghulam had been a soldier and driver for Masood, the charismatic assassinated leader of the Northern Alliance. He was a good driver and mechanic, and fearless.

We left Kabul on Sunday morning, June 24, and immediately entered the mountains that surround the city. We climbed the Hindu Kush mountains and traversed Salang Pass. We drove through miles and miles of irrigated fields and passed Afghanistan's answer to Carhenge—four Russian tanks parked vertically in the soil. We hit dusty Kunduz, the center of the German development effort in Afghanistan, and pushed north for the border crossing. Outside the windows, the fertile plains turned to sand dunes, nearly denuded of vegetation by overgrazing, a potential window into Afghanistan's future if overgrazing is left unchecked. Soon enough, we reached Sher Khan Bandar—Afghanistan's "port" with Tajikistan.

The Panj River forms the northern border of Afghanistan, its waters flowing from Lake Zorkul in the heart of Wakhan. Just east of Sher Khan Bandar, the Panj is joined by the Vakhsh to form Central Asia's greatest river, the Amu Darya, which flows nearly 2,574 kilometers (1,600 miles) to what remains of the Aral Sea.

The Aral Sea, once the world's fourth-largest inland sea, located between Kazakhstan and Uzbekistan, was now nearly dry. It was Central Asia's worst environmental disaster. Stalin, seeking to make the Soviet Union self-sufficient in cotton and later rice, led the development of massive irrigation projects in the 1950s that diverted the waters of the Amu Darya and its sister river, the Syr Darya, to irrigate Uzbekistan's desert to grow "white gold." For a short time, Uzbekistan became the world's largest exporter of cotton. As part of these projects, huge amounts of pesticides (DDT) and fertilizers were used, much of which ran off back into the Aral Sea. But as the Aral Sea shrank and dried, salt, pesticides, and fertilizer became airborne, damaging human health and agriculture throughout the region. What remained rendered the former seabed unusable. Moreover, Vozrozhdeniye Island, in the middle of the Aral Sea, was an abandoned former Soviet biological weapons lab that weaponized anthrax, smallpox, brucellosis, tularemia, and the bubonic plague. The waters of the seas—which had been a natural barrier to any escape of rats, ticks, and fleas that carried weaponized pathogens and protected the site from those with nefarious intentions—dried up, leaving the island connected to a large city to its south.

The Amu Darya's spring floods, full of the snowmelt from the Pamir glaciers, once caused the Aral Sea to overflow its boundaries. But now the river is so heavily taxed by irrigation withdrawals that it sinks into the sandy desert before it reaches the sea. The legacy of Soviet environmental mismanagement has humbled a mighty river.

The port where we crossed the Amu Darya, Sher Khan Bandar, took its name from a tragic figure in Afghan history. Sher Khan Nashir was a Ghaznavid khan, born in the 1890s in what is the city of Ghazni in present-day Afghanistan. Sher Khan founded Spinzar Cotton Company, one of Afghanistan's most storied companies, and turned his vast land holdings into cotton fields—and in the process, founded the modern-day city of Kunduz. As a hereditary khan of the Ghilzai Kharot, one of the largest tribes of the Pashtuns, and governor of the whole Kunduz District and the greater Baghlan area, Sher Khan's growing financial wealth and political influence soon became a threat to the king's power. Ultimately, he was poisoned by a royal assassin while recovering from minor surgery in a hospital. He supposedly heard his own death announced on the radio minutes before the poison took effect.

The port of Sher Khan is not quite as romantic or dramatic as the story of the assassination. A few dilapidated buildings, a guardhouse, and a construction site for the new bridge that would connect Afghanistan to Tajikistan (to the horror of the Tajiks, it seemed, but essential for the Afghan economy). A small guardhouse and a few tree trunks that fashioned into a gateway greeted arrivals to the port—along with a barrier across the road. We had to work to get the guards' attention; they didn't seem to be expecting anyone. A border guard clad in an ill-fitting Afghan army uniform and Chinese flip-flops approached our vehicle, toting an AK-47. We told him we were taking the ferry to Tajikistan. He seemed a bit surprised.

"I think the ferry is closed today," he responded, puzzled at our request.

This was bad news. We only had two full working days in Tajikistan before I had to head back to catch my flight to a conference in South

Africa (via Dubai and then Ethiopia). I would be flying via Ethiopian Airlines, which had just one flight per week to South Africa, and our two days in Tajikistan provided the only window we had to lay the groundwork for the second peace park meeting. Without approval and support in Tajikistan, there would be no meeting and possibly no park.

We asked the guard why the ferry was closed. His answer was simple. "The Tajiks are picnicking today."

This made little sense. Can an international border close? It was fun to imagine the entire Tajik population, picnic baskets in hand, in the middle of fields surrounded by high snow-covered mountains. But picnic or not, we needed to get across the border, and soon.

The guards explained that the Afghan side of the port was open, but attempting to cross the river toward a closed crossing on the Tajik side would have been frowned upon, so the border was effectively closed. It pointed to an essential difference between the countries. In Afghanistan, people sought to make things possible. But across the border, Tajikistan's Soviet history created a legacy of bureaucratic paralysis. A history of war taught Afghans to find solutions to survive, but in Tajikistan, helping others or bending the rules meant risking your career. Historical explanations were cold comfort; we were going to lose a half day of our trip, at the very least.

We pleaded our case to the guards; we were traveling on behalf of the governments of Afghanistan and the United States to set up an international preserve, and we needed to get across that night. As with most things in Afghanistan, the guards were accommodating, helpful, and kind. They suggested we go to the customs office to see what could be done. After some prolonged discussion at the customs office, we headed to the ferry operator's house. The ferryman said that he would call over to the Tajik side to see if anyone there would allow us to cross. He also reconfirmed what we were told by the guards: we could leave Afghanistan, but we couldn't enter Tajikistan. Static answered his repeated calls on the radio. It was hard not to imagine those picnickers.

At this point, our only choice was to drive sixty kilometers across the desert dunes back to Kunduz, find a guesthouse, and come back in the morning. Kunduz was not a particularly safe place to spend the night; potential risks included vehicle theft, robbery, kidnapping, or all of the above. This was the last Taliban stronghold in Afghanistan to fall to the Northern Alliance and American troops, and a feeling of threat still permeated the air.

Kunduz wasn't a particularly attractive place to spend the night either. The prewar bright colors of Kunduz have been enveloped with a heavy, chalky, beige layer of dust. Sunlight struggles to penetrate to the street as its bright rays suffocate in dust clouds. It has the feel of an old town in the Wild West, with two-story-high mud buildings with wooden verandas, waiting for a gunfight.

We hadn't made advance arrangements, an essential for finding safe lodging in Afghanistan's few safe locations. On previous trips through Kunduz, WCS staff stayed at the guesthouse of the German development agency. But their guesthouse was full, and the guards there sent us to the agency's national office, where we might find the acting country director.

We weren't well suited for a formal sit-down. The Germans were typically put together—wearing crisply pressed business attire. Even their offices, in the middle of a dust-choked city, were immaculate. On our end, we fit the part of field biologists. We looked like we had been dragged through the desert by an Asiatic wild ass, with a few head-butts from a Marco Polo sheep thrown in for good measure. I probably had some of my lunch in my hair as well, having never managed competency at eating on the ground. I did my best to look distinguished, smoothing out my wrinkles with my hands—as befits the chief of party and Afghanistan country director of the WCS—and combing the rice out of my hair, and it worked well enough to secure a meeting with the development agency's acting country director. After initial skepticism, he was nonetheless kind enough to allow us the use of their guesthouse.

I went to bed that night worrying about whether we would make it across in the morning. We would have no more than a day and a half in Tajikistan, assuming the border was actually open. *If* we could get into Tajikistan, we had no idea whether any of the meetings we'd requested would happen or if the Tajiks would even assent to host the second meeting about the peace park. And there was another bureaucratic mousetrap waiting for us; it was recommended that we register with the Department of Visas and Registration of the Ministry of Internal Affairs (known by its acronym, OVIR, and part of the state security apparatus), but the process took considerable time that we no longer had. We weren't going to be there long enough to be required to register; registration only kicked in when you would be in the country for three days or more, but without registering, if we got delayed, we could be in serious trouble, including being subject to fines, deportation, or possible imprisonment.

We left the German guesthouse at 7:00 a.m. to get back to the border crossing by 8:00. Our first stop at the port was a dusty row of small mud buildings housing the Afghan roads authority, who gave us the necessary permits to drive in Tajikistan with Afghan plates. Next came a check with Afghan customs to ensure that we weren't exporting any opium from the country, and then we headed to the crossing. The Tajik border was open, and now all we had to do was cross the Panj—a river formidable enough to form the border of empires.

Sher Khan Bandar isn't much of a port, apart from a battered ferry barge moored to a tree. A small group of Afghan officials sat in plastic lawn chairs under a dusty canvas canopy, erected to block the intense sun. Apart from the officials, there was very little to distinguish this particular stretch of river from the rest of the border. But this "port" helped millions of dollars flow into Afghanistan's small, growing economy (outside of the financial flows from reconstruction, which tended to create an economy in an economy).

We pulled our Land Cruiser up to the canopy tent and got out to greet all the officials. The Afghan commander in charge of the port bade me to sit next to him. He offered glasses of green tea, already poured and ready for us. Like most former mujahideen, he looked friendly, but with a fierceness lurking in his eyes. After warm greetings, we had a friendly discussion (in broken Farsi and Dari) about what WCS was doing in Afghanistan, what we proposed to do in Tajikistan, and my own background—before we were interrupted by the loud explosion and thick black smoke from the ferry. More precisely, the eruption came from the dilapidated tugboat that pulled the ferry barge across. Even without a load, the tugboat was struggling. This was our ride.

Qais, Ghulam, and I eyed the boat skeptically. We weren't very optimistic about this craft making a half-mile crossing of fast-moving water without a load, to say nothing about pulling a Land Cruiser. The tug's tired-looking hull consisted of warped planks and rusty nails, and the cabin on top was painted sky blue, a ubiquitous color in Afghanistan—perhaps inspired by the Soviet-built Zavod Imeni Likhacheva trucks so often seen on the country's roads. The captain of the tug wore a dirty white skullcap, a well-kempt beard, and a jungle-green camouflage T-shirt matched with formal dress pants. He was frantically yelling directions to his assistants, who were tying up the barge to the trees onshore. The captain's chair was a pink plastic lawn chair, although he stood for most of the operations. A low, rusty rail and a faded Afghan flag completed the tug's regalia.

The barge behind the tug itself was heavily battered and dented, only big enough for two vehicles. Disconcerting dark puncture marks punched through the metal barely above the waterline, and rust had metastasized the entire hull. The upper portions of the ferry bore the same light blue paint job as the tug. A knot of gnarled metal cables tied a much-abused tire to the bow of the barge. We would share the tiny barge with a second Land Cruiser carrying the governor of an undisclosed Afghan province and his assistant. The governor was polite but not friendly when we greeted him. He didn't want to be recognized by foreigners who might take interest in his activities in Tajikistan.

We loaded our SUV on the ferry by driving across two dubious-looking wooden planks lain haphazardly from ship to shore. I took the liberty of straightening out the planks before we drove six thousand pounds of engine, chassis, ballistic blankets, extra-large gas tanks, reinforced cargo racks, winches, and other modifications across these inch-thick hunks of geriatric wood. Somehow both Land Cruisers survived the loading process. The two vehicles covered almost the entirety of the surface of the barge. I imagined the border unit would use these planks until they broke and dumped a vehicle into the river. Life in Afghanistan felt like a lottery where the grand prize was avoiding disaster.

We steamed off for the far shore, and the tug groaned into the river's strong, glacier-fed current. After fifteen long minutes, we reached the Tajik side. A much larger barge—clearly meant for freight trucks—waited there. Most commerce at the port went from Tajikistan to Afghanistan, so it made sense that the bigger, safer-looking barge was on this shore. The Tajik port was in better shape than the Afghan side, but not by much. Out came the planks again, and we drove off the ferry into the muddy bank and into Tajikistan.

The immigration post was in a trailer rather than under a sheet of canvas. Languages mingle across the borders of Afghanistan, Tajikistan, and Iran, but there are enough differences to create confusion if you aren't paying attention. The woman at the customs house remembered Ghulam from his previous visits when he was part of the Northern Alliance, and he thankfully spoke some words of Tajik, which immediately earned her attention and kindness. She dressed in Tajik fashion, with a long dress and a matching patterned kerchief on her head but not covering it. We were no longer in the Islamic Republic of Afghanistan.

The provincial governor quickly passed through the customs, and his driver unscrewed their Land Cruiser's Afghan plates and replaced them with Tajik tags. They drove off into the country, bypassing customs altogether. I wasn't sure if this was diplomatic privilege in action or something less official, but it was the last we saw of him either way. We had to navigate customs and the road authority to get through. After visiting a series of offices (each more elaborate than the previous) inside a dilapidated building and gratefully accepting countless cups of tea, we got the needed authorization and rolled into Tajikistan.

In my initial impressions of the Tajik countryside, I felt like I were watching a Soviet propaganda movie—a beautiful romance of collectivization. Women, all wearing kerchiefs and flowing dresses in vivid floral patterns straight out of 1970s window drapery, worked in wide, golden fields of wheat side by side with men, with old Soviet tractors completing the panorama. It was a beautiful, bucolic scene, but it felt like time had forgotten this place and people. The fact that the Cold War had ended and the Soviet Union had collapsed over a decade earlier didn't seem to make a difference in their lives.

The romance quickly came to an end. About three miles down the road from the port, we came upon our first policeman standing at the edge of the road. He immediately waved us over. Our bright green Afghan tags with their Dari script were noticeable in a country that used Cyrillic script. Persian script had been banned in the country since 1939. The Tajik policeman looked eager to increase his meager salary. Ghulam calmly handed over our authorization documents, and the policeman disappointedly let us go after a few minutes.

Back on track, our excitement for the work ahead grew until we encountered a second policeman after a few more miles down the road. He waved us to the side of the road and asked for our documentation. Ghulam repeated the drill. After an obligatory review, we resumed the journey. Another five miles down the road, we encountered a third policeman, who waved us over to the side of the road. This scene replayed a dozen times on the road to Dushanbe, and each stop dealt a blow to our hopes for the trip. Some policemen inspected our documentation thoroughly, hoping for an error that would be worthy of a bribe; others barely glanced at it. Each was an interruption that slowed us down. We passed through towns with well-paved roads; it was clear that the Tajiks were better off than the Afghans, and perhaps slightly freer—but not by much. Underneath the Soviet facade of stability, a decay permeated the country, one that no amount of officious policing could hide.

For a national capital, Dushanbe is small. The name translates to "Monday" in Tajik, as the city began as a humble mountain village known for its Monday market. The village became a city in the 1920s, along lines laid out by Bolshevik-minded architects and urban planners from Saint Petersburg. Buildings in the tsarist baroque style of Saint Petersburg mingle with Soviet apartment blocks and private houses. The village roots still show in the green, leafy feeling of the capital.

We had two business cards to guide us on our mission to accomplish our goals—these were from members of the Tajik delegation in Ürümqi. One belonged to Vice President Abdulvohid Karimov, the chairman of the State Committee on Environmental Protection and Forestry of the Ministry of Agriculture and Nature Protection of the Republic of Tajikistan. The second belonged to Kokul Kasirov, the chief of the State Department of Natural Protected Areas in the Ministry of Agriculture and Nature Protection of the Republic of Tajikistan. Although we had been e-mailing and calling their offices for some time, we hadn't made much progress, which meant a face-to-face meeting would make or break the plans for the peace park summit.

I had met both Karimov and Kasirov in Ürümqi the previous year but hardly knew or interacted with them other than a few formal exchanges in poor Farsi and even worse Russian. I started the work of making the necessary arrangements with Kasirov. Kasirov wore a heavy black mustache under a dark mop of hair and eyes that seemed to hunt for hidden meanings and potential profit in every encounter. This relentless scheming would have been useful during the Soviet era and perhaps hadn't lost its value. He was fairly quiet and did not seem particularly enthusiastic about the environment, despite being the director of Tajikistan's national parks system.

We couldn't find Kasirov's offices, and he offered to escort us there by meeting us where we pulled over. He showed up in a dull white LADA from the mid-1980s that looked like it was made of secondhand sardine tins and rode on tiny bald tires twelve inches off the ground. But Kasirov navigated the streets of Dushanbe like a rally car driver, using babushkas overburdened with bags of vegetables as human slalom poles. We followed him to his offices, which we never would have found otherwise. The complex for the State Department of Natural Protected Areas looked like an abandoned repair shop. A thick layer of dust blanketed the hall leading to Kasirov's office. A small television tuned to Tajik news muttered in the corner, and uncomfortable metal chairs awaited Qais and me. Kasirov settled in and yelled for tea, which his assistants brought immediately. I launched right into the matter at hand. We wanted to build on the success of the Ürümqi meeting with a second summit right here in Tajikistan, but we'd need a conference venue big enough for 110 attendees, government permissions, and a local liaison.

Kasirov listened carefully and without comment, busily considering what benefit he could extract from the scenario. He soon started making calls on the multiple phones on his desk, arranging meetings for the next day. I wound up spending the evening with Kasirov on the heights of Victory Park, at a South Pacific–themed restaurant that seemed very out of place. The restaurant was also decorated with camouflage netting, probably surplus from the country's civil war. Now it provided atmosphere over a kitchen and speakers blasting Soviet-sounding techno. Men in tracksuits (an unfortunate, almost trite uniform of post-Soviet fashion) gathered at tables, but Kasirov led us to an isolated spot. His twenty-two-year-old son joined us—a nice young man who ran his own ecotourism concern and drove a high-end BMW. Kasirov ordered food for us and spoke about his own plans to open a restaurant. He was largely uninterested in talking about conservation efforts or the peace park. However, at the end of the evening, he promised to support our efforts. I worked late into the night putting together documents for a proper proposal to the government, tired but glad to be making progress.

Over the next day, Kasirov and I did a grand tour of meetings in his LADA. He insisted on driving. Riding with him was terrifying, and I tried to distract myself with figuring out how to get my seat belt fastened. I settled on tying it—I doubt my knot skills would have made much of a difference in a crash, but I felt a vague reassurance just the same. Kasirov took traffic circles and tight corners at startlingly high speeds, sending me bouncing into the passenger-side door, which I expected to fly open at any moment. As he careened down the bumpy streets, he talked to me in a mix of Farsi and Russian, urging me to agree with what he was saying. He often turned and looked right at me, awaiting a response to a question or proposal while completely ignoring the road. My responses came in Farsi, less grammatically correct than usual because of my mounting stress about an impending collision. As we screeched from meeting to meeting, I tried to offer my front seat to my traveling companions, but Kasirov insisted I take the front as the guest of honor. The few times I did manage to escape to the back seat, I curled up into a ball and braced myself. For all their many failings, LADAs are made to last—which meant lots of metal, usually sticking out at angles ideally suited to impale passengers in the event of a crash. Maybe this was actually a way of discouraging reckless driving.

If so, it was the only such discouragement I saw. The same Tajik traffic police who had delighted in pulling over our WCS Land Cruiser completely ignored Kasirov's LADA with its government plates, even when it egregiously ignored traffic signals. The automotive terror served to break up a day of endless meetings with bureaucrats—some productive, some not—before we concluded at Karimov's office. This office was the largest we had visited that day, and the size of his desk seemed proportional to his power. While Kasirov's desk was modest, Karimov's desk was enormous and had a fifteen-foot-long table that abutted perpendicularly against the desk and could seat almost twenty people in a classic Soviet "T" configuration. The arrangement focused the room on the man at the big desk.

Karimov was a heavy, gray relic of the Soviet era, as much as the tractors and apartment blocks I had seen. His very appearance seemed to embody bureaucratic intransigence. But Karimov proved kind, grandfatherly, and bemused by my efforts to describe our activities in my broken Farsi (it was clear that Russian was the language of command in Tajikistan). He agreed to sponsor the request for yet another meeting that would get us closer to the necessary presidential approval, with Kasirov as the official government liaison to WCS. I asked about the possibility of hiring an independent representative and mentioned the name of the outspoken female Tajik environmentalist I had met. That almost got us thrown out of the office. The officials quickly came to a consensus: Eldar, Kasirov's assistant, would be our "independent" representative. Eventually, WCS would need to station a proper representative in Dushanbe, but for now, we would have to rely on Eldar, who would almost certainly have the government's interest in mind.

It wasn't perfect, but we had officially achieved our three goals for the trip. There was also the unspoken goal of getting back to Kabul, the fourth task, but that could wait until tomorrow.

Qais, Ghulam, and I made evening plans to meet at the square in front of the Ayni Opera & Ballet Theatre to celebrate our success. A beautiful fountain sits in the center of the square, in front of the neo-classical Roman columns of the opera house, on landscaped grounds, surrounded by kabob houses and beer gardens. Qais arrived a half hour late, hauling what looked like a Walmart-size stock of soaps and other toiletries for his wife. When I pointed out some of these things could be found in the stores in Kabul, Qais just laughed and shrugged.

The important thing in Afghanistan was not to return empty-handed, he explained. Afghan travelers are obligated to return laden with gifts. Their purchases, however mundane, obtain their exoticness simply from being purchased abroad. We spent the night drinking beer and munching kabobs. The Russian waitresses spoke no Farsi and bullied Qais and Ghulam with surly impatience. We joked right back with them, though. Ghulam shared stories of life with Masood and the Northern Alliance, and eventually we headed back to our lodgings.

We left Dushanbe early in the morning, our spirits high at the success of our trip. We stopped at a market for a greasy breakfast of eggs and bread and picked up provisions for the drive. As soon as I returned to Kabul, I would leave for South Africa, and preparations for the conference were already filling my head. I noticed that festive decorations were going up in every town square we passed through, but I didn't make much of it.

On the road to the port, the police seemed too preoccupied with preparations for a festival to stop us, which seemed strange. We zipped through numerous checkpoints without stopping. Finally, at a larger town, we were told that we would have to detour around the town square due to a celebration. Ghulam did his best to find a path, but we got lost more than once. I asked why he didn't follow street signs; Qais quietly informed me that Ghulam, due to the civil war, never learned to read and navigated entirely by memory. Eventually, we got directions from a local policeman. Qais asked the policeman about the upcoming festival, and the policeman explained that today was June 27, the day of national unity, another holiday, even bigger than the previous one.

This didn't bode well for crossing the border. I asked Qais to find out if this meant the border would be closed, and the officer responded with an uncertain yes. We got back on the road toward Sher Khan, driving fast and in utter silence. Maybe we could get there before the port closed for the holiday. I didn't want to miss my trip to South Africa, but more urgently, today was the third and final day of our visas, and we had not registered ourselves in the country—a major problem if we had to spend another night. There were no cars driving toward the port as we got closer.

The port was desolate. Not a single other vehicle was visible. We jumped out of the car and ran to the customs building. It appeared locked and empty. It was sinking in that the Tajiks were going on another, much bigger picnic, and that this one would have more serious consequences. If we were stuck at Sher Khan overnight, there was almost no chance of making the daisy chain of connecting flights to Port Elizabeth. The speech I was to give at the conference was important; so was a chance to get away from the stress and risk of the Afghanistan program for a few days. But avoiding a Tajik prison or complications with the government was even more important.

After a frantic few minutes, we found the single remaining official and asked if we could cross.

"The border is closed. There is no one here," he replied.

Qais, Ghulam, and I promptly ganged up on him. We argued, cajoled, complimented, and begged. When none of that worked, we threatened; keeping us at the border for a night would draw the ire of the senior political leadership in Dushanbe. We mentioned the Tajik president. We even pulled out Karimov's card and pretended to dial, although of course no one would answer on a national holiday.

Likely tired of our pleading, the border official directed us to a nearby military installation. "Go and talk to the army base assigned to the border crossing. Perhaps the commander would grant you permission to cross."

We drove over to the gate of the small base guarding the border crossing. A young boy of maybe nineteen guarded the entrance, nervously pointing an aging AK-47 at us. I offered my friendliest American greeting in English, trying the classic lost-tourist strategy. It had once helped me get into the KGB building in Moscow, by feigning the part of a Texan sightseer in the early 1990s. Here at the ferry crossing, I hoped I could at least get the soldier to aim his gun elsewhere.

"Howdy! How're ya doing?"

The boy soldier didn't seem reassured. In fact, his hands were shaking, and the gun was still aimed at my gut.

I tried another tack. "I am an American. I am here to see your boss."

That didn't help. He continued to stare at me, fear crossing his face at the word *American*.

"We need to cross the border."

No response. Gun still pointed at my gut. I tried not to think about how easily stomach wounds lead to sepsis.

I tried Farsi. *"Boro Raisee-shomah begeree."* (Go get your director.)

No response.

Qais and Ghulam joined in but didn't push the issue too hard, as the young soldier was obviously scared, and the gun was very obviously still pointed my way. My switching languages had probably made the situation a bit tougher to fathom. A self-proclaimed American rolling up in a Land Cruiser with Afghan plates and starting to speak in Farsi wasn't a great security bet in a country that is concerned about its own Islamic insurgency.

I kept repeating myself in a jumble of Farsi and Russian, nearly yelling at him to go get his commander.

Finally, he lowered his weapon and walked cautiously away from the gate, his eyes constantly darting back to us. After a few minutes, the imposingly tall Tajik commander—his shaved head and severe face creating a fearsome impression—approached the gate. We tried to explain our situation to him, using every possible detail to argue that ours was an exceptional case. We had to cross to catch a plane, we were in Tajikistan at the request of the government and had its support, and our program was funded by the US government.

The commander took that to mean that I was a diplomat.

He asked, "Do you have a diplomatic passport?"

In the heat of the moment, I nodded, perhaps unwisely. Qais instantly looked worried; he knew I wasn't a diplomat.

"Let me see it, then."

For ages, I'd been carrying a canceled black diplomatic passport, a souvenir from my days with the State Department that they had let me keep. I had a vague notion it might come in handy. And it finally did. The passport had been canceled, as indicated by the two holes punched through the front cover and a bright blue stamp reading CANCELED on the first page. But the soldier had only asked if I had a diplomatic passport, not whether I was a diplomat or whether the passport was valid, so I had some (shaky) ground to stand on.

I handed the canceled passport over, and the commander examined carefully. He flipped it open and peered at me through the punch holes. Qais looked surprised, confused, and nervous.

"Why are there two holes in the front cover?"

"Well, it validates the passport," I responded.

He then turned to the photo. I had grown a beard in Afghanistan but was clean shaven in the photo. There was nothing I could do about that, so I pointed again at the cover and the DIPLOMATIC PASSPORT label, trying to avert the soldier's eyes from the big blue CANCELED. It was too late; he had noticed the stamp. As a Tajik, he read either Arabic or Cyrillic script, but not Roman. But he knew some English and tried to sound out the word.

"Caaaaa-nnncelll, cancellllllll, cancelllllllleeeeed, caannncceellll."

Thankfully, his grasp of the Roman alphabet was about as good as my command of Farsi script. Finally, he turned to Qais and me and asked in Farsi, "*Canceled chi-ye?*" (What does *canceled* mean?)

Qais had caught on to my ruse and played along perfectly. He explained that *canceled* was English for *approved*. We were now officially on shaky ground.

The commander seemed to accept the translation and started paging through the passport, looking for a Tajik visa, which he wasn't going to find.

"You have no visa. How did you get in the country?"

I pulled out my regular blue American passport and opened it to the page with the Tajik visa. I pointed out that the photo in the civilian passport was the same as the diplomatic passport. The commander looked very confused, with a crease of worry flashing across his forehead. Qais's forehead developed a line of its own. Big cracks were forming in the shaky ground under our story.

"Why do you have two passports?"

"For safety reasons. Sometimes I have to travel on my civilian passport."

He looked at me deeply and finally concluded I was in fact an American on a diplomatic mission of some kind, or at best a spy, which seemed acceptable. We sat down together on a log next to the gate of the base.

"I hate Americans," he announced.

Oh no. I nodded at him, trying not to agree or disagree but simply acknowledge his opinion. I wanted to cross the border. He wanted to continue his diatribe against the US.

"All Americans are fat, especially your women."

I allowed that as a country we did have an obesity problem but pointed out that we were hardly alone in this.

The commander then said that he had been to the United States. This surprised me. He had traveled to New Mexico and received training from US forces there. During his sojourn in the Southwest, he claimed, he had slept with a number of "fat" American women and described the encounters in graphic language. He opined that the American military training was ineffectual compared to Russian instruction.

But he mostly wanted to talk about New Mexico, an evident source of fond memories, particularly Walmart, despite his disgust at the obese fellow shoppers. Eventually, it became clear his first statement of hatred was a provocation rather than a reflection of his actual feelings. We had cleared another obstacle. Permission to leave Tajikistan was within our grasp.

The commander called to a staffer to lift the barrier arm that would give us access to the port, but just before we could get through, a rapidly moving convoy of four white Land Cruisers appeared, heading for the base. This border crossing had a deserved reputation for drug and weapons smuggling, and June 27, National Unity Day of all days, just happened to be the date for a surprise inspection by the Organization for Security and Co-operation in Europe. You might ask what a European international security agency was doing in Tajikistan, which is very much not in Europe.

OSCE is the world's largest multilateral security organization, made up of fifty-seven member states. Their mission is early warning, conflict prevention, crisis management, and post-conflict rehabilitation. They take the concept of Europe expansively, encompassing nearly all of Central Asia and the Caucasus, as well as the United States and Canada. One of their core functions is helping countries with their border management, with a commitment to "balance between the need to maintain security against cross-border threats and the freedom of movement for persons, goods, services and commerce." We were about to shift the scale heavily in favor of free movement, but we couldn't do so as long as the inspection team was there.

As the inspectors approached, the commander hurriedly urged us to hide our vehicles and ourselves behind a tree about fifty feet away. The tree in question was no more than a foot in diameter, but we duly parked our enormous Land Cruiser behind it. Ghulam, Qais, and I peered around the tree trunk like curious cartoon characters. The OSCE team went into the base, but not before they marveled over a lizard that seemed to fascinate them more than the group of "Afghans" in a blue Land Cruiser with Afghan NGO plates peering at them from behind a tree in what was supposed to be a closed, secure border. They spent the next ten minutes inspecting the lizard rather than the border crossing, snapping photos and gawking. I was the biologist here—why wasn't I the one photographing the lizard? The next hour and a half vanished as we waited for the inspectors to finish meeting with the Tajik border security.

I was getting frustrated; I had no idea when the OSCE team would finish or whether we would make it through the border. Driving in Afghanistan after sundown carried a much greater risk of attack by insurgents. Usually, we traveled in two-vehicle convoys in case something went wrong. We had no such backup plan on this trip.

Finally, the OSCE group reemerged and drove down to the port. We decided to follow them, and we annexed ourselves to their convoy, our dark blue SUV standing out from their official white ones. At the gate, a suspicious OSCE agent hopped out and took photos of us. We waved and posed for the camera.

The commander rushed to our vehicles and told us that we had to wait behind the customs buildings until the OSCE team left, admonishing us not to be so visible. After all, the border was closed, and nobody should be crossing it. We were making him look bad, and he was trying to help us. We lounged about the customs area in consternation and boredom for the next two hours until the OSCE team finally left. The OSCE team didn't seem to notice that we were about to breach the security of the border that they were assiduously inspecting and declaring secure.

After the surprise inspection finally concluded, the commander took us to customs. He started filling out our visas but informed us that Ghulam and the Land Cruiser would have to wait until morning. It turned out that the Tajik tug that would take us over could only carry people, not vehicles, as there was no barge. We could go back to Afghanistan, but our ride couldn't.

This was another disaster. We worried that the Tajiks might take Ghulam and the SUV hostage. If Qais and I went on alone, we'd have to hire a taxi for the long drive and then have a WCS vehicle meet us on the road into Kabul. There was also the possibility that the taxi driver might just sell us to criminals who would in turn sell us to the Taliban. We duly called the WCS Afghanistan office, and they dispatched another Land Cruiser to try to meet us halfway.

The commander, with the help of the first customs official we had pleaded with hours before, processed our visas and had us sign to affirm the fact that we had formally departed the Republic of Tajikistan. Except we were very much still in Tajikistan. Still, we were just a ferry ride away from ending our three-day Tajik odyssey. I should have known it wouldn't be that simple. Down at the port, the captain of the small tug ferry informed us that he didn't have any diesel fuel, and we wouldn't be crossing as a result. We asked about the larger truck ferry. No, no diesel for that either, and the tug captain couldn't operate it in any case.

At this point, the entire ordeal might have seemed at least a little funny if the attitude of the Tajik commander hadn't suddenly darkened. He told us we would have to spend the night in the Land Cruiser here in no-man's-land and wait until morning since our single-entry visas were now expired and we couldn't reenter the country. If we did that, there would be no way to make the flight to South Africa, and there was nothing stopping him from putting us all in prison for being in Tajikistan now without a visa or permission.

We pleaded with him, offering to fill up a fifty-gallon drum with diesel at our expense if he would permit us to drive to a petrol station that was only a few miles away. He refused. Then we suggested that Ghulam go, with the commander tagging along, and that Qais and I would wait here. Again, the commander refused. We tried to pressure the commander by threatening to go over his head to Dushanbe. This backfired a bit, as the Tajik commander got angry. He noted that he had done everything he could to get us across, but now, for our ingratitude, he would put us in prison. We were making him look foolish, after all; he now had to explain how two Afghans and an American wound up trapped in between borders at a crossing that was supposed to be closed.

The work of science diplomacy often requires navigating tricky boundaries between neighbors with complicated histories. That navigation was usually more figurative than literal. But at the Sher Khan Bandar border crossing, I was literally stuck between Tajikistan and Afghanistan, and my experience as a diplomat with the State Department was failing me here. Qais, Ghulam, and I were confined to the fifty meters of soggy soil between the Tajik entry point and the murky water of the Amu Darya. I needed to get not just back to Kabul but on a plane to Africa.

Qais and I walked to the river's edge. It was still very much a half mile wide and still high with snowmelt from the Pamirs. I thought about swimming the glacier-fed river by putting our passports and money into plastic bags, grabbing a log, and kicking my way over—but the Amu Darya was freezing cold and fast moving. We could also very easily drown attempting the crossing.

Qais's face scrunched in deep concentration. When I asked him what he was thinking about, he said that he was considering how to reach the Aga Khan Foundation and borrow their helicopter. I was giving up hope of getting to South Africa, but in a last-ditch effort, we tried the commander on the Afghan side, who had given me his number on the crossing over. He didn't answer, so we left a message. And then a few more.

After ten excruciating minutes, we saw and heard the Afghan tugboat and barge suddenly belch into action. The engine groaned and coughed up a thick black ball of smoke and then slowly headed our way, struggling against the current. It was also pulling the battered barge. We all let out a cheer, including the Tajik commander. I took out a box of chocolates that I had bought in Tajikistan as a gift for the Kabul staff and repurposed it as a gift of gratitude for the border commander, who had never asked for a bribe or seemed to expect one. He seemed touched. Ghulam quickly processed his departure paperwork, got customs clearance for the vehicle, and pulled up to the larger Tajik ferry. We could use the bigger boat as a ramp onto the Afghan barge, although we still had to drive across the wooden planks to get from one boat to the other.

We thanked the commander and the customs official for their help and shook hands, with broad smiles all around. The political tension was gone, but the tension of getting safely across the river awaited. The tug captain was working solo, so we all pitched in to bring in the tug and its towed ferry barge even against the larger Tajik ferry, which we were using to board the smaller ferry barge. Qais, Ghulam, and I boast plenty of skills, but we're not longshoremen. Tying up the barge in the fast current took a number of tries, but we got the job done. Ghulam drove the Land Cruiser across the large ferry onto the small barge. We had finally, completely left Tajik soil. I didn't feel entirely safe— or confident that I'd make it to South Africa—until we were halfway across the river. I had never been so happy to see the Afghan flag and the national spirit of possibility that it represented.

By this stage of the adventure, I should have realized that something could always go wrong. The captain wasn't used to running the tug and the barge without help. As the tug crept to the Afghan shore, the powerful current somehow tangled its connection with the barge. The ferry barge, loaded down and full of momentum, was spinning and crashed into the tug. The collision punched a large hole in the tug's hull and then smashed the small craft into the riverbank. If the tug sank, it might take the barge and our Land Cruiser to the bottom of the Amu Darya.

The spinning creating a second issue. Always-alert Ghulam noticed that the metal cable connecting the barge to the tug had also snagged on a low guardrail, and tension was building as the barge spun. He called out a warning in Farsi, pointing to the cable. If the cable came free, its tension would snap across the corner of the barge, precisely where we were standing, and possibly cut off our feet or otherwise injure us seriously. Qais, Ghulam, and I took off just as the cable came free from the rail and whipped across the barge. The whole barge jerked as the cable regained tension and faced upriver again.

Now it was starting to seem funny. We couldn't help ourselves from laughing out loud. Afghans are quick to acknowledge the good luck required to survive in a difficult situation, even upon avoiding of maiming or worse. Ghulam, a man of very few words, turned to me, stretched out his hands to show the increasing tension on the cable, and said, "Cable . . . phooof."

The captain screamed at the Afghans on the shore for help as we neared the "port." We unhooked the troublesome cable from the tug and threw it ashore. One of the people on the shore hitched the barge to a tree stump. The heavy current immediately yanked the stump right out of the ground and pulled it into the water. Now we were floating downstream without an engine or a tug or any way to steer.

But the tug came racing after us, and we secured ourselves once again. The captain excoriated the people on the shore, scolding them to tie the barge to something sturdier. Soon enough, we were driving onto Afghan soil, and an old man at the border crossing was writing our names into a schoolboy's notebook. He provided a scrap of paper in lieu of an entry stamp, and we were officially back from the CCCP.

CHAPTER 11

THE SNOW LEOPARD COMFORTER

L OTS OF TRAVEL to and from Afghanistan meant lots of waiting around, and thus a lot of monotony. Eventually, I bought a Sony PlayStation Portable (PSP, for short) for distraction during the long waits in airport lounges, on tarmacs, and during flights. Little did I realize that this gaming device would jump-start a critical conservation project by way of a friendly airline steward and a home movie starring endangered raptors.

It started on a Kam Air flight from Dubai back to Kabul. I was traveling solo, without Kara or any colleagues. The steward, a friendly twentysomething wearing a crisp white shirt and boyish features, stopped in the aisle when he saw me playing games.

"I have a Sony PSP too," he said enthusiastically.

"Nice," I responded, not expecting the conversation to go much further.

"I use it not only for playing games, but I have also uploaded videos onto it. Have you tried that? Do you want to see?" He was clearly proud of his PSP.

"Sure," I responded out of politeness more than genuine interest. "I didn't know you could put videos on it."

The steward pulled out his own PSP, loaded up a video, and handed the device over.

The video seemed to have been shot on the very same plane, but not on a regular commercial flight. Eight men, wearing off-white or tan dishdashas, some covered by a jacket, with red-checked kaffiyeh—the male head scarfs worn in the Persian Gulf—were singing an Arab song in the front of the plane. Some were standing, others sitting. Some of the men were smoking, which struck me as odd. The filmmaker focused on the singers for a minute before turning to take in the rest of the cabin, which appears mostly empty. The cameraperson then moved down the aisle, passing a Kam Air stewardess, and then the same steward who had just handed me his game player walked by the camera.

As the camera moved through the rows of seats, I saw that the cabin was not in fact empty. But the passengers weren't human. Perched on armrests and on wooden platforms wedged between seats sat dozens of massive birds. The raptors were brown with streaks of white on their breasts, and I recognized them as falcons, as many as seven to a row. The birds wore hoods, each labeled with a number marked on pieces of tape. As the camera scanned row after row, I could see that nearly every seat held a bird of prey. Perhaps forty falcons in all. I kept watching the video unbelievingly.

As the camera approached the rear of the plane, it came across two men sitting across each other in the aisle, smoking, and leaning in toward each other, in animated conversation. Falcons were seated next to them and behind them. One of the men abruptly stopped talking, lowered his cigarette, and stared upward with unwavering menace into the camera. The dirty look was enough to unnerve the unknown filmmaker. An Afghan-accented voice nervously announced, "Movie, movie," in English, explaining the obvious. For a few seconds, the man held his stare, his face framed by cigarette smoke. Soon the camera turned to the second man, who was also staring darkly. This man took a slow, deep draw on his cigarette without shifting his gaze or saying a word. The camera quickly was spun around, and the filmmaker hurried back to the front of the plane. Roll credits.

I was thunderstruck. It was surprising enough to see a passenger jet full of falcons, but the birds in the video were not just any falcons; they were an endangered species—Saker falcons—and someone had rented an entire commercial plane to fly them into Afghanistan. Saker falcons are highly valued hunting birds in Arabian Peninsula states, part of a tradition that stretches back thousands of years. The historical record shows that hunting with falcons (and sometimes with domesticated cheetahs for ground support) dates as far back as 3500 BC. These birds helped find food in unforgiving Arabian and West Asian deserts and became a key part of the nomadic Bedouin culture. Today, falconry is less about finding dinner and more about maintaining identity in a rapidly changing Middle East. The birds are a connection to a simpler (and often idealized) past and to the environments that shaped civilizations in Arabia and Central Asia. In 2010, UNESCO added falconry to its representative list of Intangible Cultural Heritage, joining a list of humanity's most treasured cultural activities. But the UNESCO seal of approval does not guarantee that traditional falconry is good for falcons, especially endangered ones.

Saker falcons live in a vast area stretching from Spain to Western China, their range roughly following the path of the Silk Road. They are exceptional hunters and thus prized by falconers in the Gulf. Habitat destruction and the loss of prey, exacerbated by wildlife trafficking servicing the falconry trade, has pushed Sakers into danger. International conservation groups categorize the Saker falcon as endangered, particularly in Western and Central Asia. Falcons can be bred in captivity, but the perception among falconers is that captive-bred birds are inferior hunters. This preference for wild-caught birds has led to outlandish prices for prized falcons, from thousands of dollars to as much as a million dollars for the most prized hunters. Such prices have only increased demand for wild-caught birds that are trapped in Afghanistan, Pakistan, and Iran, which in turn puts the species at even greater risk.

I suspected that these falcons were on their way to hunt for a fellow endangered species. The prized prey of Gulf Arab falconers is the Asian houbara bustard (*Chlamydotis macqueenii*). This gawky, long-legged, tawny bird resembles a turkey in shape, with a messy white tuft of feathers on its head, and long plumes of black and white feathers that drape over its blue-gray foreneck. The houbara bustard stands over two feet tall (65–75 centimeters) with a nearly five-foot (1.5-meter) wingspan. While its stature is magnificent, it is the bustard's flamboyant mating display that sets it apart among its avian brethren. In the presence of a female, the male bustard slowly puffs up the ornate white feathers on its crest, chest, and neck while simultaneously raising its wings to each side of his head, creating two black standing epaulets of feathers. Dressed in this exotic martial attire, the bustard struts regally in front of its proposed mate. After a few minutes of strutting, the suitor dramatically buries its head into its crest and further puffs its white breast feathers so that the plumes curl around over its hunched head. Looking like a giant volleyball on stilts, the bustard launches into an erratic, high-stepping, zigzagging run, literally blinded to any obstacles in its path by its own plumage.

This mating ritual, impressive as it is, has not been enough to keep up the population, thanks to falcon hunting. With the houbara hunted nearly to extinction in the Arab states of the Persian Gulf, Arab falconers have turned to the deserts of Iraq, Afghanistan, and Pakistan, where the bird winters and mates and where oversight and regulation are limited and often easily corrupted. The International Union for Conservation of Nature (IUCN) has designated the houbara bustard as vulnerable to extinction due to these hunting pressures. According to one study, the bustard population has declined by 35 percent since the mid-1980s. Arab sheiks hunting in Pakistan were rumored to have killed two thousand bustards on a single twenty-one-day hunting permit, senseless carnage reminiscent of nineteenth-century American buffalo hunts.

The airline steward grew increasingly nervous at my barrage of questions. "Where did you get this? When did it happen? Had this happened before? Where were you flying to?" I learned the plane in the video was en route to Kandahar, an area colored bloodred on ANSO security maps, one of the most dangerous areas in a not especially safe country. Despite the presence of important wildlife in Afghanistan's south and large areas like the Registan Desert that were barely surveyed (if at all), the WCS didn't dare to work or even travel in the south. The Pakistani-Afghan border areas were dangerous enough for our teams, but the hunting party in the video had chartered a McDonnell Douglas MD-83 from a commercial airline to carry a million dollars or more of hunting birds deep into the Taliban-held desert. Such a hunting trip could last weeks, supported by an elaborate encampment of tents, generators, four-wheel-drive vehicles, and staff. This meant they likely had secured the permission and protection of all groups in southern Afghanistan, including the insurgency that was hunting US troops. In some cases, the sheiks actually leased hunting grounds, turning Afghan or Pakistani soil into exclaves of Saudi Arabia or the Emirates. At least one such expedition to Afghanistan was notorious for reasons far bigger than bustards.

On February 9, 1999, the CIA had tracked Osama bin Laden to the Sheikh Ali hunting camp in southern Afghanistan. Bin Laden's host was a member of the Emirati royal family. According to the 9/11 Commission Report, because of the presence of the Emirati and a lack of specifics on bin Laden's location within the camp, the CIA decided not to launch a cruise missile to take out the al-Qaeda leader. Collateral damage—perhaps killing the Emirati and family—would have had serious political consequences. By February 12, bin Laden had moved on, and the opportunity was lost. In the two years that followed, bin Laden planned and orchestrated massive terrorist attacks on New York and Washington, and many lamented the hunting trip as a missed chance to save thousands of lives and perhaps change the course of history.

I asked the Kam Air steward for his contact information, which he reluctantly gave me. His concern was understandable. The video placed him at risk; his face was shown in the movie, in fact. Over the next three months, I frequently attempted to reach him, but he didn't respond to e-mails, phone calls, or letters left on visits to the Kam Air office. In my messages, I promised that we would protect him and only use the video to protect Afghanistan's wildlife. Finally, we received a call that someone had left a package for us in the Kam Air office. It was a DVD. The flight steward had given us the video, along with a request that we not contact him again. We wound up using the home movie to highlight for US and Afghan authorities the trafficking and trade of Saker falcons (even carrying them across international borders is illegal) and illegal hunting of the houbara bustard, as promised, but in order to protect the steward the video was never duplicated, put on the web, or turned over to authorities.

The young flight attendant had, by sheer chance, shown off the video storage capacity of his PSP to the head of the only international conservation NGO working in Afghanistan, one of the few organizations with the interest, capability, and opportunity to address wildlife trafficking. The video awakened us to the problem that Afghanistan's wildlife was a source population for illegal trade. We soon discovered an even bigger driver: the international humanitarian community and US and international military forces.

WE HAD COME across a fur factory near Chicken Street that had reported to us that an American soldier had placed an order for one hundred lynx and snow leopard comforters (this was also the same factory where we had found the cheetah jacket that led to our expedition to Herat). The size of the supposed order was difficult to believe. Given that each comforter would require roughly one hundred lynx pelts, such an order could require up to ten thousand lynx to fill, with an unknown number of snow leopards. According to the IUCN, the Eurasian lynx (which ranges to Afghanistan) has a population of nine thousand to ten thousand individuals, but in Afghanistan, it could be as low as two hundred to four hundred individuals. Our initial estimates indicated that Afghanistan's snow leopard population had been reduced to roughly seventy to one hundred animals. Accordingly, this one order could wipe out the Eurasian lynx across its entire range, including all the lynx in Afghanistan, as well as wiping out all the Afghan snow leopards. The order was unlikely to ever be filled, but it suggested a hidden threat we had missed, and it was concerning for a few reasons.

First, such comforters were a lucrative luxury item—each one could fetch thousands. Moreover, as the population of these cats declined with hunting, their rarity would raise the value of each pelt, increasing demand for the fur. Even a few comforters could mean a grave risk to Afghanistan's endangered cat species. Second, that a US soldier placed this rumored order suggested that the international presence in Afghanistan was driving the illegal trade. The soldier's request also demonstrated a frightening reality: a single individual has the potential to wipe out an entire species. There are many such people with the means to do so in the world, particularly in emerging economies that may not have reliable enforcement of conservation laws. We needed to stop the trade before the big cats went extinct in Afghanistan. Thus was born our Snow Leopard Project.

Wildlife trade was not new in Afghanistan. In the 1970s, the hippie trail passed through Afghanistan. Travelers came for the cheap hashish and rich culture and left with an exotic skin. The trade died off as Afghanistan fell into war and conflict. However, the aftermath of the 2001 US invasion brought a massive influx of humanitarians, war tourists, development workers, and military personnel from all over the world. And much like the hippies before them, these visitors wanted to bring home Afghan souvenirs. The demand for furs was climbing, and they were widely for sale on Chicken Street, next to the rug and lapis shops. We needed to do more than just write to embassies about cracking down on illegal trade. We needed to shut down trade altogether. But how?

First, we needed to expand public outreach and education. Afghanistan's anything-goes, Wild West atmosphere granted a sense of permissiveness to people, including the idea that it was okay to cloak yourself with the fur of a wild carnivore. We needed to change the social acceptance of that. We also needed to develop an awareness campaign for the humanitarian/development and military communities about how purchasing illicit wildlife products would ultimately undermine the very identity of the country that they came to support and help rebuild. It was crucial to highlight that individuals buying products made from endangered species could be found liable in three different ways—under the laws of their home countries, under Afghan law, and under international conventions dedicated to ending trade in endangered species.

Although moral probity alone would not suffice to deter such trade, social pressure, an appeal to identity, and fear of punishment could be quite compelling. We designed posters, placed articles in expat journals, and even considered launching an Afghan television show with Tolo Television—which we wanted to call *Afghan Geographic*—that would feature Prince Mostapha Zaher as a narrator.

Second, we needed to monitor wild populations and the fur trade to understand the pressures on natural systems and the sources of the furs. We needed to know how many snow leopards, caracals, and other cats were left in Afghanistan. WCS was already undertaking the first systematic wildlife survey work in three decades, in Wakhan and Band-e-Amir, to document what had happened to wildlife in Afghanistan. However, we needed to train Afghan conservationists and build a body of expertise to carry out such surveys in the future. Simultaneously, we also needed to go undercover into the shops on Chicken Street and at the markets that sprang up around military bases to measure the trade and supply. Furs and skins weren't always on display, and it would take some goading to get a trader to show off his snow leopard, caracal, or Persian leopard pelts, which wasn't without risk.

Third, we needed to actually shut down the trade. That was a complex objective, given the many ways that people could flow in and out of the country. The reconstruction and humanitarian community flew in from Dubai and elsewhere through Kabul International Airport, so we needed to train Kabul's customs officials in international conventions governing trade in endangered species, highlight the species in Afghanistan covered by domestic and international law, and finally, teach the officials to how to spot illegal items. The airport was only the first step. Much of the trade happened at pop-up markets on military bases—the ISAF market in downtown Kabul and the market at Bagram Airfield, an hour north of Kabul. Soldiers and civilians working at Bagram could get in and out of Afghanistan without ever passing through Afghan customs. That meant we needed to work with the US and ISAF forces to shut down wildlife trade on military bases. Our pitch to the military leadership was simple: "Such trade is again illegal under Afghan law, international law, and the laws of the home countries of the ISAF forces, including the US, which you have a duty to uphold. But more importantly, you are undermining your own mission." They responded to that argument. Ultimately, we needed to train military before they came to Afghanistan, to warn them off buying illegal goods.

Finally, we needed to work with the Afghan legislature and government to improve enforcement, refine the existing Afghan endangered species legislation, and build expertise in the government and staff. We needed to work with our friends at the United Nations Environment Programme for this. Finally, once we shut down the trade, we would need to find a way to preferentially benefit those who didn't sell furs of endangered species. Our goal wasn't to hurt the shopkeepers but encourage them to develop other products that used domestic animals over wildlife.

This strategy would have two economic effects. Once illegal furs were seized at the airports (including the military ones), it would reduce demand for them in the market since there was a risk that their purchase would be taken away. The buyers themselves would put pressure on the fur traders to ensure what they would be selling could be legally taken out of the country and thus reduce demand for such products. And if we could shut down sales of furs at the ISAF markets, perhaps penalizing violators by having them kicked out of the lucrative base market, we would further collapse the demand for such products from poachers and hopefully reduce the poaching of wildlife overall.

I PARTNERED WITH Clay Miller, the embassy science fellow on detail from the EPA to NEPA for the trainings. Clay's access to embassy logistics and into the military commands as a result of his position in the embassy was critical to getting our work started. He also helped us access military newspapers like the *Stars and Stripes* to influence the demand side of trade by stopping the purchase before it happened and raising awareness of wildlife trafficking throughout the world.

Clay and I set about designing training programs and lecture materials that covered the richness and importance of Afghan biodiversity, international and Afghan legal regulations, and identification of endangered species from their skins. The owner of Baba Amir restaurant near the WCS offices continued to give us access to his extensive collection of carnivore skins, including a Persian cheetah, an Afghan tiger, a snow leopard, and a Persian leopard, among others, which we would use for the training.

One of our first tests was a trip to the airport, where we met with Afghan civil aviation authorities to discuss the wildlife trafficking. As you might expect, the Kabul airport had unusually strict security protocols. A first checkpoint reviewed your credentials and tickets and inspected the exterior of your car for vehicle-borne IEDs (VBIEDs). The second stop inspected the interior of the car for possible explosives. That meant dragging your luggage into a separate building, where it was hand-inspected. After parking your car at the airport gate, you dragged your luggage one hundred meters to the door. There, you needed to show your ticket, go through a metal detector, and submit your bags for x-rays. Finally, after checking in for your flight, your carry-on was x-rayed once more for good measure while you passed a final handheld metal detector test. Then and only then could you actually enter the airport.

This complex system wasn't foolproof. The morning of one of my many trips out of Afghanistan, Qais, the travel coordinator who had never been on a plane, insisted that we get to the airport four hours early for the first flight of the day to get through security and avoid potential delays. Qais was cautious, but with good reason. Flights out of Kabul were typically full and far less frequent than at major hubs.

We were not excited about the prospect of downtime at the airport. Even with my gaming device, it was a dull affair. The airport had not been modernized, and food and drink were limited. The departure lounge had only a few seats, which were extraordinarily uncomfortable even if you were lucky enough to get one. The toilets were unpleasant, and men were often washing their feet in the sinks as part of their ablutions for daily prayer. Not an unreasonable action, but if you were brushing your teeth at the next sink over, it wasn't very appetizing. Worst of all, there was nothing to do at the terminal other than stare at people in the torturous seats near yours. But Qais, with his kind, pleading eyes, was hard to disappoint.

Qais got us to the airport before 6:00 a.m. Our flight was the first of the day, but it didn't leave until 9:00 a.m. When we got to the first checkpoint, no one was there, so we lifted up the arm of the security barrier and drove through to the luggage inspection. That guard station was vacant as well. We lifted another security barrier and drove to the parking lot. The normal security check at the gate was also unmanned, so Qais, Sabour (our head of security), and I pushed open the gate and came to the door of the terminal itself. The airport was eerily silent—no one was around, no passengers, agents, or guards. What would normally be a crowded entrance with people bustling and talking and pushing was devoid of life. We walked through the metal detectors and the baggage x-ray at the door—all unmanned. The metal detectors screamed an alert as we passed under them, but no one was there to hear it. The ticket counters were empty too. We were curious about how far we could go before we encountered anyone. We walked through different exit gates, emigration, currency controls, and into the waiting area for the flight. A door was open to the tarmac, and we looked outside. In front of us stood my plane, darkened, unguarded. I found the whole scene terrifying, as if I had slept through a zombie apocalypse. Spooked by the emptiness, we quickly scurried back out. I dragged all my luggage back out to the car, and we drove back outside the first checkpoint. Security showed up at 7:00 a.m. and proceeded to give us a thorough search. Apparently, terrorists followed banker's hours in Afghanistan.

CLAY AND I met with the senior leadership of Kabul International Airport to talk about the potential training, and we offered them informational posters we had designed. One particular poster, written in English, Pashto, and Dari, showed an adorably cute baby snow leopard from the Bronx Zoo with a gun sight bull's-eye superimposed across the cub's face. The text announced that only one hundred snow leopards were left in Afghanistan and that purchasing wildlife skins was illegal. Although some of my colleagues snarkily remarked that some readers might interpret the image as an invitation to shoot baby snow leopards because of their rarity, the airport officials were extremely enthusiastic about the signs. For a long time, seemingly the only decorations visible upon flying in or out of Afghan airports were our wildlife trafficking posters.

The airport leadership was also extremely enthusiastic about training their staff in spotting illegal items. We returned a few days later to lead the training for the airport security staff, border police, and customs officials who inspected the luggage of departing passengers. We brought fur identification guides for airport security. The attention of the staff didn't waver during the all-day training. Their focus paid off, as each time I left Afghanistan, the airport guards showed me the ever-larger pile of seized furs. In fact, I came dangerously close to missing my flights because the rightfully proud guards insisted on showing me every fur they had seized so they could bask in approval and encouragement, which I duly provided. These customs seizures soon had an effect, but we needed to shut down the military markets and the tourist stores on Chicken Street to truly disrupt the lucrative business.

Our work in educating people about the problem wasn't limited to Afghan authorities. Soldiers serving in Afghanistan were buying illegal wildlife, violating all kinds of laws, and sustaining the illicit trade. We needed to talk to leaders of the American military initiative focused on routing the Taliban and al-Qaeda, as well as commanders at ISAF. Clay used his contacts with the US military to set up a visit to the massive air base at Bagram, a hub in the War on Terror and the gateway into Afghanistan for most US military personnel and equipment.

Bagram was the largest US military base in the country, named after an adjacent town. The settlement of Bagram was originally founded by Alexander the Great (he humbly named it Alexandria). In its long history, Bagram had been a great wine-making center and later, like other places in Afghanistan, a Buddhist stronghold. But in the twenty-first century, it largely existed to service (and profit from) Bagram Airfield, both legally and illegally. The base was sixty miles north of Kabul, roughly a one- to two-hour drive. The airfield was originally built by the Americans as part of a Cold War charm initiative in Afghanistan. Ironically, it became the hub of Red Army operations during the Soviet invasion and was then rebuilt by American forces after the US invasion of Afghanistan in 2001. The walls of the base hadn't fallen, even as armies came and went.

Clay and I traveled to Bagram Airfield via a State Department–chartered Bell UH-1 Iroquois helicopter, otherwise known as a Huey, an iconic helo from the Vietnam War. The pilot and the sharpshooter on the helicopter were South African former military. We left from a side gate at Kabul International, near where UNOPS—the operational and logistics wing of the UN—ran its flights. That gate was attacked later that same day, only hours after our departure. After a short low-altitude flight to Bagram, with the door open and our South African machine gunner scanning the countryside for threats, we swooped over the extensive nested walls protecting the base only to find ourselves in a traffic jam of C-130s and attack helicopters waiting to find a space to park on the air base's crowded apron. This was the Bagram equivalent of the morning rush hour. Soon enough, we were on the ground, and we headed for the military police building, where we looked for a Sergeant Lockhart who would be our host.

The MPs were waiting for us, and much like at Kabul International Airport, we were astonished by the enthusiasm of our audience. The DOD wanted to publicize the work to soldiers around the world. One young serviceman, perhaps twenty years old, took in photos of Afghanistan's biodiversity with rapt attention. It's possible that the boredom of being on base, with only movies, the gym, and fast-food franchises for entertainment coupled with the uniqueness and geographic specificity of our presentation won them over. But we were also providing an opportunity for soldiers to know more about the country they were in beyond the dusty landscapes that they routinely flew over or drove through. I was deeply impressed with how seriously the young airmen took in the information.

The training filled the entire day. We took a field trip with the MPs to the on-base market, where we feigned interest in wildlife skins. It was easy to find snow leopard, leopard cat, and Pallas's cat pelts on the initial inspection. Soon enough, sellers from the market were coming to us with even more skins based on our feigned interest. Some of the pelts were painted to look like leopard or even tiger, but others were real. The MP commander was alarmed at how easy it was to find the furs. After the review, Clay and I discussed next steps with the military police. The MPs would start unannounced inspections of the stalls, including all personal bags of merchandise carried by traders. The new rules were simple: the MPs would permit traders a single violation, where any furs discovered would be seized; a second violation would cost them lucrative access to the base.

The MPs took us over to the customs and departure area. We also discussed protocols for inspecting baggage of departing servicemen and contractors. Soldiers on base had their baggage inspected by MPs before they headed stateside. Packages shipped via mail were also screened. The purpose of such inspections was to catch any illicit items—war souvenirs from the battlefield (e.g., body parts, specifically fingers) or personal items of the enemy. Now the MPs would also look for endangered species. Finally, we visited the post office to make them aware of our effort and enlist their help in checking all packages that were mailed out, shutting down the final loophole for smuggling wildlife products off the base.

The training was successful, and the soldiers had lots of questions, so many that we wound up staying longer than expected. We hurried back to the terminal to catch our helicopter. When we arrived, the helicopter wasn't there. Clay called to find out the status—the helo supposedly had taken off from Kabul and was on its way. We waited more than an hour and checked in again, and again we were reassured that it would be there any minute. After another thirty minutes of waiting, we called the embassy. It seemed that the president of Pakistan was intending to come for a visit, and they had shut down the airport, and no traffic would be coming in or out, and no one bothered to contact us.

We asked when we could get another flight to Kabul and were told it wouldn't be until late the following day or perhaps later in the week, depending on availability. Our helicopter had been chartered by the State Department, which was great for skipping the hassle of base clearance and registration, but it also meant we didn't actually have permission to be on the base or have access to food or a place to sleep—which was a major downside, given that we might be stuck at Bagram for a while. I needed to get back for meetings the next day, so I looked at taking ground transport back to Kabul.

I called Shafiq to tell him about our situation, and he dispatched Khoja in one of our Land Cruisers to meet us at the gate to the base. With luck, we could be home in four hours, but we had to solve a few challenges first. For instance, I needed to figure out how to get off base, as Khoja wouldn't have permission to enter. The distance between the base itself and the outer walls was at least a half a mile. The roadway was isolated, under bright lights, lined with the Jersey barriers ubiquitous to American war zones. Those on base were further protected (and isolated) by concertina wire, anti-tank/vehicle barriers, and guard posts manned by American and Afghan soldiers with permission to shoot potential threats. Suffice it to say that this road was not pedestrian-friendly, especially in the dark, while weighed down with furs from our training session.

The second problem was Clay himself. Embassy personnel were never allowed to ride in private vehicles for safety reasons. It exposed them to danger. What we planned on doing—walking out into an Afghan street, where we would hop into a private vehicle—was definitely not sanctioned by the State Department. Technically, Clay worked at NEPA, but his schedule and movement were still tightly constrained, and he was under the authority of the embassy and its rules in Afghanistan. Clay risked substantial trouble, including losing his security clearance and permissions to leave the embassy, or even a reprimand and a trip home, if he were caught traveling with us. Moreover, if we were stopped by criminals or insurgents, and they identified Clay as a diplomat, he would make for a valuable hostage. With my ability to speak Farsi and my Persian features, I didn't stick out, but Clay, with his all-American, California looks, did. And Clay's presence would put me in that same danger by association. I told Clay that I was going to walk out of Bagram and that a WCS car would meet me at the gates.

"What do you want to do?" I asked.

Clay thought for a moment. "I'm going with you." This was one thing I loved about Clay. He was a rebel and adventurer.

Clay and I got a ride from the flight operations building to the main gate. I didn't tell the MP driver we were planning to walk off the base. On one hand, it was probably good that as many people as possible knew about our plan in case something went wrong. But telling too many people could prevent Clay from leaving or, worse, get him in trouble later. We needed to maintain OPSEC, or operational security. We approached the American checkpoint. The soldiers looked at us quizzically and stopped us. Clay showed his embassy credentials. We had to tell them that we were leaving, as there could be no other explanation for going past their checkpoint. They seemed confused when we told them we were walking off base to meet a waiting car.

"No one walks off base."

"It's okay. We have a car meeting us at the gate, and we're with an NGO. We live and work outside the wire." I didn't want to highlight that we probably didn't have permission to be on base in the first place or that Clay didn't have permission to be off it.

The soldier looked at me. "You still don't want to do it. It's almost a half mile to the gate."

"We don't have a lot of choice."

It was the end of the day, and there was a long line of Afghan base staff and merchants leaving for the night. The soldier stopped one of the Toyota Hilux pickups and asked if we could catch a lift. They said yes, and Clay and I jumped into the cargo bed, where a number of Afghans were sitting. We introduced ourselves to the others sitting in the cargo. They were driving back to Kabul for the evening and asked if we wanted to go there. We didn't know who they were, so I thanked them and said we would have a car at the gate. They were friendly and in a good mood, as they were done with work for the day. We laughed with them in the open air as we drove over the bumpy road with bright lights glaring at us. We chatted about what the WCS was doing in Afghanistan, and they seemed deeply interested. I wound up giving them my card.

At the wide roundabout that sat before the main gate to the base, we thanked them and shook hands with everyone in the truck before hopping out. Afghan soldiers guarding the outside entrance to the base were surprised to see Westerners getting out of a truck at the gate. This was the gate where a suicide bomber blew himself up, killing twenty-three people, trying to reach Cheney during his visit to Afghanistan. Clay pointed out the crater where the suicide bomber set off the bomb, and we walked over to look at it.

As we stared at the aftermath of the bomb, I looked around for our dark blue WCS Land Cruiser but didn't see it or Khoja. We walked back to the bemused Afghan soldiers guarding the outside entrance and stood next to them for about twenty minutes. We had no way to get back on the base since we didn't have permission to be there in the first place, and in any case, I didn't have any US government ID with me. I called Shafiq again. He noted that Khoja had left two hours earlier and should arrive any second. We walked out away from the gate into the town itself. Bagram wasn't known to be a source of support for the Taliban, given that so many in the town benefited from the US presence.

A small cluster of children in their early teens approached, and one started speaking to me in Dari.

"What is your name?"

"Eskandar," I told him, using the Dari variation of *Alex*.

"What is his name?"

"Clay."

"What are you doing here?"

"We are waiting for our car."

"What do you do here in Afghanistan?"

"We work on protecting wildlife in Afghanistan," I said.

"Where are you from?"

"I am from Iran," I lied, not wanting to mark myself as an American. "Where is he from?"

Just at that moment, Clay spoke to me in English. "What are you speaking about?"

"Is he American?" the boy asked. More and more children crowded around us, interested in the conversation with the two strangers.

"He is not American," I said. "He is . . ." I tried to think of a believable, nonthreatening country. "He is Swedish." I didn't want to draw attention to Clay, and having him labeled as an American by a group of loud children was a good way to get us kidnapped.

"He sounds like an American."

I needed to give the children more credit.

"What are they saying?" Clay asked again.

"We are just talking about what we are doing in Afghanistan."

"Are you Muslim?" one of the boys asked.

As I diplomat, I learned never answer the question you have been asked, but the question you wish you had been asked. "I am from Iran," I sidestepped. I didn't like where this was going.

"Why do you speak like an American with him?"

More kids came, and there were now about fifteen children around us. Some adults had shuffled over to the periphery of the gaggle of children, passively listening in.

"What is your name?" I asked the boy who had started the questioning, trying to change the subject.

"Is he Christian?" another boy asked. I found this question ironic, given that I had previously chased someone down the street in Afghanistan, yelling the same question, but this was a different context.

"I don't know," I responded. "But it doesn't matter. All people are good, and the Americans and others are here to help Afghanistan."

Clay, perhaps wondering why there were so many children staring and animatedly pointing at him as we spoke in Dari, and sensing my growing anxiety at the turn in conservation, again asked what I was talking about.

"We are talking about snow leopards," which is what I wished we were talking about.

I called Shafiq again, asking where Khoja was. "There was a problem on the way, so he is late," Shafiq responded.

"Please hurry," I responded.

"Christians are bad; they are unbelievers," my main ten-year-old inquisitor announced.

"No," I responded. "All people are good, and it doesn't matter what religion you are."

"Is he an American Christian?" The crowd leaned in closer to hear the answer. I again ignored the question.

"Americans are here to help Afghanistan. They come from a long way away to do so. There are many kinds of peoples and religions in the world, and we need to be tolerant. He cares less about religion and more about protecting the wildlife of Afghanistan."

"Are we in trouble?" Clay asked again with a hint of concern.

"Nope. Everything is good," I lied.

The boy's voice started heating up. "My father says that Christians are bad and they have caused many problems to Afghanistan." Other boys chimed in. More people were walking up to the group from farther away. People down the street were looking in our direction. Clay looked at me again, questioning the increasing chaos.

"He is fairly excited about what we are doing as conservationists," I added.

Clay looked at me skeptically. I searched the area for ways we could escape. More people were arriving, enlarging the crowd. Making a run for the Afghan guards at the Bagram gate might work, but we still couldn't reenter the base, and a rush for the guards might end up getting us shot by the guards in the towers if we seemed like a threat. I needed to tell Clay what was happening.

I turned to Clay to confess the increasing seriousness of the situation, when Khoja arrived in the Land Cruiser. I waved goodbye to the children, who looked at us silently and didn't wave back.

Traffic had been unusually heavy on the way, Khoja explained, and the road had been blocked.

In Kabul, we dropped Clay off at the embassy gate without incident, other than strange looks from the Afghan guards outside the USAID/ embassy compound as he strolled in.

WE REPEATED OUR training session at the ISAF base in Kabul. This market was not within the base walls but just outside it. We walked through the stalls with one of the commanders and pointed out snow leopard pelts and products made from leopard cat and other species.

A few weeks later, we returned to Bagram Airfield. The young soldier who had been listening so carefully to the lecture pulled me aside and showed me all the scientific papers he had found on wildlife in Afghanistan and asked me questions about species distribution. He had even memorized all the scientific names of the species.

We inspected the on-base bazaar again and the collection of material that inspection of baggage had produced. The illegal trade at the market had been completely shut down after several raids by military police. We couldn't find a single pelt or product made from snow leopard or other species of conservation interest. Even my private attempts to goad merchants into offering illicit goods failed; the opportunity to sell to a captive audience of soldiers was too valuable to risk being thrown out of the market. Our training had succeeded in shutting down one of the biggest illegal fur markets in Afghanistan, on a base that served sixteen thousand soldiers and civilians, at least temporarily. In two short weeks, the merchants had sworn off illegal wildlife products that were contributing to the decline of Afghanistan's biodiversity in favor of products that could be legitimately sold to and shipped home by soldiers.

At the departure customs area at Bagram, an MP showed me some seized furs—but not too many. The soldier explained, "After the first few furs were seized, the word got out that if you were taking home furs of endangered species, you would lose them. Paying $500 for a confiscated gift is a lot of money for a young soldier to lose."

This not only deterred soldiers from buying the furs, but those who had lost their souvenirs went back to the dealers to scold them for selling them contraband. This was having an impact on the merchants, many of whom also maintained stores on Chicken Street. We were making a difference. WCS was enthusiastic about our work on wildlife trade in Afghanistan and started arranging to train soldiers at stateside bases before they traveled to Afghanistan, with the support of military leadership there. Thanks to support and publicity from the embassy and the military, word was getting around. We were interviewed by DOD News, Voice of America, Dari and Pashto television and radio services, and National Geographic radio. Even the *New York Times* profiled the Afghanistan program with a full-page interview. The tide was turning on wildlife trade, at least for the moment.

BUT EVEN AS we garnered attention and saw real results, all was not well. During this time, I felt increasing pressure from USAID, particularly the foreign service officer overseeing the agriculture and environment program, who kept a count of the country directors that he had fired as proof of his effectiveness. The USAID mission in Afghanistan seemed to have little interest in actually protecting wildlife; their primary motive was burning money faster and faster as proof of their impact. While they put substantial pressure on our office to create reports, which soon took up two-thirds of my time, the reports were never read. The situation in Afghanistan was unraveling, and the political pressures of that collapse were felt by the WCS program and other USAID implementers. The failures I saw in Afghanistan—a lack of interest in science as a tool, the disinterest in actual impact, a focus on process over impact, the lack of technical expertise, the strange focus on burn rates—would inspire the major initiatives I took up when I joined USAID as its first chief scientist in two decades.

Not long after our second visit to Bagram, I received a telephone call. The fur merchants who sold on the different military bases wanted to meet with me. I wasn't sure how they had gotten my number, and I was concerned that they held a grudge against the person who had shut down their businesses. I had an antiquated vision of merchants coming in clutching violin cases, pulling out 1930s gangster machine guns, and riddling my body with bullets. Despite my fears, I agreed to their visiting our offices in Shahr-e Naw the next day. I instructed Sabour to check each visitor tomorrow thoroughly. I was pretty sure they wanted to kill me, with good reason. I slept fitfully that evening.

The next morning, Sabour led in six Afghan men. They told me that they owned the fur stores on Chicken Street and sold on the bases and that I had hurt their businesses. They stated that their intent was to only sell things that were legal and that wouldn't hurt Afghanistan's wildlife, but they didn't know which species were which, or much about Afghan, US, and international wildlife law. They asked whether I could run the training program for them. As it turned out, these were the men who had given Clay and me a ride out of Bagram.

The pressure from USAID was also felt at WCS headquarters, where their many different projects depended heavily on funding from the agency, and they saw the Afghanistan program as potentially undermining these other programs. I made a difficult decision; I would leave WCS's Afghanistan program. I sent my resignation to John Robinson, the senior vice president for conservation at WCS. I had intended to spend a lifetime working with WCS, and the Afghanistan program was perhaps the best job I would ever have, but this dream was over.

That night, Kara and I spent a sad evening at Delhi Darbar, an Indian restaurant in Kabul. She excoriated me for leaving Afghanistan and giving up on everything that I had built. Kara would stay on in Afghanistan for two more years, traveling back and forth from Afghanistan while I would go back to the State Department as a science diplomat.

I hadn't notified USAID of my resignation as country director, and the next day, I was informed that a $5 million grant application that I had written in an all-night writing session had been approved. The program had a financial basis to not only continue but even expand. Moreover, we were close to securing official final approval for the national parks we were proposing in Band-e-Amir, and the work in Wakhan was well under way. The request for training from the fur traders felt like the final indication of our success. We set the date for a month later.

Running the training session with the Afghan fur traders was the last thing I did in Afghanistan. They listened and participated with the same attention and even enthusiasm shown by Afghan customs officers and the military police. We spoke about the importance of wildlife to Afghanistan's identity, the decline in wild populations and the need to let them recover, and our efforts to set up national parks. We reviewed international and Afghan laws and highlighted which species they should not sell. We even discussed burning the pelts currently in their stores and setting up a certification system for stores that did not sell endangered wildlife products, which would benefit traders who complied with the wildlife ban. My last day in Afghanistan turned out to be my best.

The next morning, I left for the US. Shafiq, Qais, Zabih, Sabour, Khoja, and Kara walked me to the entrance of the airport terminal. I was deeply saddened to leave a country I realized I loved. For an Iranian immigrant who had been trapped between cultures, Afghanistan joined a long line of countries—UAE, Oman, Kuwait, Iraq, Uzbekistan, Kazakhstan, Georgia, Tajikistan—where I had searched for my Iranian identity, in the bazaars, in the waters of the Persian Gulf, in the kabob stands, and in the mountains and deserts. Although Afghanistan wasn't a perfect match, it was far closer than all the other places I had looked before. But I found something else in Afghanistan: an optimism for conservation and for the future. For all the terrible challenges that the Afghan people had faced over three decades, for the challenges that they had yet to face, they were resolute in finding joy, seeking happiness, and moving forward. These were the bravest people I have met in my life, yet also some of the kindest.

THE SNOW LEOPARD PROJECT

O UR OUTINGS IN Kabul became harder to replicate after our first year in 2006, and they reflected a growing trend we soon saw across the country. The heavily defended Serena Hotel came under attack on January 14, 2008. Three men dressed as police distracted the guards, and a fourth man walked into the hotel and detonated an explosive vest. A car bomb destroyed the main security entrance, and teams of gunmen burst into the hotel's health club and started executing foreigners. I had started working out at the Serena every night right around the time of night when the attack took place. I wasn't there the night of the attack because I had left Afghanistan only a few weeks before. And in 2014, insurgents went after the humanitarian communities' most sacred refuge. A suicide bomber killed the guards at the entrance of Kamel's Lebanese restaurant, and gunmen burst in and slaughtered many of the diners. Kamel died trying to protect his friends. Twenty-two people of nine nationalities died in the attack, including Americans, British, and Russians.

When I arrived in Afghanistan in 2006, the country was emerging from decades of war. The refuse of conflict littered the landscape—the rubble of pulverized buildings, bullet holes in the walls of the structures still standing, rusting hulks of troop carriers, tanks, and buses. You couldn't even see the most insidious remnants of war: the land mines.

The natural environment fared little better than cities and roads. The routine physical practices of war—bombings, firefights, fortifications—defaced huge portions of the land. There were conceptual realities to war as well. The collapse of state authority (and any semblance of resource management) led to heedless forest clearance. The flood of guns into an effectively lawless land allowed hungry soldiers and refugees to decimate the charismatic wildlife. The civilians who were caught in the middle or sought refuge in other countries lost touch with cultures of land and resource management. Systems in effect for hundreds of years—like the underground irrigation tunnels—were abandoned, and techniques for sustainability forgotten. Peter Zahler, author of the first rapid assessment of Afghanistan's post-conflict environment, summarized the situation well: Afghanistan was "a place where protected areas aren't even paper parks. After a quarter century of war, even the paper has been lost, looted, or burned."*

Having served in post-invasion Iraq with the State Department, I had lived through the challenges of a country staggering out of a war, and as with Iraq, I was nervous about what I would face in Afghanistan. In fact, the stress proved to drain me more so than any other work I did. But I was excited about an opportunity to reinvent the practices of both conservation and nation-building free of the inertia of bureaucracy or history. In Afghanistan, I saw a chance to practice conservation on the national level with a clean slate.

What I didn't realize was how different Iraq and Afghanistan are, both as countries and as conflict zones. Both war zones shared some similar characters: the opportunists (both Western and local), the hustlers, the adrenaline addicts and war tourists, the patriots, the idealists, all interacting in a dangerous vacuum of power. The war in Afghanistan proved different from the one in Iraq. Both countries experienced prolonged conflict over a similar period of time—the Soviet Union invaded Afghanistan in 1979, while the Iran-Iraq War started in 1980. Both

---

*Peter Zahler, "Top-Down Meets Bottom-Up: Conservation in a Post-Conflict World," *Conservation Magazine*, Winter 2003.

nations suffered in three separate wars—the Iran-Iraq War, followed by the two Gulf wars for Iraq; and the Russian invasion, a civil war, and the US invasion for Afghanistan. The citizens of both countries suffered terrible human rights abuses, oppression, and in some cases, genocide under different rulers and invaders. However, Iraq was a middle-income, heavily urban country, while 80 percent of Afghanistan's population lived in the countryside as of 2006. The wars in Afghanistan proved in some ways more brutal and devastating to the country. Neither the Russian invasion nor the bloody civil war followed the rules of war.* Iraqis were spared the indiscriminate distribution of land mines, sprinkled from helicopters, which maimed countless Afghan children. Humanity often disappeared on the battlefields of Afghanistan (as it would later under ISIS in Iraq). Wave after wave of destruction ground down a nation to dust and chunks of rubble. This was the canvas for our work in Afghanistan. War had shattered much of the country, but it hadn't defeated its people. The Afghans we met, despite all they had been through, showed kindness and care to us.

As I left Afghanistan at the end of 2007, the security situation started markedly to decline. As in Iraq, the United States would mount a "surge" with one hundred thousand troops deployed into Afghanistan by August 2010. The number of insurgent attacks on US, ISAF, and Afghan troops exceeded 1,600 per week in September 2010, with improvised explosive devices accounting for nearly half of US troop deaths. The attacks also increasingly targeted aid workers—"soft targets" less defended than military installations (or in our case, not defended at all). With NGOs pulling out and shuttering their rebuilding work, the Afghan government lost ground in the fight for "hearts and minds."

Attacks similar to the one on the Serena Hotel, where I had my memorable encounter with the Iranian ambassador, hit restaurants where we'd eaten and the motel we'd used as our first office, killing

---

*The same could be said about Saddam Hussein's use of chemical weapons, including against his own people, during the Kurdish uprising.

friends and neighbors. Activities as modest as a beer at the Gandamack Lodge or a picnic trip to Qargha Lake became too much of a risk, and most aid organizations barred nonessential travel for staff.

Some Western organizations could hunker down in fortified compounds, but WCS was based in the field, which meant greater risk. But rather than shut down the program, WCS persevered to achieve tremendous successes. In 2009, Band-e-Amir became the country's first national park. Afghanistan then created a second national park in 2014 (Wakhan National Park, which, at 4,200 square miles, is bigger than Yellowstone). Wakhan National Park encloses nearly the entire distribution range of Marco Polo sheep in Afghanistan, preserving the heartland of the population, as well as 70 percent of the country's snow leopard habitat. Kol-e-Hashmat Khan, the wetland where I bird-watched with a Talib, became Afghanistan's third protected area in 2017.

And the success didn't just come in paper designations. Ecotourism soared at Band-e-Amir. In 2017, 189,000 people, mostly Afghan citizens, visited the park's dams and dazzling blue lakes. Tourism boosted the economy, as locals provided accommodations, food, and handicrafts. The stylish ranger station (incidentally, home to Afghanistan's first female rangers) was only the beginning of infrastructure renovation at the park, with improved trails and a host of other additions. Local communities continued to help govern the park through the Band-e-Amir Protected Area Committee. WCS completed wildlife surveys in and around Band-e-Amir, documenting ibex, urials, Persian leopards, Himalayan lynx, Pallas's cats, and more. In 2017, WCS confirmed—in Bamiyan—the presence of the Southwest badger in Afghanistan, never before verified.

In Wakhan, WCS actively comanaged the development of the new national park and expanded the research on the status of Afghanistan's snow leopards and Marco Polo sheep. Using camera traps and satellite collars and by analyzing scats and signs, WCS collected enough evidence to *double* the estimated population of snow leopards in Afghanistan. This work provided a welcome cause for optimism about a species threatened by both human encroachment and climate change.

In Badakhshan, WCS scientists led by Stephane Ostrowski discovered a breeding population of the large-billed reed warbler, dubbed "the world's least-known bird," and in Wakhan, they verified the presence of brown bears and other carnivores.

Bears notwithstanding, Wakhan tourism received a huge push. In 2008, *National Geographic* declared Wakhan one of the best "new" trips in the world. The increased publicity drove visits, and WCS helped in building a tourism center in Ishkashim and an interpretative center in Qala Panja, training Wakhan residents in ecotourism work, improving facilities, and working with other organizations and the local government to promote the park's treasures. It also encouraged the development of airstrips in Wakhan, including in Ishkashim, Kret, and Chaqmaqtin in Little Pamir.

To decrease conflict between humans and snow leopards, WCS built more than 34 communal predator-proof corrals and improved 820 household corrals. Most importantly, we also aided in the creation of the democratically elected Wakhan Pamir Association to help establish and implement the rules and regulations for the protected area and the activities within it. Even the transboundary peace park would show promise. In October 2018, partners from protected areas in Afghanistan, China, Pakistan, and Tajikistan created the Bam-e-Duniya ("roof of the world") network to coordinate long-term conservation and sustainable mountain development in the Hindu Kush Karakoram Pamir Landscape. The Pamirs Transboundary Peace Park would exist in practice, even if it did not in treaty.

In the Eastern Forests Complex, we rediscovered species long thought to be extinct in Afghanistan (like the Kashmir musk deer) and found signs of snow leopards, markhor, Asiatic black bears, rhesus macaques, jackals, leopard cats, crested porcupines, yellow-throated martens, Asiatic black bears, and common palm civets, the latter previously unknown in Afghanistan. However, the deteriorating security situation led to the shutdown of WCS work in the Eastern Forests in 2009. The following year brought a tragedy that underscored the deadly risks of fieldwork in the Eastern Forests and the risks our teams were taking.

In 2010, Taliban fighters staged an ambush in Kunar Province and kidnapped Dr. Linda Norgrove and three Afghan colleagues. Norgrove had collaborated with WCS on initial efforts to create Band-e-Amir National Park in her role at the UN Office for Project Services. Though her colleagues were released, Norgrove remained a captive at a remote Taliban camp. United States Naval Special Warfare Development Group, better known as SEAL Team Six, whose members would kill Osama bin Laden only a year later, attempted a predawn rescue on the Taliban mountaintop complex. Tragically, one of the members of SEAL Team Six threw a grenade into the hut in which Linda was being held, mortally wounding her.*

The wildlife trade programs I had started continued on in force and expanded. They continued the trainings not only on the bases in Afghanistan but in the US before soldiers were deployed. WCS evicted and confiscated catches from falcon trappers in Band-e-Amir. However, ultimately, it was the security situation, coupled with the lack of demand, that reduced the levels of wildlife trade.

In the years after I left, our talented WCS staff and their families experienced challenges. Shafiq moved his family to Germany in April 2012, but they found life in a foreign environment difficult, which was too much to bear for some family members, and they returned to Kabul six months later. Qais took over Shafiq's office director job and worked assiduously to become the country director, and Zabih continued his work in managing WCS Afghanistan's finances. Zalmai finished his master's on Marco Polo sheep in India and came back to work with the teams in Badakhshan and in the Eastern Forests. He was lead author on many papers on Afghanistan and eventually earned a place at a doctoral program at University of Massachusetts–Amherst. His research focuses on human-wildlife conflict in Wakhan, and he will be a leader in a new generation of Afghan conservationists.

---

*You can help continue the work she did through the Linda Norgrove Foundation.

Haqiq, our highly talented GIS director, started his PhD at the University of Florida, doing research on snow leopard ecology using camera-trap and telemetry data.

Ayub worked with WCS for a few more years on Band-e-Amir before starting to work with a local Afghan conservation organization. Many of the drivers and guards have stayed on with WCS, some moving into administrative roles.

Mohammad Reza Bahrami, who loved serving in Afghanistan as the Iranian ambassador but was dismissed by President Ahmadinejad after finding out that my request to combat wildlife trade was not an opportunity to resume negotiations with the United States, had his ambassadorship to Afghanistan restored after the election of President Rouhani in 2013. It was ironic that my own work post-Afghanistan led me to the US State Department team under the leadership of Ambassador Dennis Ross, which started the engagement with Iran. I used conservation of the Iranian cheetah and other forms of science diplomacy, many focused on the environment, as ways to build the foundation for trust in the lead-up to the nuclear deal. Ambassador Bahrami and I missed our timing by a year.

Although I didn't meet Ismail Khan in Afghanistan, I did end up meeting him at a high-level diplomatic event in DC convened by President Bush. The Afghan delegation, including Mostapha Zaher, created official credentials as part of the delegation for me so we could have a boisterous reunion over an official lunch. This led to our table getting shushed several times by high-ranking ministers of multiple European countries. The Afghans, who had persevered through wars and invasion, weren't going to suffer through boring speeches when there were friends to meet. I later watched President Bush shake hands with Ismail Khan. Bush had no idea that the older man in a turban and crisp white robe had fiercely fought the mighty Soviet army with shoulder-launched missiles supplied by the CIA, headed by his own father.

After Afghanistan, I went back to work for the State Department, just as the government weathered the changing of presidential administrations. In his first inauguration speech, President Obama committed the country to "restor[ing] science to its rightful place," to development and to international diplomacy. This put me in a unique place to lead a transformation around harnessing science and technology to further US diplomacy and development efforts.

After returning from Afghanistan, I started working with the Office of the Science and Technology Adviser to the Secretary of State and was soon busy shaping the scientific aspects of President Obama's Cairo Initiative for larger engagement with the Muslim world. Science could become a way to reset American relationships with the Middle East. The Cairo Initiative represented an approach to the Middle East fundamentally different from previous administrations. A year into Obama's first term, I was appointed the chief scientist of USAID—the first person to hold that post in thirty years. My mission wasn't simple. I was to help restore science, technology, and innovation to their rightful places within international development. This work meant programming (the Grand Challenges for Development); launching new initiatives, including building an innovation lab within the agency, modeled on the Defense Advanced Research Projects Agency, which had created the internet, self-driving cars, and drones; and substantially increasing the number of scientists and engineers working for the agency. My work was in part driven by the failures I saw on the ground in Afghanistan. USAID's job was to nation-build, but it had lacked the tools, expertise, and incentives to succeed.

In Washington, there were many reminders of my work in Afghanistan. The young, brash foreign service officer David Jea, who was stationed at the Bamiyan PRT, moved back to DC, living a block from my house. Many other friends from NGOs, State, and USAID lived only blocks away, and we would met up at barbecues, weddings, and parties and recount stories. Some of the WCS Afghanistan staff on study tours visited with us in Washington, and we maintained close contact with them. Many of my colleagues from Iraq and Afghanistan rose to leadership positions in their governments.

Other reminders existed as well. One day, I walked into the Afghanistan/Pakistan conference room for a meeting on how we could use science and technology to advance the efforts there. A panoramic photo of Band-e-Amir stretched across the wall of the conference room, which had been named after the national park. I made sure the imagery of Band-e-Amir was in my public speeches. USAID's magazine *Front-Lines* dedicated an issue in part to the work my group and others were doing in science and innovation across the agency. Unintentionally, the editors used an image of Afghans working on solar panels, with Band-e-Amir's lakes in the background. Our lives aren't a single straight line; sometimes the threads are braided together.

Many of my colleagues took tremendous risks in the name of the program, particularly our Afghan staff and their families. I faced no greater danger than anyone else in the program and far less than others. I don't know if the young man who met me at the Kol-e-Hashmat Khan wetlands really was a Talib or just trying to scare a Westerner. It hardly matters, as there were enough threats in Afghanistan—some obvious, some hidden. But for every cause for fear, there were a thousand reminders of Afghanistan's amazing hospitality, resiliency, and beauty. Ten years after I left the country, the snowy mountains, the sweet taste of the mulberries, and the goodness of the people remain vivid in my mind. I understand completely why so many Afghans who have suffered tragedy and lost friends and family still want to return. It is as if Afghanistan merges into your DNA.

Officially, the Iranian cheetah is thought to be extinct in Afghanistan, but I am sure a population remains. Dare mighty things. Go and find it.

ACKNOWLEDGMENTS

The successes of WCS in Afghanistan came about through the hard work and sacrifices of many men and women—some Afghan, some overseas guests, all brave and bright and hardworking and honest. All deserve the deepest gratitude. Neither the book nor this project would have been done without them.

First among them, I am deeply grateful for the extraordinary patience of my partner, Kara, and our children, Fynn and Cylus, as I wrote and revised the book over multiple years. These were days and weeks taken away from them that I cannot repay. Kara bore a burden in managing the family as a "single" parent, for which I am grateful. She was also critical in helping me to recall people, places, and events, and in reminding me to be humble. She was also a core part of the team in Afghanistan whose diplomatic and conservation work with the Afghan government and people was critical to our success.

This story began with Peter Zahler, whose tireless dedication to a forgotten region for conservation launched the Afghanistan program—without him, none of this would have occurred, and he deserves the credit for the success of the program. I am deeply grateful to him for his leadership and for the extraordinary opportunity to help stand up Afghanistan's first national parks. This would be a defining opportunity in my life: not only to work in Afghanistan, but to have the honor of working with him. I have rarely met anyone so devoted to conservation. He inspires me.

I am deeply grateful to the people of Afghanistan, and its government, for their welcome and hospitality, and for sharing their country with me.

The Snow Leopard Project wouldn't exist but for them and because of them. We were lucky to work with amazing leadership in the Afghan government and in our partner organizations: Parliamentarian Haji Aworang, Governor Habiba Sarābi, Ghulam Malikyar, Wali Modaqiq, Ghani Ghurriani, Eng. Hazrat Hussain Khaurin, Eng. Hashim Barakzai, Sulaiman Shah Sallari, and Fauzia Assifi. Most of all, I am incredibly indebted to His Excellency Prince Mostapha Zaher for his leadership and friendship and support.

We were lucky to have great supporters and collaborators at the Department of State and USAID, including Bill Taliaferro and David Jea. I am also incredibly grateful to Mary Melnyk, who was our chief cheerleader at USAID and a great champion for the environment. Clay Miller, the incredibly humble embassy science fellow, helped me with recalling events for the book, but even more so, and was a friend and collaborator in Afghanistan and long after. Clay also introduced me to Paul Bunje, who as my co-founder at Conservation X Labs, like the rest of my team, was deeply supportive of my writing the book. I was deeply impressed by the countless American men and women in uniform who worked with us to protect Afghanistan's wildlife. Countless other international experts drove the effort to protect Afghanistan's environment—people like Belinda Bowling, David Jea, Erin Hannan, Chris Shepard, Sergeant Lockhart, Senior Custom NCOIC Sergeant First Class Gualberto Gonzalez, Asif Zaidi, Ali Azimi, and the late Linda Norgrove. There are many more who should be mentioned who came after and deserve much credit.

The WCS team, both in Washington and in Afghanistan, were indispensable to the execution of the Afghanistan Biodiversity Conservation Project. WCS is an outstanding institution filled with dedicated men and women who work to protect wildlife and wildlands in the world's toughest places. Without an amazing team of Afghans and international experts and WCS leadership and staff at the Bronx Zoo, this project would have not been as successful as it has been.

WCS Afghanistan's subsequent country directors Peter Smallwood, David Lawson, and Richard Paley—assisted greatly by Peter Bowles and Kara Stevens—provided admirable continued leadership to the project that led to the designation of the new national parks. Stephane Ostrowski helped WCS create a scientific juggernaut through his careful mentoring of Afghan scientists and conservationists. Chris Shank, Rich Harris, John Winnie, Anthony Simms, Don Bedunah, Inayat Ali, John Mock, David Bradfield, Anthony Fitzherbert, Bilal Habib, Raffael Aye, Maria Karlstetter, McKenzie Johnson, and Ted Callahan also boldly led programs in science, exploration, and community-driven conservation in the farthest and most challenging reaches of Wakhan and Bamiyan, doing the work that defines WCS. But the most credit should go to the incredible Afghans who worked directly for WCS—people like Shafiq, Qais, Zabih, Sabour, Ayub, Zalmai, Dr. Farid and Dr. Esmael, Inayatollah (Jeff), Haqiq, Rohullah, Sweeta, Nuristani, Dr. Ali Madad, Dr. Hafizullah, Sharbat Khan, Deen Mohammad, Naquibullah, Ghulam, Khoja, Khalil, Ali, Karim, Naqib, Gul Makai, Seemin, and Tamkeen. There are many more people who helped us who deserve recognition and inclusion on this list. My failure to mention them in no way is meant to undercut their work and importance.

I also want to thank the WCS leadership in New York—John Cavelli, John Robinson, Robert Cook, Billy Karesh, Luke Hunter, George Schaller, Steve Osofsky, Josh Gingsberg, David Wilkie, George Amato, Kent Redford, Kelly Aylward, John Delaney, Steve Fairchild, Natalie Cash, Laura Perozo, and Peggy O'Shaughnessy—for their incredible help and support to the project and for their friendship. Ullas Karanth was a critical partner to the Afghanistan program as a leader of WCS India and as an eminent conservation scholar who shared his expertise with us generously. The WCS Asia program did very well under the leadership of Colin Poole and Peter Zahler, and with the support of Lisa Yook and Rose King. Rose was many times our secret advocate and friend. Heidi Kretser did a spectacular job running wildlife trade training sessions for US soldiers at Fort Drum and elsewhere.

There were many people who were very helpful in the writing of this book. At WCS, these include Shafiq, Ayub, Qais, Inayat Ali, Inayatollah, Stephan Owstrowski, Etienne Delattre, Ted Callahan, and Zalmai, who answered endless questions. I also want to thank WCS Asia for permitting the use in the book of some of the photos that were taken by WCS staff during my tenure in Afghanistan. Special thanks to Sana Masood and Anh Tuan Tran for their help in securing permissions.

Peter Lange, the former provost at Duke, working with Michael Merson, created the David M. Rubenstein Fellowship to allow me to accelerate my progress in writing this book. The fellowship gave me the opportunity to build a company as well. The support of Peter, Mike, Matt Nash, and Duke University is gratefully acknowledged.

I am grateful to the entire team at PublicAffairs, particularly my wonderful editor, Colleen Lawrie, who ultimately created the opportunity for this book by believing in its potential. She has had spectacular insight and judgment that have been critical to shaping the book. I also want to thank Stephanie Summerhays and Collin Tracy, my production editors; the copyediting team Sara and Chris from Scriptacuity; the marketing team, Lindsay Fradkoff and Miguel Cervantes; and the publicity team, especially Kristina Fazzalaro, publicist for PublicAffairs. Finally, thanks to Pete Garceau for the extraordinary jacket design and Trish Wilkinson for the interior design of the print book.

I worked with Pete Beatty, who provided independent editorial review and edits to the text of the book. Pete's insights were invaluable and extremely helpful. As a first-time author, his insights, experience, skill, and feedback helped me substantially. Tamara Wilson, a writer and colleague at USAID, pushed me to make this book a reality and spent hours working with me on the book.

Finally, I would like to thank my agent, Jessica Papin, and the team at Dystel, Goderich, & Bourrett, LLC. I don't think I could have found a better agent anywhere, especially one better matched for my work and interests. Jessica has been a forceful advocate for this book and myself, but even more than that, she helped me better understand the themes in my writing with brilliance and insight in the early days of writing the proposal. I am honored to work with her every day.

Alex Dehgan
Washington, DC
October 2018

ABBREVIATIONS

ADB	Asian Development Bank
ANSO	Afghan NGO Security Office
BAPAC	Band-e-Amir Protected Area Committee
CERF	Commander Emergency Relief Funds
CPA	Coalition Provisional Authority
CTO	cognizant technical officer
DOD	Department of Defense
DOS	Department of State
EPA	Environmental Protection Agency
EU	European Union
FAA	Federal Aviation Administration
FAO	Food and Agriculture Organization
GIS	geographic information systems
ICS	Iranian Cheetah Society
IED	improvised explosive device
ISAF	International Security Assistance Force
ISIS	Islamic State in Iraq and Syria
IUCN	International Union for Conservation of Nature
MAIL	Ministry of Agriculture, Irrigation and Livestock
MRE	meal ready to eat
NATO	North Atlantic Treaty Organization
NEPA	National Environmental Protection Agency
NGO	nongovernmental organization

OSCE	Organization for Security and Co-operation in Europe
PRT	provisional reconstruction team
PSP	PlayStation Portable
RPG	rocket-propelled grenade
UAE	United Arab Emirates
UDCA	ursodeoxycholic acid
UNEP	United Nations Environment Programme
UNESCO	United Nations Educational, Scientific and Cultural Organization
UNOPS	United Nations Office for Project Services
USAID	United States Agency for International Development
UXO	unexploded ordnance
VBIED	vehicle-borne improvised explosive device
WCS	Wildlife Conservation Society

INDEX

Abdul, Muhammad Afzal, 73
Abu Ghraib, 15n
Acinonyx jubatus venaticus. See Asiatic
    cheetah
ADB. *See* Asian Development Bank
Afghan NGO Security Office (ANSO),
    37–38, 230
Afghan urial (*Ovis vignei cycloceros*), 158. *See
    also* urial
Afghanistan
    Arab invasion of, 22
    Asiatic cheetah in, 57, 169–170, 172–176,
        179–189
    biodiversity of, 2, 23–25, 41–42, 63, 82,
        103, 107, 127, 129–132, 142, 147–148,
        235, 239, 246
    black market in, 34–36
    British in, 22, 116, 180–181
    Buddhism in, 21–22, 63, 115–116, 118,
        126, 133–134, 137, 150, 155, 238
    burkas in, 70–71
    China and, 48, 51, 137, 196–197
    civil war in, 23, 25–26, 48, 52–53, 73, 79,
        90–91, 95, 133, 251–253
    civil war in, environmental impact of,
        25–26, 52–53
    conservation in, 20–21, 41–42, 44, 49–51,
        58, 63, 107, 127, 129
    deforestation in, 78, 147–148, 158, 168
    extinction in, 4, 57, 74, 97–98, 119, 148,
        255, 259
    government organizations of, 40–42
    government organizations of, WCS and,
        41–42, 63
    history of, 20–23, 25

housing in, 29–33
IEDs in, 31, 36, 66, 176, 236
intelligence agency of, 141, 144
Iran and, 72, 80–86, 96, 128–129, 130,
    149, 177–178, 180
Iraq compared with, 124, 252–253
Ismaili in, 38, 60, 66, 87–89, 101–103,
    117, 149
Kyrgyz in, history of, 89–91
Madagascar compared with, 7
minefields in, 16, 18–21, 26, 31, 36, 39,
    59, 73, 88, 92–97, 99–100, 107–109,
    120, 129, 133, 137–138, 142, 180, 182,
    184, 186, 251, 253
Mongols in, 22, 117, 140–141, 177, 180
Montanans in, 54–55
mujahideen in, 74, 91–92, 94, 101, 152,
    178, 183, 208
national parks in, 3, 5, 15–16, 40, 49, 55,
    142–143, 173, 249, 252, 254
NGOs in, 15–16, 32–34, 37, 63–65, 68,
    92, 96, 104, 109, 125, 127, 153, 176,
    194, 232, 253
in Pakistan, nationals of, 38, 90, 96, 133,
    155
Pakistan and, 148–149, 152, 191, 195,
    199, 259
preliminary rapid assessment of, 15, 26,
    55, 120, 175, 252
real estate in, 29–30
redevelopment in, 127–128
refugees of, 1, 5, 20, 23, 38, 90, 94, 96,
    107, 120, 133, 154–156, 252
Russia and, 22, 55, 91–92
Saur Revolution in, 90

Afghanistan *(continued)*
 security in, 15–16, 36–40, 43, 59–62,
  66–68, 91, 94–95, 105, 123–124,
  164–166, 168, 176, 188, 221, 230–231,
  236–237, 239, 243, 251, 253–256, 259
 southern, hunting in, 230–231
 Soviet Union in, 48–49, 52, 56, 73, 79,
  90–91, 93–96, 105, 107, 130, 133,
  152, 155–156, 177–178, 181, 186, 189,
  238–239, 252–253, 257
 Tajikistan border with, 47–48, 99–102,
  106, 203–210, 216–225
 under Taliban, 38–39, 66, 107, 116–117,
  119–120, 133, 156, 177, 181–182
 terrain of, 23, 47–51, 147
 timber trafficking in, 78
 Turkmenistan and, 173, 176, 178, 183,
  189
 UNESCO World Heritage sites in, 126
 US Defense Department in, 44–45,
  128–129, 239
 US in, 23, 44–45, 64, 73, 91, 128–129,
  152, 164, 167, 177, 184, 196, 233, 239,
  253
 US State Department and, 31, 45, 81,
  142, 241
 weddings in, 69–72
Afghanistan Biodiversity Conservation
 Program, 2
Afghanodon mustersi. See Paghman stream
 salamander
African cheetah, 169, 172
Aga Khan, 101
 Hazara following, 38, 117
 hotel built by, 66
 Wakhi following, 60, 88–89, 117
Aga Khan Development Network, 101
Aga Khan Foundation, 88, 110, 127–128,
 194, 223
Ahmadi, Said Ahmad, 142
Ahmadinejad, Mahmoud, 81, 86, 257
Ajar Valley, 118–119, 121–122
Akbar (Mughal ruler), 169
Aleppo, Syria, 125
Alexander the Great, 22, 150, 177, 180
Ali, Hazrat, 102, 118
Ali, Inayat, 91
Ali, Rita, 167–168
Amanullah (king), 73
American Museum of Natural History, 157
Amin, Hafizullah, 90
Amur leopard, 170
Anglo-Afghan wars, 22, 34, 65
ANSO. *See* Afghan NGO Security Office

Arabs, 22, 169, 229–231
Aral Sea, 204–205
Ariana Afghan Airlines, 196
Armenia, 75, 98
Arthaud, Pascal, 156
Asian Development Bank (ADB), 121, 125,
 128
 Band-e-Amir and, 129, 132, 138–139,
  144
 transboundary park and, 194
Asian houbara bustard (*Chlamydotis
 macqueenii*), 183–184, 229–232
Asiatic black bear (*Ursus thibetanus*),
 158–159, 167, 255
Asiatic cheetah (*Acinonyx jubatus venaticus*)
 in Afghanistan, finding, 170, 172–176,
  179–189
 in Afghanistan, historically, 57, 169,
  173–174
 endangered, 170–171, 170–172
 in Herat, search for, 181–182, 184–189
 in Iran, 81, 169–170, 173, 175, 182, 185,
  189, 257
 NEPA and, 179, 181
 wide range of, 172–173
Asiatic lion, 57
Atef, Ezatullah, 73
Ayub, 140
 Ajar and Band-e-Amir surveys of,
  121–122
 Band-e-Amir national park and, 122,
  139, 141–142, 257
Azerbaijan, 75, 98

Babur, 97
bacha bazi (playboys), 71
Bactrian deer, 119
Badakhshan, Afghanistan, 89, 98–99,
 255–256
Bagram airfield, 35
 suicide bombing at, 243
 traveling to, 239–248
 wildlife trafficking and, 234, 238–240,
  246–247
Bahadery, Torialai, 29–30
Bahrami, Mohammad Reza
 dismissal of, 86, 257
 meeting with, 82–86
 restored as ambassador, 257
Baluch, 149
Bam-e-Duniya (roof of the world), 47
Bamiyan, Afghanistan
 Buddhas of, 115–117, 126, 133–134,
  136–138

Buddhism in, 63, 115–116, 133–134,
137
Genghis Khan in, 140–141
governor of, 132–136, 142
Hazara in, 116–117
history of, 115–116
minefields in, 120, 133, 137–138
national park in, 113, 133
NEPA and, 143
PRT in, 179, 258
WCS and, 113, 132–133, 254,
259
Band-e-Amir, 117, 259
ADB and, 129, 132, 138–139, 144
Agriculture Ministry and, 132–133, 136,
141–142
Buddhas in, 118
ecotourism and, 129, 254
international organizations in, 125
minefields in, 129
national park for, 119–120, 122, 129–130,
132–133, 137, 139–140, 142, 145–146,
246, 248, 254–255, 259
NEPA and, 141
Persian leopard in, 118, 122
Sarābi and, 132–133, 135–136, 139,
142–144
surveying, 121–122
UNEP and, 125, 127, 132
UNESCO World Heritage list and, 118,
118n, 125–127
WCS and, 119–122, 132–133, 138–145,
234, 248, 254–257
Zaher and, 132, 146
See also Bamiyan, Afghanistan
Band-e-Amir Protected Area Committee
(BAPAC), 254
Ayub and, 122, 141
first meeting of, 136–137, 141–144
Band-e-Haibat, 138
BAPAC. *See* Band-e-Amir Protected Area
Committee
Barakzai, Hashim, 42, 134, 136, 139, 142
bear bile, 158–159, 159n
Bedunah, Don, 54–55
Band-e-Amir survey of, 122
Wakhan expedition and, 60–61
behavior plasticity, 7
Bernini, Gian Lorenzo, 118
Biden, Joe, 145
big game hunting. *See* hunting
Big Pamir, 49, 89
Big Pamir Wildlife Reserve, 49, 89, 106
bin Laden, Osama, 116, 231, 256

biodiversity
of Afghanistan, 2, 23–25, 41–42, 63, 82,
103, 107, 127, 129–132, 142, 147–148,
235, 239, 246
donor-coordinating committee for,
130–132
of Eastern Forests Complex, 147–148
in Madagascar, 67
Bowles, Peter, 91, 112
Bowling, Belinda, 132
Brezhnev, Leonid, 48
Britain, 22, 116, 124–125, 180–181
British India. *See* India
Bronx Zoo. *See* Wildlife Conservation
Society in New York
Buddhism
in Afghanistan, 21–22, 63, 115–116, 118,
126, 133–134, 137, 150, 155, 238
in Bamiyan, 63, 115–116, 133–134, 137
in Band-e-Amir, 118
in Hadda, 155
in Nuristan, 150
Taliban and, 116, 126, 133–134, 137
burka, 70–71
burn rate, 44–45, 247
Bush, George W., 35, 84, 257
Bush Market, Kabul, 35–36
Byron, Robert, 181

Cairo Initiative, 258
Callahan, Ted, 91, 103–104, 111–112
Canada, 120–121
Capra falconeri falconeri. See markhor
capture myopathy, 53–54
Caspian tiger (*Panthera tigris virgata*), 97–98
CERF. *See* Commander Emergency Relief
Funds
Cheney, Dick, 243
CHF International, 27, 38
Chicken Street. *See* Kabul
China, 50, 60, 98, 121
Afghanistan and, 48, 51, 137, 196–197
bear bile and, 158–159
Islam in, 193, 197
Kyrgyz and, 89–90
Marco Polo sheep in, 51, 55
Pakistan and, 199
transboundary park and, 89, 191,
193–194, 196–201
Uyghurs in, 194, 197–200
WCS program for, 197–198
See also Ürümqi; Xinjiang
Chlamydotis macqueenii. See Asian houbara
bustard

City of Screams (Shahr-e Gholghola),
140–141
civets, common palm, 255
Coalition Provisional Authority (CPA), 10,
12, 14
cognizant technical officers (CTO), 44–45
Cold War, 202, 239
Columbia University. *See* Society for
Conservation Biology
Commander Emergency Relief Funds
(CERF), 128–129
Cooperative Threat Reduction Program, 11
CPA. *See* Coalition Provisional Authority
CTO. *See* cognizant technical officers
Curzon, George, 51

Danziger, Nick, 178
Defense Advanced Research Projects
Agency, 258
Defense Department, US (DOD)
in Afghanistan, 44–45, 128–129, 239
in Iraq, 10, 12–14
deforestation
in Afghanistan, 78, 147–148, 158, 168
in Eastern Forests Complex, 148
in Madagascar, 7–8
Delattre, Etienne, 28–29, 34
democracy, 143–145
Dionysus, 150
DOD. *See* Defense Department
DOS. *See* State Department
Dresden Elbe Valley, Germany, 126
Dubai, 16, 107
Terminal 2 in, 17–19
wildlife trafficking and, 227, 234
See also United Arab Emirates
Duncan, Alex, 109–110
Dupree, Louis, 154–155
Dupree, Nancy, 22, 79, 115, 154–155, 176
Durand Line, 148–149, 195
Dushanbe, Tajikistan
transboundary park meeting in, 201–203,
207–208, 212–214
traveling to, 203–204, 210–225

Eastern Forests Complex, Afghanistan
biodiversity of, 147–148
dangers of, 148, 151–153, 156
deforestation in, 148
Pashtun in, 148–149
species rediscovered in, 255
WCS in, 148, 152–153, 255–256
ecotourism, 213
Band-e-Amir and, 129, 254

in transboundary park discussions, 194
in Wakhan, 105–106, 255
effective population size, 171–172
Elphinstone, Mountstuart, 150
Esmael, Dr., 157
Eurasian lynx, 232
Eurasian Pole of Inaccessibility, 194
extinction
in Afghanistan, 4, 57, 74, 97–98, 119,
148, 255, 259
houbara bustard vulnerable to, 230
in Madagascar, 5, 7–8, 186
extinction vortex, 170–172

Faizabad, Afghanistan, 59, 98–99
FAO. *See* Food and Agriculture
Organization
Farhadinia, Mohammad, 182–183
Farid, Dr., 157, 166
Field Museum, 173
Fitzherbert, Anthony, 52
flying squirrels, 16, 24
Food and Agriculture Organization, UN
(FAO), 52, 90, 119, 158
Forest and Rangeland Department,
Afghanistan, 42
Franklin, Ian Robert, 170
FrontLines (magazine), 259

gazelle
in Afghanistan, 24, 98, 173, 181–183,
185, 189
Asiatic cheetah and, 181–183, 185
in Iran, decline of, 182
gene flow, 162, 170
Genghis Khan, 31, 38, 116–117, 140–141.
See also Mongols
George W. Bush Market, 164
Germany
Dresden Elbe Valley of, 126
in Kunduz, development agency of,
207–208
ghormeh sabzi, 85–86
Ghulam
in Northern Alliance, 203, 210, 215
on Tajikistan trip, 203, 209–211,
215–217, 220–221, 223–224
Ghurriani, Abdul Ghani, 42
Gilgit, Pakistan, 90, 107
GIS, 29, 44–45, 157, 257
goitered gazelle, 98, 173, 181, 189. *See also*
gazelle
Gorbachev, Mikhail, 48
GPS units, 161–164

Grand Challenges for Development, 258
Grand Trunk Road, Afghanistan, 153–154
Great Game, 48
Great Pamir Mountain Range. *See* Big Pamir
Great Patriotic War, 92
Green Zone, Iraq, 9–12, 12n

Hadda, Afghanistan, 155
Halim (doctor), 156–157
HALO Trust, 92, 96
Haqiq, 29, 34, 157, 257
Hassinger, Jerry, 173
Hazara, 38, 116–117, 133, 145
Hazarajat Plateau Project, 120
Helmand River basin, 128–129
Herat, Afghanistan, 175–176
    Asiatic cheetah search in, 181–182,
        184–189
    bazaar of, 181
    drug trafficking in, 180, 188
    Dupree, Nancy, on, 176
    governor of, 177–179
    history of, 176–178, 180–181
    monuments of, 180–181
    PRT in, 179–180
    Silk Road in, 181
Himalayan lynx, 122, 254
Himalayas, 47–48, 57, 59, 108
Hindu Kush, 16, 48, 73, 118, 149
    markhor in, 158
    Persian leopards of, 74–75
    salamanders of, 74
    Salang Pass tunnel crossing, 91–94
Hitler, Adolf, 92
Hunter, Luke, 157
hunting
    big game, 55–57, 149, 158
    of houbara bustard, 229–232
    by Kyrgyz, 103–104
    of Marco Polo sheep, 52–53, 55–57,
        103–104
    of snow leopard, 57–58, 104
    in southern Afghanistan, 230–231
    Tajikistan and, 103
    in Wakhan, 102–104
    by Wakhi, 104
    Zahir Shah and, 1–2, 49, 56, 102, 173
Hussein, Saddam, 10–11, 14, 253n

ibex, 25, 118
    in Ajar Valley, 119, 121–122
    Siberian, 121
    snow leopard and, 57, 104
    in Wakhan, 52, 100, 104, 106–107, 112

ICS. *See* Iranian Cheetah Society
improvised explosive devices (IEDs)
    in Afghanistan, 31, 36, 66, 176, 236
    in Iraq, 10, 12, 123
    vehicle-borne, 236
Inayatollah, 176, 179–180, 183
India
    British, 22, 48, 149
    transboundary park and, 195–196
    WCS program for, 157
Indonesia, 123
Intelligence Ministry, Afghanistan, 136
International Security Assistance Force,
        Afghanistan (ISAF), 45, 79, 164, 253
    Kabul base of, 246
    PRT of, 179–180, 258
    wildlife trafficking and, 234–235,
        238–239, 246
International Union for Conservation of
        Nature (IUCN), 158–159, 230, 232
Iran, 68, 70–71, 74–75, 101
    Afghanistan and, 72, 80–86, 96, 128–129,
        130, 149, 177–178, 180
    Asiatic cheetahs in, 81, 169–170, 173,
        175, 182, 185, 189, 257
    Taliban and, 81, 83–84, 129
    US and, 80–84, 129, 257
    US State Department and, 257
Iranian cheetah. *See* Asiatic cheetah
Iranian Cheetah Society (ICS), 182
Iranian revolution, 64, 72
Iran-Iraq War, 252–253
Iraq, 15n, 40, 54–55, 67
    Afghanistan compared with, 124,
        252–253
    Green Zone in, 9–12, 12n
    IEDs in, 10, 12, 123
    redirection program in, 11–14
    scientists in, 11–12, 14
    US Defense Department in, 10, 12–14
    US State Department and, 9–10,
        13–14, 252
    wars of, 252–253, 253n
ISAF. *See* International Security Assistance
        Force
ISAF Provincial Reconstruction Team (PRT)
    in Bamiyan, 179, 258
    in Herat, 179–180
Ishkashim, Afghanistan, 100–101, 106, 255
ISIS, 14, 253
Islam
    in China, 193, 197
    in Nuristan, 150–152
    opium and, 110

Islam *(continued)*
  Shi'a, 84, 88–89, 117
  Sunni, 14, 88–89, 117
  in Tajikistan, 192, 201
  US and, Cairo Initiative on, 258
  Wahhabi, 152
Ismael (shah), 89
  home of, 102, 106
  meeting with, 103–107
Ismaili, 91
  in Afghanistan, 38, 60, 66, 87–89,
    101–103, 117, 149
  Aga Khan of, 38, 60, 66, 88–89, 101, 117
  Hazara, 38, 117
  Wakhi, 60, 87–89, 102–103, 149
  See also Islam
IUCN. *See* International Union for
  Conservation of Nature

Jalalabad, Afghanistan, 153–157
Jathanna, Devcharan, 157, 161–162
Jawad, Ahmad, 60–61
Jea, David, 144, 258
Jouvenal, Peter, 65

Kabul, Afghanistan, 43, 75–77, 91
  arrival in, 19, 25–26
  Bush Market in, 35–36
  Chicken Street in, 78–79, 232–234, 238,
    247–248
  conservation in, 63
  expatriates in, 64–68, 72
  golf club in, 72–73
  ISAF base in, 246
  Karzai and, 132–133
  Kol-e-Hashmat Khan and, 1
  minefields in, 18–19, 73, 95
  Qual-e-Fatullah guesthouse in, 33–34
  Shahr-e Naw Park in, 162–164
  Wazir Akbar Khan neighborhood of, 99
  WCS in, 4, 25–26, 30–34, 36, 60, 63–64,
    72, 113, 161–162, 236, 248
Kabul International Airport
  attack on, 239
  wildlife trafficking and, 237–238
Kabul University, Afghanistan Center at, 155
Kafiristan. *See* Nuristan
Kafirs, 150–151, 167
Kaka, 68–69, 72, 130
Kam Air
  trafficking on, 227–228, 231–232
  traveling on, 18–19
Kamel. *See* Taverna du Liban
Kandahar, Afghanistan, 230

Karanth, Ullas, 157
Karim, 38–39
Karimov, Abdulvohid, 212, 214, 216
Karzai, Hamid, 64, 88, 134, 143, 146
  Khan, Ismail, and, 179
  limited power of, 132
  WCS and, 132
Kasirov, Kokul, 212–214
Kennedy, John Fitzgerald, 43
Khalilzad, Zalmay, 84
Khan, Ismail, 177–179, 257
Khan, Rahman Gul, 90
Khaurin, Hazrat Hussain, 42
Khoja
  hiring of, 28
  at WCS, 28–29, 37, 75–76, 91, 97, 123,
    241, 243, 245–246, 249
Khyber Pass, 154–155
Kol-e-Hashmat Khan, 1–2, 63, 102, 254, 259
Koshk-e Kohneh, Afghanistan, 183
Kuchi, 94, 189
Kunduz, Afghanistan, 204–208
Kushan Empire, 115
Kyrgyz, 51, 53, 105
  in Afghanistan, history of, 89–91
  China and, 89–90
  fleeing Soviet Union, 89
  hunting by, 103–104
  leaders of, 87–88, 90, 103
  in Pakistan, 90
  in Pamirs, 50, 89–90
  society of, 60, 89

Lamb, Rob, 40
large-billed reed warbler, 255
Larsson, John, 119, 149, 158, 160–161
lemurs, 5, 7–8, 67, 164
Linda Norgrove Foundation, 256n
Little Pamir, 50, 90, 108, 112, 255
Logan Act, 81
lynx, 24, 167
  Eurasian, 232
  Himalayan, 122, 254

Madagascar, 68
  Afghanistan compared with, 7
  biodiversity in, 67
  deforestation in, 7–8
  expedition to, 7–9
  extinction in, 5, 7–8, 186
  lemurs in, 5, 7–8, 67, 164
Madera, 153, 155–156
MAIL. *See* Ministry of Agriculture,
  Irrigation, and Livestock

Malikyar, Ghulam, 134, 136
Manhattan, federal court in, 6
Marco Polo sheep (*Ovis ammon polii*), 49,
    199, 256
  capture myopathy of, 53–54
  in China, 51, 55
  decline of, 52–53
  FAO survey of, 90
  hunting of, 52–53, 55–57, 103–104
  overgrazing and, 58, 104
  in Pamirs, 50–52, 56, 60
  petroglyphs of, 52, 100, 112
  Schaller studying, 55–56, 175
  surveying, 51, 53–55, 62, 112–113,
    186, 254
  in Tajikistan, 55–56, 103
  transboundary park for, 55, 191, 193
  UNEP assessment of, 52
  in Wakhan, 106–107, 186
  WCS and, 50–51, 53–55, 57, 62, 87,
    89–90, 103–104, 112–113, 254
markhor (*Capra falconeri falconeri*), 158,
    167–168, 193
Masood, Ahmad Shah, 92, 107, 108, 203, 215
Maurya, Chandragupta, 22
meals ready to eat (MREs), 35–36
Michelangelo, 118
Miller, Clay, 122–123, 134–136
  at Bagram airfield, 239–246, 248
  wildlife trafficking and, 235–244
Minaret of Jam, 126
minefields
  in Afghanistan, 16, 18–21, 26, 31, 36,
    39, 59, 73, 88, 92–97, 99–100,
    107–109, 120, 129, 133, 137–138,
    142, 180, 182, 184, 186, 251, 253
  in Bamiyan, 119–120, 133, 137–138
  in Band-e-Amir, 129
  in Kabul, 18–19, 73, 95
  near Noshaq, 108–109
  in Salang Pass tunnel, 92–93
  Soviets and, 95–96
  strategy for, 184
Ministry of Agriculture, Irrigation, and
    Livestock, Afghanistan (MAIL), 75,
    125, 176
  Band-e-Amir and, 132–133, 136, 141–142
  Nuristan and, 157
  Stevens at, 43, 123
  WCS and, 40–44, 57, 99, 125,
    141–142, 162
Ministry of Defence, British, 124–125
Ministry of Energy and Water,
    Afghanistan, 41

Ministry of Information and Culture,
    Afghanistan, 125–126
Ministry of Women's Affairs,
    Afghanistan, 133
Mock, John, 52
Mohammad, Jan, 167–168
Mongolia, 16, 55
Mongols, 22, 117, 140–141, 177, 180
Montana, 54–55
Moschus cupreus. See musk deer
Moscow Zoo, 6
Mountain Wilderness International, 109
MREs (meals ready to eat), 35–36
Mughals, 116, 169
mujahideen, Afghan, 74, 91–92, 94, 178
  former, 101, 183, 208
  in Nuristan, 152
Musalla Complex, 181
musk deer (*Moschus cupreus*), 148, 255
  musk of, 160–161, 167
  surveying, 159–160, 167–168

Namibia, 91
Nangarhar University, 156
Nashir, Sher Khan, 205
National Army, Afghan, 179
National Democratic Institute, 144–145
National Environmental Protection Agency,
    Afghanistan (NEPA), 43–44, 75, 99
  Asiatic cheetah and, 179, 181
  Bamiyan and, 143
  Band-e-Amir and, 141
  Miller of, 122–123, 134–136,
    235–246, 248
  Nuristan and, 157
  WCS and, 40–41, 122–125, 179, 235
  wildlife trafficking and, 235
national park
  in Afghanistan, 3, 5, 15–16, 40, 49, 55,
    142–143, 173, 249, 252, 254
  in Bamiyan, 113, 132–133
  for Band-e-Amir, 119–120, 122,
    129–130, 132–133, 137, 139–140, 142,
    145–146, 248, 254–255, 259
  Zaher and, 146
National Police, Afghan, 136, 139, 144, 179
NATO, 152
Naval Special Warfare Development Group,
    US (SEAL Team Six), 256
NEPA. *See* National Environmental
    Protection Agency
Nepal, 17, 36, 78, 105
New Zealand Provincial Reconstruction
    Team, 135, 138

NGOs
  in Afghanistan, 15–16, 32–34, 37, 63–65,
    68, 92, 96, 104, 109, 125, 127, 176,
    194, 232, 253
  security of, 15–16, 37, 176, 253
  Taliban and, 64–65
9/11 attacks, 9, 79, 84
9/11 Commission Report, 231
Norgrove, Linda, 256, 256n
North Korea, 159
Northern Alliance, 186, 210
  Masood of, 107, 108, 203, 215
  Taliban and, 95, 107–108, 184, 207
Northwest Afghanistan Game Reserve, 173,
    187–189
Noshaq, 108–109
Nuristan, Afghanistan, 149
  Agriculture Ministry and, 157
  Buddhism in, 150
  culture of, 150–151
  dangers of, 156, 164–166, 168
  history of, 150–152
  as Kafiristan, 150
  Kafirs of, 150–151, 167
  Madera in, 153, 155–156
  mujahideen in, 152
  NEPA and, 157
  Persian leopard in, 158, 167
  religion in, 150–152
  resistance of, 152
  survey team of, 156–165
  trafficking and, 152
  UNEP in, 158
  urial in, 158, 167
  WCS and, 152–153, 156–168
Nuristan Provincial Reconstruction Team,
    164
Nuristani, Abdullah Mayar, 157, 162

Obama, Barack, 258
Oman, 126
Omar (mullah), 116
onager, 173, 182, 188–189
opium, 101, 110–111, 180, 192
Organization for Security and Co-operation
    in Europe (OSCE), 220–221
Ostrowski, Stephane, 167, 255
overgrazing, 58, 122
Ovis ammon polii. See Marco Polo sheep
Ovis vignei cycloceros. See Afghan urial

Paghman stream salamander (*Afghanodon
    mustersi*), 74

Pakistan, 16, 183
  Afghanistan and, 148–149, 152, 191, 195,
    199, 259
  Afghans in, 38, 90, 96, 133, 155
  China and, 199
  Kyrgyz in, 90
  transboundary park and, 191–192, 198,
    201–202
Pamirs, 63, 194
  Big, 49, 89
  Big, wildlife reserve for, 49, 89, 106
  Kyrgyz in, 51, 89–90
  Little, 50, 90, 108, 112, 255
  Marco Polo sheep in, 50–52, 56, 60
  Silk Road and, 60, 112
  traveling in, 59–60
  Wakhi in, 50, 88–89
Panthera pardus saxicolor. See Persian leopard
Panthera tigris virgata. See Caspian tiger
Panthera uncia. See snow leopard
Pashtun, 2, 16, 34, 163, 205
  in Eastern Forests Complex, 148–149
  language of, 151, 159
Peace Corps, 17, 36, 43
peace park. *See* transboundary park
Persian leopard (*Panthera pardus saxicolor*)
  in Band-e-Amir, 118, 122
  of Hindu Kush, 74–75
  in Nuristan, 158, 167
Petocz, Ron, 90, 149, 158, 160–161
petroglyphs, 52, 60, 100, 112
Philips, Carl, 11
Pinelli, Carlo Alberto, 108
playboys (bacha bazi), 71
Polo, Marco, 48, 50, 106
poppy, 98–99
PRT. *See* ISAF Provincial Reconstruction
    Team
PSP. *See* Sony PlayStation Portable

al-Qaeda, 9, 116, 149, 231
Qais, 28–29, 75, 176, 236–237
  as country director, 256
  hiring of, 27
  as refugee, 38
  in security test, 39
  on Tajikistan trip, 203, 209, 212,
    215–221, 223–224
Qala Panja, Afghanistan, 103, 106, 108
Qargha Lake, 73, 162, 254

Rahmon, Emomali, 202
Rashid Khan, Abdul, 87–88, 91, 103–106

Razaq, Abdul, 176, 183, 187
redirection programs, US, 11
RMSI, 40, 61
The Road to Oxiana (Byron), 181
Robinson, John, 248
roof of the world (Bam-e-Duniya), 47
Ross, Dennis, 257
Rouhani, Hassan, 257
Route Irish, Iraq, 10
Russia
  Afghanistan and, 22, 55, 91–92
  post-Soviet, 5–6, 67, 92, 202, 217
  Wakhan Corridor and, 48

Sabour, 38–39, 248
Safi Landmark tower, 33
Saker falcon
  endangered, 229–230
  in history, 229
  trafficking of, 183, 227–229, 231–232,
    256
Salang Pass tunnel, 91–94
Sarābi, Habiba
  Band-e-Amir and, 132–133, 135–136,
    139, 142–144
  tourism and, 133
Saur Revolution, 90
Scarth, Richard, 29–30, 74
Schaller, George, 198
  Asiatic cheetah and, 175, 186–189
  Marco Polo sheep studied by, 55–56, 175
Science and Technology Adviser to the
  Secretary of State, Office of, 258
SEAL Team Six. *See* Naval Special Warfare
  Development Group
Serena Hotel, 80–82, 144
  Aga Khan and, 66
  attack on, 251, 253
Shafiq
  Asiatic cheetah and, 174
  emigration, return of, 256
  hiring of, 28–29
  at WCS, 28–29, 37–38, 40, 72–73, 75,
    79–80, 123, 174, 241, 243, 245
Shāhnāmah, 169
Shahr-e Gholghola. *See* City of Screams
Shahr-e Naw Park, 162–164
Shakespeare, William, 97
Shank, Christopher, 120, 144
  at Band-e-Amir, 121–122
  report of, 119, 122
Sharif, Mohammad (deputy minister), 134,
  136, 139

Sher Khan Bandar crossing, 200
  name of, 205
  traveling through, 205–206, 208–210,
    216–225
Shi'a, 84, 88–89, 117
Siberian ibex, 121. *See also* ibex
Silk Road, 16–17, 19, 47, 141
  biological, of Afghanistan, 107
  Caspian tigers on, 98
  in Herat, 181
  Kushan Empire and, 115
  Pamirs and, 60, 112
  Saker falcons and, 229
  Ürümqi and, 194
Smithsonian Institution, 145–146
smuggling. *See* trafficking
snow leopard (*Panthera uncia*), 25, 90, 175
  fur market in, 79, 232–234, 237–238,
    240, 246
  hunting of, 57–58, 104
  ibex and, 57, 104
  overgrazing and, 58
  protecting, 58, 89, 103, 104–105, 233, 255
  transnational park for, 191, 193
  WCS and, 51, 58, 87, 89, 103, 104,
    112–113, 158, 167, 187, 233, 254–255
Snow Leopard Project, 233
Society for Conservation Biology, Columbia
  University, 15, 121, 203
Sony PlayStation Portable (PSP), 227, 232
South Africa, 91, 112, 203, 206, 239
South West Africa. *See* Namibia
Southwest badger, 254
Soviet Union, 5–6, 23, 98
  in Afghanistan, 48–49, 52, 56, 73, 79,
    90–91, 93–96, 105, 107, 130, 133,
    152, 155–156, 177–178, 181, 186,
    189, 238–239, 252–253, 257
  Aral Sea disaster of, 204–205
  Cooperative Threat Reduction Program in
    former, 11
  Kyrgyz fleeing, 89
  minefields and, 95–96
  See also Russia; Tajikistan
Stalin, Joseph, 204
State Department, US (DOS), 68
  Afghanistan and, 31, 45, 81, 142, 241
  Iran engagement of, 257
  Iraq and, 9–10, 13–14, 252
  return to, 248, 257–258
  USAID and, 43–44
  See also Science and Technology Adviser
    to the Secretary of State

Stevens, Kara, 18
    in Afghanistan, 29, 36, 43, 69–72, 75–76,
        81, 90, 112, 123, 141–142, 146, 154,
        156–157, 248–249
    at Agriculture Ministry, 43, 123
    background of, 17, 36
Stuart, Rory, 154
suicide bombing, 243, 251
Sultan, Omar, 125–127
Sunnis, 14, 88–89, 117

Tajikistan
    Afghan border with, 47–48, 99–102, 106,
        203–210, 216–225
    hunting and, 103
    Islam in, 192, 201
    Marco Polo sheep in, 55–56, 103
    officials of, 212–214
    OSCE in, 220–221
    police in, 211, 215
    transboundary park and, 89, 191–193,
        198, 201–203, 205–208, 211–214
    traveling to, 203–204, 209–225
    WCS in, 214
Taliaferro, Bill, 122
Taliban, 2–3, 16, 146
    Afghanistan under, 38–39, 66, 107,
        116–117, 119–120, 133, 156, 177,
        181–182
    Buddhas destroyed by, 116, 126,
        133–134, 137
    Hazara and, 38, 116–117
    Iran, US and, 81, 83–84, 129
    NGOs and, 64–65
    Norgrove kidnapped by, 256
    Northern Alliance and, 95, 107–108,
        184, 207
    rise of, 23
    after US invasion, 21, 74, 81, 83–84, 91,
        94, 108, 149, 154, 155, 164, 183, 231
Tamerlane, 150
Tanala, 8
Taraki, Nur Muhammad, 90, 177
Tarzi, Zemaryalai, 137
Taverna du Liban, 65, 251
Terminal 2. *See* Dubai
Tethys Sea, 47
Timurid Empire, 177
Tolo Television, 234
Tourism Organization, Afghan, 56–57,
    125, 149
trafficking
    Bagram and, 234, 238–240, 246–247
    of drugs, 180, 188, 192, 219

    in Herat, 180, 188
    by humanitarian community, 232–233
    ISAF and, 234–235, 238–239, 246
    Kabul International Airport and, 237–238
    on Kam Air, 227–228, 231–232
    NEPA and, 235
    Nuristan and, 152
    of Saker falcons, 183, 227–229, 231–232,
        256
    timber, 78, 148–149
    UNEP and, 235
    US, international military and, 232–235,
        238–240, 246–247
    WCS and, 78–82, 85, 233–243, 246–249,
        256
    wildlife, 78–82, 85, 113, 148, 159,
        159n, 174–175, 183, 199, 227–243,
        246–249, 256
    See also opium
transboundary park
    ADB and, 194
    China and, 89, 191, 193–194, 196–201
    Dushanbe meeting for, 201–203,
        207–208, 212–214
    India and, 195–196
    Marco Polo sheep and, 55, 191, 193
    mountain ranges of, 192–193
    Pakistan and, 191–192, 198, 201–202
    as peace park, 55, 89, 198–199
    political issues of, 191–193, 195–200
    snow leopard and, 191, 193
    Tajikistan and, 89, 191–193, 198,
        201–203, 205–208, 211–214
    Ürümqi meeting for, 193–202, 212–213
    Wakhan and, 195
    Zaher and, 198
transect, 161–163, 165, 167–168
Transitional Administration, Afghan, 178
travertine, 117–118, 125, 132
Turkey, 90
Turkmenistan, 173, 176, 178, 183, 189
Turquoise Mountain Foundation, 154
Twelvers, 88

UDCA. *See* ursodeoxycholic acid
Ulan Bator, Mongolia, 16
UN Environmental Program Post-Conflict
    Assessment Unit, 26, 55, 59, 120, 127
UN Mine Action Program for Afghanistan,
    96
UNEP. *See* United Nations Environment
    Programme
UNESCO Intangible Cultural Heritage list,
    229

UNESCO World Heritage sites
in Afghanistan, problems of, 126
Band-e-Amir as, 118, 118n, 125–127
unexploded ordnance (UXO), 95
United Arab Emirates (UAE), 183, 231
United Nations Environment Programme
(UNEP), 41–42
Band-e-Amir and, 125, 127–128, 132
Marco Polo sheep assessment of, 52
in Nuristan, 158
wildlife trafficking and, 235
United Nations Office for Project Services
(UNOPS), 125, 127–128, 129,
239, 256
United States (US)
in Afghanistan, 23, 44–45, 64, 73, 91,
128–129, 152, 164, 167, 177, 184, 196,
233, 239, 253
in Afghanistan, Defense Department of,
44–45, 128–129, 239
Afghanistan and State Department of, 31,
45, 81, 142, 241
Iran and, 80–84, 129, 257
in Iraq, Defense Department of, 10, 12–14
Iraq and State Department of, 9–10,
13–14, 252
Islam and, Cairo Initiative of, 258
military of, wildlife trafficking and,
232–235, 238–240, 246–247
SEAL Team Six of, 256
Taliban and, 81, 83–84, 129
See also US Agency for International
Development
UNOPS. *See* United Nations Office for
Project Services
urial, 57, 182–183, 185
in Ajar Valley, 119, 121
in Band-e-Amir, 118, 254
in Eastern Forests Complex, 148
in Northwest Afghanistan Game Reserve,
189
in Nuristan, 158, 167
ursodeoxycholic acid (UDCA), 159, 161
Ursus thibetanus. See Asiatic black bear
Ürümqi, China
remoteness of, 194–195
Silk Road and, 194
transboundary park meeting in, 193–202,
212–213
US. *See* United States
US Agency for International Development
(USAID)
Afghanistan staff of, 40–41
burn rate and, 44–45, 247

as chief scientist of, 247, 258
CTO of, 44–45
establishment of, 43
magazine of, 259
State Department and, 43–44
WCS and, 3–4, 16, 26–27, 29, 43–44, 51,
65, 80–81, 84–85, 98, 128, 142, 156,
186–187, 192, 247–248
UXO. *See* unexploded ordnance
Uyghurs, 194, 197–200
Uzbekistan, 204

Vaidyanathan, Srinivas, 157, 161–162
vampire deer. *See* musk deer
vehicle-borne IEDs (VBIEDs), 236
Vietnam, 92, 159, 159n
Virgil, 97

Waghjir Valley, 49–51, 60
Wahhabism, 152
Wahid Khan, Mir Abdul, 101, 104, 109,
112–113
Wakhan Corridor, 24, 50, 58, 63, 256
ecotourism in, 105–106, 255
habitat of, 49, 51
health in, 109–110
history of, 47–49
hunting in, 102–104
ibex in, 52, 100, 104, 106–107, 112
Marco Polo sheep in, 106–107, 186
national park for, 87, 89, 99, 103, 113
opium in, 101, 110–111
petroglyphs of, 52, 60, 100
Russia and, 48
transboundary park and, 195
traveling to, 59–62, 91–102, 107–108,
111–113
WCS in, 49, 87, 105–108, 113, 234, 248,
254–255
See also Badakhshan; Faizabad; Himalayas
Wakhan National Park, 254
Wakhan Pamir Association, 255
Wakhi, 53, 108–110, 117, 194
hunting by, 104
as Ismaili, 60, 87–89, 102–103, 149
in Pamirs, 50, 88–89
Shah Ismael of, 89, 102–107
society of, 60, 88–89
villages of, 60
Wald, Beth, 186
Wildlife Conservation Society in New York
(WCS), 2, 5, 7
Afghan government organizations and,
41–42, 63

Wildlife Conservation Society in New York
    (WCS) *(continued)*
  Afghanistan staff of, 27–29, 37, 256–257,
    258–259
  Agriculture Ministry and, 40–44, 57, 99,
    125, 141–142, 162
  in Ajar Valley, 118–119, 121–122
  Asiatic cheetah search of, 170, 172–176,
    179–189
  in Badakhshan, 98–99, 255
  Bamiyan and, 113, 132–133, 254, 258
  Band-e-Amir and, 119–122, 132–133,
    138–145, 234, 248, 254–257
  biodiversity group of, 130–132
  China program of, 197–198
  in Eastern Forests Complex, 148,
    152–153, 255–256
  ecotourism and, 105–106, 194, 254–255
  India Program of, 157
  Ismaili, Kyrgyz leaders and, 87–88
  joining, 15–16
  in Kabul, 4, 25–26, 30–34, 36, 60, 63–64,
    72, 113, 161–162, 236, 248
  Karzai government and, 132
  leaving, 248–249
  Marco Polo sheep and, 50–51, 53–55, 57,
    62, 87, 89–90, 103–105, 112–113, 254
  NEPA and, 40–41, 122–125, 179, 235
  Nuristan and, 152–153, 156–168
  Paghman stream salamander and, 74
  snow leopard and, 51, 58, 87, 89, 103,
    104–105, 112–113, 158, 167, 187,
    233, 254–255
  south Afghanistan avoided by, 231
  in Tajikistan, 214
  timber trafficking and, 78
  transboundary park proposed by, 55, 89,
    191–203, 207–208, 212–214
  USAID and, 3–4, 16, 26–27, 29, 43–44,
    51, 65, 80–81, 84–85, 98, 128, 142,
    156, 186–187, 192, 247–248

  in Wakhan, 49, 87, 105–108, 113, 234,
    248, 254–255
  Wakhan expedition and, 59–62
  wildlife trafficking and, 78–82, 85,
    233–243, 246–249, 256
  Zaher and, 40–41, 122–123
wildlife trafficking. *See* trafficking
World War II, 11, 92, 95

Xi'an, China, 60
Xinjiang, China, 193
  ethnic groups of, 194–195, 197–198
  Uyghurs in, 194, 197–200
Xuanzang, 137

Yale School of Forestry, 9
Yama, 187

Zabih, 28–29, 69, 77, 174, 256
Zaher, Mostapha (prince), 124, 234, 257
  in Bamiyan, 134–136
  Band-e-Amir national park and,
    132, 146
  first meeting with, 41
  transboundary park and, 198
  WCS and, 40–41, 122–123
Zahir Shah, Mohammed (king)
  death of, 134–135
  hunting programs and, 56
  nature reserves of, 1–2, 49, 102, 173
  Zaher and, 40, 134–135
Zahler, Peter, 17, 27, 29, 176, 198
  in Post-Conflict Assessment Unit, 26, 55,
    59, 120, 127
  preliminary rapid assessments of, 15, 26,
    55, 59, 120, 175, 252
  recruitment by, 15
  Western and Central Asia focus of, 16
Zalmai, 186–187, 256
Zoroastrianism, 21, 70

Credit: Les Todd, Duke University

Alex Dehgan is the cofounder and CEO of Conservation X Labs, which is focused on transforming the field of conservation through technology, entrepreneurship, and innovation. Previously, he was USAID's first chief scientist in twenty years; during his tenure he sought to restore science to its rightful place in the agency. Prior to joining USAID, Alex worked in multiple positions within the Office of the Secretary of State and the Bureau of Near Eastern Affairs at the US Department of State; his work included efforts to rebuild science in Iraq under the Coalition Provisional Authority and, under Ambassador Dennis Ross and as a liaison to the late Ambassador Richard Holbrooke, developing the Obama administration's science diplomacy strategy with Iran. Alex received his PhD from the Committee on Evolutionary Biology at the University of Chicago; a JD from the University of California, Hastings; and a BS from Duke University. He was chosen as an "Icon of Science" by *Seed Magazine* in 2005, received the World Technology Award for Policy in 2011, and has been recognized through multiple awards from USAID and the Departments of State and Defense. Alex currently teaches at Duke University. He has worked and traveled in more than eighty countries across five continents. Follow him on Twitter @lemurwrangler.

PublicAffairs is a publishing house founded in 1997. It is a tribute to the standards, values, and flair of three persons who have served as mentors to countless reporters, writers, editors, and book people of all kinds, including me.

I. F. STONE, proprietor of *I. F. Stone's Weekly*, combined a commitment to the First Amendment with entrepreneurial zeal and reporting skill and became one of the great independent journalists in American history. At the age of eighty, Izzy published *The Trial of Socrates*, which was a national bestseller. He wrote the book after he taught himself ancient Greek.

BENJAMIN C. BRADLEE was for nearly thirty years the charismatic editorial leader of *The Washington Post*. It was Ben who gave the *Post* the range and courage to pursue such historic issues as Watergate. He supported his reporters with a tenacity that made them fearless and it is no accident that so many became authors of influential, best-selling books.

ROBERT L. BERNSTEIN, the chief executive of Random House for more than a quarter century, guided one of the nation's premier publishing houses. Bob was personally responsible for many books of political dissent and argument that challenged tyranny around the globe. He is also the founder and longtime chair of Human Rights Watch, one of the most respected human rights organizations in the world.

•   •   •

For fifty years, the banner of Public Affairs Press was carried by its owner Morris B. Schnapper, who published Gandhi, Nasser, Toynbee, Truman, and about 1,500 other authors. In 1983, Schnapper was described by *The Washington Post* as "a redoubtable gadfly." His legacy will endure in the books to come.

Peter Osnos, *Founder*